M Train

M Train

Patti Smith

ALFRED A. KNOPF

New York Toronto

2015

THIS IS A BORZOI BOOK
PUBLISHED BY ALFRED A. KNOPF
AND ALFRED A. KNOPF CANADA

www.aaknopf.com
www.penguinrandomhouse.ca

Library of Congress Cataloging-in-Publication Data
Smith, Patti.
M train / Patti Smith.
pages cm
ISBN 978-1-101-87510-0 (hardcover : alk. paper)—
ISBN 978-1-101-87511-7 (eBook)
1. Smith, Patti.
2. Women rock musicians—United States—Biography.
3. Rock musicians—United States—Biography.   I. Title.
ML420.S672A3   2015   782.42166092—
dc23   [B]   2015012904

Library and Archives Canada Cataloguing in Publication
Smith, Patti, author
M train / Patti Smith.
Issued in print and electronic formats.
ISBN 978-0-345-81545-3
eBook ISBN 978-0-345-81547-7
1. Smith, Patti.   2. Rock musicians—United States—Biography.
I. Title.
ML420.S672A3   2015   782.42166092   c2015-903822-7

Front-of-jacket photograph © Claire Alexandra Hatfield
Cover design by Carol Devine Carson

Manufactured in the United States of America
Published October 6, 2015
Reprinted Six Times
Eighth Printing, November 2015

for Sam

Stations

M Train

It's not so easy writing about nothing.

That's what a cowpoke was saying as I entered the frame of a dream. Vaguely handsome, intensely laconic, he was balancing on a folding chair, leaning backwards, his Stetson brushing the edge of the dun-colored exterior of a lone café. I say lone, as there appeared to be nothing else around except an antiquated gas pump and a rusting trough ornamented with a necklace of horseflies slung above the last dregs of its stagnant water. There was no one around, either, but he didn't seem to mind; he just pulled the brim of his hat over his eyes and kept on talking. It was the same kind of Silverbelly Open Road model that Lyndon Johnson used to wear.

—But we keep on going, he continued, fostering all kinds of crazy hopes. To redeem the lost, some sliver of personal revelation. It's an addiction, like playing the slots, or a game of golf.

—It's a lot easier to talk about nothing, I said.

He didn't outright ignore my presence, but he did fail to respond.

—Well, anyway, that's my two cents.

—You're just about to pack it in, toss the clubs in a river, when you hit your stride, the ball rolls straight in the cup, and the coins fill your inverted cap.

The sun caught the edge of his belt buckle, projecting a flash that shimmered across the desert plain. A shrill whistle sounded, and as I stepped to the right I caught sight of his shadow spilling a whole other set of sophisms from an entirely different angle.

—I been here before, haven't I?

He just sat there staring out at the plain.

Son of a bitch, I thought. He's ignoring me.

—Hey, I said, I'm not the dead, not a shade passing. I'm flesh and blood here.

He pulled a notebook out of his pocket and started writing.

—You got to at least look at me, I said. After all, it is my dream.

I drew closer. Close enough to see what he was writing. He had his notebook open to a blank page and three words suddenly materialized.

Nope, it's mine.

—Well, I'll be damned, I murmured. I shaded my eyes and stood there looking out toward what he was seeing—dust clouds flatbed tumbleweed white sky—a whole lot of nothing.

—The writer is a conductor, he drawled.

I wandered off, leaving him to expound on the twisting track of the mind's convolutions. Words that lingered then fell away as I boarded a train of my own that dropped me off fully clothed in my rumpled bed.

Opening my eyes, I rose, staggered into the bathroom, and splashed cold water on my face in one swift motion. I slid on my boots, fed the cats, grabbed my watch cap and old black coat, and headed out toward the road many times taken, across the wide avenue to Bedford Street and a small Greenwich Village café.

Café 'Ino

+ ㅤ⇥◈⇤ +

F OUR CEILING FANS spinning overhead.
The Café 'Ino is empty save for the Mexican cook
and a kid named Zak who sets me up with my usual order
of brown toast, a small dish of olive oil, and black coffee. I
huddle in my corner, still wearing my coat and watch cap. It's
9 a.m. I'm the first one here. Bedford Street as the city awakens. My table, flanked by the coffee machine and the front
window, affords me a sense of privacy, where I withdraw into
my own atmosphere.

The end of November. The small café feels chilly. So why
are the fans turning? Maybe if I stare at them long enough my
mind will turn as well.

It's not so easy writing about nothing.

I can hear the sound of the cowpoke's slow and authori-
tative drawl. I scribble his phrase on my napkin. How can
a fellow get your goat in a dream and then have the grit
to linger? I feel a need to contradict him, not just a quick
retort but with action. I look down at my hands. I'm sure I

could write endlessly about nothing. If only I had nothing to say.

After a time Zak places a fresh cup before me.

—This is the last time I'll be serving you, he says solemnly.

He makes the best coffee around, so I am sad to hear.

—Why? Are you going somewhere?

—I'm going to open a beach café on the boardwalk in Rockaway Beach.

—A beach café! What do you know, a beach café!

I stretch my legs and watch as Zak performs his morning tasks. He could not have known that I once harbored a dream of having a café of my own. I suppose it began with reading of the café life of the Beats, surrealists, and French symbolist poets. There were no cafés where I grew up but they existed within my books and flourished in my daydreams. In 1965 I had come to New York City from South Jersey just to roam around, and nothing seemed more romantic than just to sit and write poetry in a Greenwich Village café. I finally got the courage to enter Caffè Dante on MacDougal Street. Unable to afford a meal, I just drank coffee, but no one seemed to mind. The walls were covered with printed murals of the city of Florence and scenes from *The Divine Comedy*. The same scenes remain to this day, discolored by decades of cigarette smoke.

In 1973 I moved into an airy whitewashed room with a small kitchen on that same street, just two short blocks from Caffè Dante. I could crawl out the front window and sit on the fire escape at night and clock the action that flowed through the Kettle of Fish, one of Jack Kerouac's frequented bars.

There was a small stall around the corner on Bleecker Street where a young Moroccan sold fresh rolls, anchovies packed in salt, and bunches of fresh mint. I would rise early and buy supplies. I'd boil water and pour it into a teapot stuffed with mint and spend the afternoons drinking tea, smoking bits of hashish, and rereading the tales of Mohammed Mrabet and Isabelle Eberhardt.

Café 'Ino didn't exist back then. I would sit by a low window in Caffè Dante that looked out into the corner of a small alley, reading Mrabet's *The Beach Café*. A young fish-seller named Driss meets a reclusive, uncongenial codger who has a so-called café with only one table and one chair on a rocky stretch of shore near Tangier. The slow-moving atmosphere surrounding the café so captivated me that I desired nothing more than to dwell within it. Like Driss, I dreamed of opening a place of my own. I thought about it so much I could almost enter it: the Café Nerval, a small haven where poets and travelers might find the simplicity of asylum.

I imagined threadbare Persian rugs on wide-planked floors, two long wood tables with benches, a few smaller tables, and an oven for baking bread. Every morning I would wipe down the tables with aromatic tea like they do in Chinatown. No music no menus. Just silence black coffee olive oil fresh mint brown bread. Photographs adorning the walls: a melancholic portrait of the café's namesake, and a smaller image of the forlorn poet Paul Verlaine in his overcoat, slumped before a glass of absinthe.

In 1978 I came into a little money and was able to pay a security deposit toward the lease of a one-story building on

East Tenth Street. It had once been a beauty parlor but stood empty save for three white ceiling fans and a few folding chairs. My brother, Todd, supervised repairs and we white-washed the walls and waxed the wood floors. Two wide sky-lights flooded the space with light. I spent several days sitting beneath them at a card table, drinking deli coffee and plotting my next move. I would need funds for a new toilet and a coffee machine and yards of white muslin to drape the windows. Practical things that usually receded into the music of my imagination.

In the end I was obliged to abandon my café. Two years before, I had met the musician Fred Sonic Smith in Detroit. It was an unexpected encounter that slowly altered the course of my life. My yearning for him permeated everything—my poems, my songs, my heart. We endured a parallel existence, shuttling back and forth between New York and Detroit, brief rendezvous that always ended in wrenching separations. Just as I was mapping out where to install a sink and a coffee machine, Fred implored me to come and live with him in Detroit. Nothing seemed more vital than to join my love, whom I was destined to marry. Saying good-bye to New York City and the aspirations it contained, I packed what was most precious and left all else behind—in the wake, forfeiting my deposit and my café. I didn't mind. The solitary hours I'd spent drinking coffee at the card table, awash in the radiance of my café dream, were enough for me.

Some months before our first wedding anniversary Fred told me that if I promised to give him a child he would first take me anywhere in the world. Without hesitation I chose

Saint-Laurent-du-Maroni, a border town in northwest French Guiana, on the North Atlantic coast of South America. I had long wished to see the remains of the French penal colony where hard-core criminals were once shipped before being transferred to Devil's Island. In *The Thief's Journal* Jean Genet had written of Saint-Laurent as hallowed ground and of the inmates incarcerated there with devotional empathy. In his *Journal* he wrote of a hierarchy of inviolable criminality, a manly saintliness that flowered at its crown in the terrible reaches of French Guiana. He had ascended the ladder toward them: reform school, petty thief, and three-time loser; but as he was sentenced the prison he'd held in such reverence was closed, deemed inhumane, and the last living inmates were returned to France. Genet served his time in Fresnes Prison, bitterly lamenting that he would never attain the grandeur that he aspired to. Devastated, he wrote: *I am shorn of my infamy.*

Genet was imprisoned too late to join the brotherhood he had immortalized in his work. He was left outside the prison walls like the lame boy in Hamelin who was denied entrance into a child's paradise because he arrived too late to enter its doors.

At seventy, he was reportedly in poor health and most likely would never go there himself. I envisioned bringing him its earth and stone. Though often amused by my quixotic notions, Fred did not make light of this self-imposed task. He agreed without argument. I wrote William Burroughs, whom I had known since my early twenties. Close to Genet and possessing his own romantic sensibility, William

promised to assist me in delivering the stones at the proper
time.

Preparing for our trip Fred and I spent our days in the
Detroit Public Library studying the history of Suriname
and French Guiana. We looked forward to exploring a place
neither of us had been, and we mapped the first stages of
our journey: the only available route was a commercial flight
to Miami, then a local airline to take us through Barbados,
Grenada, and Haiti, finally disembarking in Suriname. We
would have to find our way to a river town outside the capital city and once there hire a boat to cross the Maroni River
into French Guiana. We plotted our steps late into the night.
Fred bought maps, khaki clothing, traveler's checks, and a
compass; cut his long, lank hair; and bought a French dictionary. When he embraced an idea he looked at things from

every angle. He did not read Genet, however. He left that up to me.

Fred and I flew on a Sunday to Miami and stayed for two nights in a roadside motel called Mr. Tony's. There was a small black-and-white television bolted near the low ceiling that worked by inserting quarters. We ate red beans and yellow rice in Little Havana and visited Crocodile World. The short stay readied us for the extreme heat we were about to face. Our trip was a lengthy process, as all passengers were obliged to deplane in Grenada and Haiti while the hold was searched for smuggled goods. We finally landed in Suriname at dawn; a handful of young soldiers armed with automatic weapons waited as we were herded into a bus that transported us to a vetted hotel. The first anniversary of a military coup that overthrew the democratic government on February 25,

1980, was looming: an anniversary only a few days before our own. We were the only Americans around and they assured us we were under their protection.

After we spent a few days bending in the heat of the capital city of Paramaribo, a guide drove us 150 kilometers to the town of Albina on the west bank of the river bordering French Guiana. The pink sky was veined in lightning. Our guide found a young boy who agreed to take us across the Maroni River by pirogue, a long, dugout canoe. Packed prudently, our bags were quite manageable. We pushed off in a light rain that swiftly escalated into a torrential downpour. The boy handed me an umbrella and warned us not to trail our fingers in the water surrounding the low-slung wooden boat. I suddenly noticed the river teeming with tiny black fish. Piranha! He laughed as I quickly withdrew my hand.

In an hour or so the boy dropped us off at the foot of a muddy embankment. He dragged his pirogue onto land and joined some workers taking cover beneath a length of black oil-cloth stretched over four wooden posts. They seemed amused by our momentary confusion and pointed us in the direction of the main road. As we struggled up a slippery knoll, the calypso beat of Mighty Swallow's "Soca Dance" wafting from a boom box was all but drowned by the insistent rain. Completely drenched we tramped through the empty town, finally taking cover in what seemed to be the only existing bar. The bartender served me coffee and Fred had a beer. Two men were drinking calvados. The afternoon slipped by as I consumed several cups of coffee while Fred engaged in a broken French-English conversation with a leathery-skinned fellow who presided over the nearby turtle reserves. As the rains subsided, the owner of the local hotel appeared offering his services. Then a younger, sulkier version emerged to take our bags, and we followed them along a muddied trail down a hill to our new lodgings. We had not even booked a hotel and yet a room awaited us.

The Hôtel Galibi was spartan yet comfortable. A small bottle of watered-down cognac and two plastic cups were set on the dresser. Spent, we slept, even as the returning rain beat relentlessly upon the corrugated tin roof. There were bowls of coffee waiting for us when we awoke. The morning sun was strong. I left our clothes to dry on the patio. There was a small chameleon melting into the khaki color of Fred's shirt. I spread the contents of our pockets on a small table. A wilting map, damp receipts, dismembered fruits, Fred's ever-present guitar picks.

Around noon a cement worker drove us outside the ruins of the Saint-Laurent prison. There were a few stray chickens scratching in the dirt and an overturned bicycle, but no one seemed to be around. Our driver entered with us through a low stone archway and then just slipped away. The compound had the air of a tragically defunct boomtown—one that had mined the souls and shipped their husks to Devil's Island. Fred and I moved about in alchemical silence, mindful not to disturb the reigning spirits.

In search of the right stones I entered the solitary cells, examining the faded graffiti tattooing the walls. Hairy balls, cocks with wings, the prime organ of Genet's angels. Not here, I thought, not yet. I looked around for Fred. He had maneuvered through the high grasses and overgrown palms, finding a small graveyard. I saw him paused before a headstone that read *Son your mother is praying for you.* He stood there for a long time looking up at the sky. I left him alone and inspected the outbuildings, finally choosing the earthen floor of the mass cell to gather the stones. It was a dank place the size of a small airplane hangar. Heavy, rusted chains were anchored into the walls illuminated by slim shafts of light. Yet there was still some scent of life: manure, earth, and an array of scuttling beetles.

I dug a few inches seeking stones that might have been pressed by the hard-calloused feet of the inmates or the soles of heavy boots worn by the guards. I carefully chose three and put them in an oversized Gitanes matchbox, leaving the bits of earth clinging to them intact. Fred offered his handkerchief to wipe the dirt from my hands, and then shaking it out he made a little sack for the matchbox. He placed it in my hands, the first step toward placing them in the hands of Genet.

We didn't stay long in Saint-Laurent. We went seaside but the turtle reserves were off-limits, as they were spawning. Fred spent a lot of time in the bar, talking to the fellows. Despite the heat, Fred wore a shirt and a tie. The men seemed to respect him, regarding him without irony. He had that effect on other men. I was content just sitting on a crate outside the bar staring down an empty street I had never seen and might never see again. Prisoners once were paraded on this same stretch. I closed my eyes, imagining them dragging their chains in the intense heat, cruel entertainment for the few inhabitants of a dusty, forsaken town.

As I walked from the bar to the hotel I saw no dogs or children at play and no women. For the most part I kept to myself. Occasionally I caught glimpses of the maid, a barefoot girl with long, dark hair, scurrying about the hotel. She smiled and gestured but spoke no English, always in motion. She tidied our room and took our clothes from the patio, then washed and pressed them. In gratitude I gave her one of my bracelets, a gold chain with a four-leaf clover, which I spotted dangling from her wrist as we departed.

There were no trains in French Guiana, no rail service at all. The fellow from the bar had found us a driver, who carried himself like an extra in *The Harder They Come*. He wore aviator sunglasses, cocked cap, and a leopard-print shirt. We arranged a price and he agreed to drive us the 268 kilometers to Cayenne. He drove a beat-up tan Peugeot and insisted our bags stay with him in the front seat as chickens were normally transported in the trunk. We drove along Route Nationale through the continuing rains interrupted by fleeting sun, listening to reggae songs on a station riddled with static. When the signal was lost the driver switched to a cassette by a band called Queen Cement.

Every once in a while I untied the handkerchief to look at the Gitanes matchbox with its silhouette of a Gypsy posturing with her tambourine in a swirl of indigo-tinged smoke. But I did not open it. I pictured a small yet triumphal moment passing the stones to Genet. Fred held my hand as we wordlessly wound through dense forests, and passed short, sturdy Amerindians with broad shoulders, balancing iguanas squarely on their heads. We traveled through tiny communes like Tonate that had just a few houses and one six-foot crucifix. We asked the driver to stop. He got out and examined his tires. Fred took a photograph of the sign that read *Tonate. Population 9,* and I said a little prayer.

We were unfettered by any particular desire or expectation. The primary mission accomplished, we had no ultimate destination, no hotel reservations; we were free. But as we approached Kourou we sensed a shift. We were entering a military zone and hit a checkpoint. The driver's identity card was inspected and after an interminable stretch of silence we were ordered to get out of the car. Two officers searched the front and back seats, finding a switchblade with a broken spring in the glove box. That can't be so bad, I thought, but as they knocked on the back of the trunk our driver became markedly agitated. Dead chickens? Maybe drugs. They circled around the car, and then asked him for the keys. He threw them in a shallow ravine and bolted but was swiftly wrestled to the ground. I glanced sidelong at Fred. He'd had trouble with the law as a young man and had always been wary of authority. He betrayed no emotion and I followed his lead.

They opened the trunk of the car. Inside was a man who looked to be in his early thirties curled up like a slug in a rusting conch shell. He seemed terrified as they poked him with a rifle and ordered him to get out. We were all herded to the police headquarters, put in separate rooms, and interrogated in French. I knew enough to answer their simplest questions, and Fred, installed in another room, conversed in bits of barroom French. Suddenly the commander arrived and we were

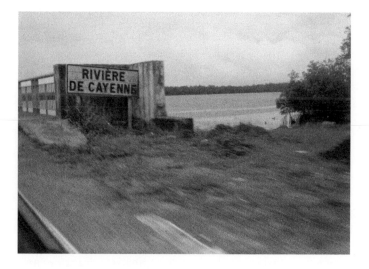

brought before him. He was barrel-chested with dark, sad eyes and a thick mustache that dominated his careworn face browned by sun. Fred quickly took stock of things. I slipped into the role of compliant female, for in this obscure annex of the Foreign Legion it was definitely a man's world. I watched silently as the human contraband, stripped and shackled, was led away. Fred was ordered into the commander's office. He turned and looked at me. Stay calm was the message telegraphed from his pale blue eyes.

An officer brought in our bags, and another wearing white gloves went through everything. I sat there holding the handkerchief sack. I was relieved I was not asked to surrender it, for as an object it had already manifested a sacredness second only to my wedding ring. I sensed no danger but counseled myself to hold my tongue. An interrogator brought me a black coffee on an oval tray with an inlay of a blue butterfly and entered the commander's office. I could see Fred's profile. After a time they all came out. They seemed in amiable spirits. The commander gave Fred a manly embrace and we were placed in a private car. Neither of us said a word as we pulled into the capital city of Cayenne, situated on the banks of the estuary of the Cayenne River. Fred had the address of a hotel given to him by the commander. We were dropped off at the foot of a hill, the end of the line. It's somewhere up there, he motioned, and we carried our bags up the stone steps that led to the path to our next dwelling place.

—What did you two talk about? I asked.

—I really can't say for sure, he only spoke French.

—How did you communicate?

—Cognac.

Fred seemed deep in thought.

—I know that you are concerned about the fate of the driver, he said, but it's out of our hands. He placed us in real jeopardy and in the end my concern was for you.

—Oh, I wasn't afraid.

—Yes, he said, that's why I was concerned.

The hotel was to our liking. We drank French brandy from a paper sack and slept wrapped in layers of mosquito netting. There was no glass in the windows—neither in our hotel nor in the houses below. No air conditioners, just the wind and sporadic rain providing relief from the heat and dust. We listened to the Coltrane-like cries of simultaneous saxophones wafting from the cement tenements. In the morning we explored Cayenne. The town square was more of a trapezoid, tiled black-and-white and framed with high palms. It was Carnival time, unbeknownst to us, and the city was all but deserted. The city hall, a nineteenth-century whitewashed French colonial, was closed for the holiday. We were drawn to a seemingly abandoned church. When we opened the gate, rust came off on our hands. We dropped coins into an old Chock Full O' Nuts can with the slogan *The Heavenly Coffee* placed at the entrance for donations. Dust mites dispersed in beams of light then formed a halo above an angel of glowing alabaster; icons of saints were trapped behind fallen debris, rendered unrecognizable under layers of dark lacquer.

All things seemed to flow in slow motion. Although strangers we moved about unnoticed. Men haggled over a price for a live iguana with a long, slapping tail. Overcrowded ferries departed for Devil's Island. Calypso music poured from a mammoth disco in the shape of an armadillo. There were a few small souvenir stands with identical fare: thin, red blankets made in China and metallic blue raincoats. But mostly there were lighters, all kinds of lighters, with images of parrots, spaceships, and men of the Foreign Legion. There was nothing much to keep one there and we thought of applying for a visa to Brazil, having our pictures taken by a mysterious Chinaman called Dr. Lam. His studio was filled with large-format cameras, broken tripods, and rows of herbal remedies in large glass vials. We picked up our visa pictures yet we stayed in Cayenne until our anniversary as if bewitched.

On the last Sunday of our journey, women in bright dresses and men in top hats were celebrating the end of Carnival. Following their makeshift parade on foot, we ended up at Rémire-Montjoly, a commune southeast of the city. The revelers dispersed. Rémire was fairly uninhabited and Fred and I stood mesmerized by the emptiness of the long, sweeping beaches. It was a perfect day for our anniversary and I couldn't help thinking it was the perfect spot for a beach café. Fred went on before me, whistling to a black dog somewhat up ahead. There was no sign of his master. Fred threw a stick into the water and the dog fetched it. I knelt down in the sand and sketched out plans for an imaginary café with my finger.

An unwinding spool of obscure angles, a glass of tea, an opened journal, and a round metal table balanced with an empty matchbook. Cafés. Le Rouquet in Paris, Café Josephinum in Vienna, Bluebird Coffeeshop in Amsterdam, Ice Café in Sydney, Café Aquí in Tucson, Wow Café at Point Loma, Caffe Trieste in North Beach, Caffè del Professore in Naples, Café Uroxen in Uppsala, Lula Cafe in Logan Square, Lion Cafe in Shibuya, and Café Zoo in the Berlin train station.

The café I'll never realize, the cafés I'll never know. As if reading my mind, Zak wordlessly brings me a fresh cup.

—When will your café open? I ask him.

—When the weather changes, hopefully early spring. A couple of buddies and me. We have to get some things together, and we need a little more capital to buy some equipment.

I ask him how much, offer to invest.

—Are you sure, he asks, somewhat surprised, for in truth we don't know each other very well, complicit solely through our daily coffee ritual.

—Yeah, I'm sure. I once thought about having a café of my own.

—You'll have free coffee for the rest of your life.

— God willing, I say.

I sit before Zak's peerless coffee. Overhead the fans spin, feigning the four directions of a traversing weather vane. High winds, cold rain, or the threat of rain; a looming continuum of calamitous skies that subtly permeate my entire being. Without noticing, I slip into a light yet lingering malaise. Not a depression, more like a fascination for melancholia, which I turn in my hand as if it were a small planet, streaked in shadow, impossibly blue.

Roberto Bolaño's chair, Blanes, Spain

Changing Channels

I CLIMB THE STAIRS to my room with its lone skylight, a worktable, a bed, my brother's Navy flag, bundled and tied by his own hand, and a small armchair draped in threadbare linen set back in the corner by the window. I shed my coat, time to get on with it. I have a fine desk but I prefer to work from my bed, as if I'm a convalescent in a Robert Louis Stevenson poem. An optimistic zombie propped by pillows, producing pages of somnambulistic fruit—not quite ripe or overripe. Occasionally I write directly into my small laptop, sheepishly glancing over to the shelf where my typewriter with its antiquated ribbon sits next to an obsolete Brother word processor. A nagging allegiance prevents me from scrapping either of them. Then there are the scores of notebooks, their contents calling—confession, revelation, endless variations of the same paragraph—and piles of napkins scrawled with incomprehensible rants. Dried-out ink bottles, encrusted nibs, cartridges for pens long gone, mechanical pencils emptied of lead. Writer's debris.

I skip Thanksgiving, dragging my malaise through December, with a prolonged period of enforced solitude, though sadly without crystalline effect. In the mornings I feed the cats, mutely gather my things, and then make my way across Sixth Avenue to Café 'Ino, sitting at my usual table in the corner drinking coffee, pretending to write, or writing in earnest, with more or less the same questionable results. I avoid social commitments and aggressively arrange to spend the holidays alone. On Christmas Eve I present the cats with catnip-enhanced mice toys and exit aimlessly into the vacant night, finally landing near the Chelsea Hotel at a movie theater offering a late showing of *The Girl with the Dragon Tattoo*. I buy my ticket and a large black coffee and a bag of organic popcorn at the corner deli, and then settle in my seat in the back of the theater. Just me and a score of slackers, comfortably isolated from the world, attaining our own brand of holiday well-being, no gifts, no Christ child, no tinsel or mistletoe, only a sense of complete freedom. I liked the looks of the movie. I had already seen the Swedish version without subtitles but hadn't read the books, so now I would be able to piece together the plot and lose myself in the bleak Swedish landscape.

It was after midnight when I walked home. It was a relatively mild night and I felt an overriding sense of calm that slowly bled into a desire to be home in my own bed. There were few signs of Christmas on my empty street, just some stray tinsel embedded in the wet leaves. I said goodnight to the cats stretched out on the couch, and as I headed upstairs to my room, Cairo, an Abyssinian runt with a coat the color of the pyramids, followed at my heels. There I unlocked a glass cabinet and carefully unwrapped a Flemish crèche consisting of Mary and Joseph, two oxen, and a babe in his cradle, and arranged them on the top of my bookcase. Carved from bone, they had developed a golden patina through two centuries of age. How sad, I thought, admiring the oxen, that they are only displayed at Christmastide. I wished the babe a happy birthday and removed the books and papers from my bed, brushed my teeth, turned down the coverlet, and let Cairo sleep on my stomach.

New Year's Eve was pretty much the same story with no particular resolution. As thousands of drunken revelers disbursed in Times Square, my little Abyssinian circled the floor with me as I paced, wrestling with a poem I was aiming to finish to usher in the New Year, in homage to the great Chilean writer Roberto Bolaño. In reading his *Amulet* I noted a passing reference to the hecatomb—an ancient ritualistic slaughter of one hundred oxen. I decided to write a hecatomb for him—a hundred-line poem. It was to be a way to thank him for spending the last stretch of his brief life racing to finish his masterpiece, *2666*. If only he could have been given special dispensation, been allowed to live. For *2666* seemed set up to go on forever, as long as he wished to write. Such a sad portion of injustice served to beautiful Bolaño, to die at the height of his powers at fifty years old. The loss of him and his unwritten denying us at least one secret of the world.

As the last hours of the year ticked away I wrote and

rewrote then recited the lines aloud. But as the ball dropped in Times Square I realized I had written 101 lines by mistake and couldn't face figuring which one to sacrifice. It also occurred to me that I was inadvertently invoking the slaughter of the kin of the glowing bone oxen watching over the Christ child in the crèche on my bookcase. Did it matter the ritual was in word only? Did it matter my oxen were carved in bone? After a few minutes of looping rumination I temporarily laid aside my hecatomb and switched over to a movie. While watching *The Gospel According to Saint Matthew,* I noticed that Pasolini's young Mary resembled the equally young Kristen Stewart. I placed it on pause and made a cup of Nescafé, slipped on a hoodie, and went outside and sat on my stoop. It was a cold, clear night. A few drunken kids, probably from New Jersey, called out to me.

—What the fuck time is it?

—Time to puke, I answered.

—Don't say that around her, she's been doing it all night.

She was a barefoot redhead wearing a sequined minidress.

—Where's her coat? Should I get her a sweater?

—She's all right.

—Well, happy New Year.

—Did it happen yet?

—Yeah, about forty-eight minutes ago.

They hastily disappeared around the corner, leaving a deflating silver balloon hovering above the sidewalk. I walked over to rescue it just as it limply touched ground.

—That about sums it up, I said aloud.

·

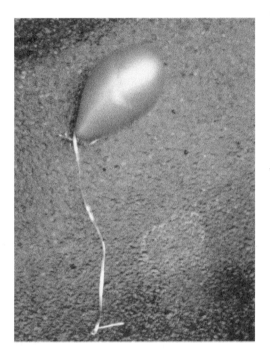

Snow. Just enough snow to scrape off my boots. Donning my black coat and watch cap, I trudge across Sixth Avenue like a faithful postman, delivering myself daily before the orange awning of Café 'Ino. As I labor yet again on variations of the hecatomb poem for Bolaño, my morning sojourn lengthens well into the afternoon. I order Tuscan bean soup, brown bread with olive oil, and more black coffee. I count the lines of the envisioned one-hundred-line poem, now three lines shy. Ninety-seven clues but nothing solved, another cold-case poem.

I should get out of here, I am thinking, out of the city. But where would I go that I would not drag my seemingly incurable lethargy along with me, like the worn canvas sack of an angst-driven teenage hockey player? And what would become of my mornings in my little corner and my late nights scanning the TV channels with an obstinate channel changer that needed to be tapped several times into awareness?

—I changed your batteries, I say pleadingly, so change the damn channel.

—Aren't you supposed to be working?

—I'm watching my crime shows, I murmur unapologetically, not a trifling thing. Yesterday's poets are today's detectives. They spend a life sniffing out the hundredth line, wrapping up a case, and limping exhausted into the sunset. They entertain and sustain me. Linden and Holder. Goren and Eames. Horatio Caine. I walk with them, adopt their ways, suffer their failures, and consider their movements long after an episode ends, whether in real time or rerun.

The haughtiness of a small handheld device! Perhaps I should be concerned as to why I have conversations with inanimate objects. But as it has been part of my waking life since I was a child I have no problem with that. What really bothers me is why I have spring fever in January. Why the coils of my brain seem dusted with a vortex of pollens. Sighing, I meander around my room scanning for cherished things to make certain they haven't been drawn into that half-dimensional place where things just disappear. Things beyond socks or glasses: Kevin Shields's EBow, a snapshot of a sleepy-faced Fred, a Burmese offering bowl, Margot Fonteyn's ballet slippers, a misshapen clay giraffe formed by my daughter's hands. I pause before my father's chair.

My father sat at his desk, in this chair, for decades, writing checks, filling out tax forms, and working fervently on his own system for handicapping horses. Bundles of *The Morning Telegraph* were stacked against the wall. A journal wrapped in jeweler's cloth, noting wins and losses from imaginary bets, kept in the left-hand drawer. No one dared touch it. He never spoke about his system but he labored over it religiously. He was neither a betting man nor had the resources to bet. He was a factory man with a mathematical curiosity, handicapping heaven, searching for patterns, and a portal of probability opening up onto the meaning of life.

I admired my father from a distance. He seemed dreamily

estranged from our domestic life. He was kind and open-minded, having an inner elegance that set him apart from our neighbors. Yet he never placed himself above them. He was a decent man who did his job. A runner when young, a superb athlete and acrobat. In World War II he was stationed in the jungles of New Guinea and the Philippines. Though he opposed violence he was a patriotic soldier, but the atomic bombings of Hiroshima and Nagasaki broke his heart and he mourned the cruelty and weakness of our material society.

My father worked the night shift. He slept in the day and left while we were at school and returned late at night when we were sleeping. On the weekends we were obliged to give him some privacy as he had little time for himself. He would sit in his favorite chair watching baseball with the family Bible on his lap. He often read passages aloud attempting to provoke discussion. Question everything, he would tell us. Through the seasons he dressed in a black sweatshirt, worn dark pants rolled up to his calves, and moccasins. He was never without moccasins, as my sister, my brother, and I would save our coins throughout the year to buy him a new pair every Christmas. In his last years he fed the birds so consistently, in all manner of weather, that they came to him when he called, alighting upon his shoulders.

When he died I inherited his desk and chair. Inside the desk was a cigar box containing canceled checks, nail clippers, a broken Timex watch, and a yellowed newspaper cutting of my beaming self in 1959, being awarded third prize in a national safety-poster contest. I still keep the box in the top right-hand drawer. His sturdy wooden chair that my mother irreverently decorated with decals of burnished roses is against the wall facing my bed. A cigarette burn scarring the seat gives the chair a feel of life. I run my finger over the burn, conjuring his soft pack of Camel straights. The same brand John Wayne smoked, with the golden dromedary and palm tree silhouette on the pack, evoking exotic places and the French Foreign Legion.

You should sit on me, his chair urges, but I can't bring myself to do it. We were never allowed to sit at my father's desk, so I don't use his chair, just keep it near. I did once sit in the chair of Roberto Bolaño when visiting his family's home in the seacoast town of Blanes, in northeast Spain. I immediately regretted it. I had taken four pictures of it, a simple chair that he superstitiously carried with him from one dwelling place to another. It was his writing chair. Did I think that sitting in it would make me a better writer? With a shiver of self-admonishment, I wipe dust from the glass protecting my Polaroid of that same chair.

I go downstairs, then carry two full boxes back to my room and dump the contents onto my bed. Time to face up to the last mail of the year. First I sift through brochures for such things like time-sharing condos in Jupiter Beach, unique and lucrative methods of senior-citizen investing, and full-color illustrated packets on how to cash in my frequent-flier miles for exciting gifts. All left unopened for the recycle bin yet producing a pang of guilt, considering the amount of trees necessary to churn out this mound of unsolicited crap. On the other hand there are some good catalogues offering nineteenth-century German manuscripts, memorabilia of the Beat generation, and rolls of vintage Belgium linen to stack by the toilet for future diversion. I saunter past my coffeemaker that sits like a huddled monk on a small metal cabinet storing my porcelain cups. Patting its head, avoiding eye contact with the typewriter and channel changer, I reflect on how some inanimate objects are so much nicer than others.

Clouds move past the sun. A milky light pervades the skylight and spreads into my room. I have a vague sense of being summoned. Something is calling to me, so I stay very still, like

Detective Sarah Linden, in the opening credits of *The Killing,* on the edge of a marsh at twilight. I slowly advance toward my desk and lift the top. I don't open it very often, as some precious things hold memories too painful to revisit. Thankfully I need not look inside, as my hand knows the size, texture, and location of each object it contains. Reaching beneath my one childhood dress, I remove a small metal box with tiny perforated holes in the cover. I take a deep breath before I open it, as I harbor the irrational fear that the sacred contents may dissipate when confronted with a sudden onrush of air. But no, everything is intact. Four small hooks, three feathered fishing lures, and another composed of soft purple transparent rubber, like a Juicy Fruit or a Swedish Fish, shaped like a comma with a spiraled tail.

—Hello, Curly, I whisper, and am instantly gladdened.

I lightly tap him with my fingertip. I feel the warmth of recognition, memories of time spent fishing with Fred in a rowboat on Lake Ann in northern Michigan. Fred taught me to cast and gave me a portable Shakespeare rod whose parts fit like arrows in a carrying case shaped like a quiver. Fred was a graceful and patient caster with an arsenal of lures, bait, and weights. I had my archer rod and this same little box holding Curly—my secret ally. My little lure! How could I have forgotten our hours of sweet divination? How well he served me when cast into unfathomable waters, performing his persuasive tango with slippery bass that I later scaled and panfried for Fred.

The king is dead, no fishing today.

Gently placing Curly back in my desk, I tackle my mail with new resolve—bills, petitions, invitations for gala events past, imminent jury duty. Then I swiftly set aside one item of particular interest—a plain brown envelope stamped and sealed with wax with the raised letters CDC. I hurry to a locked cabinet, choosing a slim bone-handled letter opener, the only proper way to open a precious piece of correspondence from the Continental Drift Club. The envelope contains a small red card with the number twenty-three stenciled in black and a handwritten invitation to deliver a talk of my choosing at the semi-annual convention to take place in mid-January in Berlin.

I experience a wealth of excitement, but I have no time to lose, as the letter is dated some weeks ago. I hastily write a response in the affirmative, then rummage through my desk for a sheet of stamps, grab my cap and coat, and drop the letter into the mailbox. Then I cross over Sixth Avenue to 'Ino. It is late afternoon and the café is empty. At my table I attempt to write a list of items to take on my journey but am immersed in a particular reverie taking me back through a handful of years through the cities of Bremen, Reykjavík, Jena, and soon Berlin, to meet again with the brethren of the Continental Drift Club.

Formed in the early 1980s by a Danish meteorologist, the CDC is an obscure society serving as an independent branch of the earth-science community. Twenty-seven members, scattered across the hemispheres, have pledged their dedication to *the perpetuation of remembrance,* specifically in regard to Alfred Wegener, who pioneered the theory of continental drift. The bylaws require discretion, attendance at the biannual conferences, a certain amount of applicable fieldwork, and a reasonable passion for the club's reading list. All are expected to keep abreast of the activities of the Alfred Wegener Institute for Polar and Marine Research, in the city of Bremerhaven in Lower Saxony.

I was granted membership into the CDC quite by accident. On the whole, members are primarily mathematicians, geologists, and theologians and are identified not by name but by a given number. I had written several letters to the Alfred Wegener Institute searching for a living heir in hopes of obtaining permission to photograph the great explorer's boots. One of my letters was forwarded to the secretary of the Continental Drift Club, and after a flurry of correspondence I was invited to attend their 2005 conference in Bremen, which coincided with the 125th anniversary of the great geoscientist's birth and thus the seventy-fifth of his death. I attended their panel discussions, a special screening at City 46 of *Research and Adventure on the Ice,* a documentary series containing rare footage of Wegener's 1929 and 1930 expeditions, and joined them for a private tour of the AWI facilities in nearby Bremerhaven. I am certain I didn't quite meet their criteria, but I suspect that after some deliberation they welcomed me due to my abundance of romantic enthusiasm. I became an official member in 2006, and was given the number twenty-three.

In 2007 we convened in Reykjavík, the largest city in Iceland. There was tremendous excitement, as that year certain members had planned to continue to Greenland for a CDC spinoff expedition. They formed a search party hoping to locate the cross that was placed in Wegener's memory in 1931 by his brother, Kurt. It had been constructed with iron rods some twenty feet high, marking his resting place, approximately 120 miles from the western edge of the Eismitte encampment where his companions last saw him. At the time its whereabouts were unknown. I wished I could go, as I knew the great cross, were it found, would inspire a remarkable photograph, but I hadn't the constitution required for such an endeavor. Yet I did stay on in Iceland, as Number Eighteen, a thoroughly robust Icelandic Grandmaster, surprised me by asking me to preside in his stead over a highly anticipated local chess match. My doing so would enable him to join the search party into the Greenland interior. In exchange I was promised three nights in the Hótel Borg and permission to photograph the table used in the 1972 chess match between Bobby Fischer and Boris Spassky, currently languishing in the basement of a local government facility. I was a bit wary about the idea of monitoring the match, seeing as my love of chess was purely aesthetic. But the opportunity to photograph the holy grail of modern chess was consolation enough for staying behind.

The following afternoon I arrived with my Polaroid camera just as the table was unceremoniously delivered to the tournament hall. It was quite modest in appearance but had been signed by the two great chess players. As it turned out my duties were actually quite light; it was a junior tournament and I was merely a figurehead. The winner of the match was a thirteen-year-old girl with golden hair. Our group was

photographed, after which I was given fifteen minutes to shoot
the table, unfortunately bathed in fluorescent light, anything
but photogenic. Our picture fared much better and graced the
cover of the morning newspaper, the famed table in the fore-
ground. After breakfast I went to the countryside with an old
friend and we rode sturdy Icelandic ponies. His was white
and mine was black, like two knights on a chessboard.

When I returned I received a call from a man identifying
himself as Bobby Fischer's bodyguard. He had been charged
with arranging a midnight meeting between Mr. Fischer and
myself in the closed dining room of the Hótel Borg. I was to
bring my bodyguard, and would not be permitted to bring
up the subject of chess. I consented to the meeting and then

crossed the square to the Club NASA where I recruited their head technician, a trustworthy fellow called Skills, to stand as my so-called bodyguard.

Bobby Fischer arrived at midnight in a dark hooded parka. Skills also wore a hooded parka. Bobby's bodyguard towered over us all. He waited with Skills outside the dining room. Bobby chose a corner table and we sat face-to-face. He began testing me immediately by issuing a string of obscene and racially repellent references that morphed into paranoiac conspiracy rants.

—Look, you're wasting your time, I said. I can be just as repellent as you, only about different subjects.

He sat staring at me in silence, when finally he dropped his hood.

—Do you know any Buddy Holly songs? he asked.

For the next few hours we sat there singing songs. Sometimes separately, often together, remembering about half the lyrics. At one point he attempted a chorus of "Big Girls Don't Cry" in falsetto and his bodyguard burst in excitedly.

—Is everything all right, sir?

—Yes, Bobby said.

—I thought I heard something strange.

—I was singing.

—Singing?

—Yes, singing.

And that was my meeting with Bobby Fischer, one of the greatest chess players of the twentieth century. He drew up his hood and left just before first light. I remained until the servers arrived to prepare the breakfast buffet. As I sat across from his chair I envisioned members of the Continental Drift Club still sleeping in their beds, or unable to sleep, filled with emotional expectation. In a few hours they would rise and embark into the icy Greenland interior in search of memory in the form of the great cross. It occurred to me, as the heavy curtains were opened and the morning light flooded the small dining area, that without a doubt we sometimes eclipse our own dreams with reality.

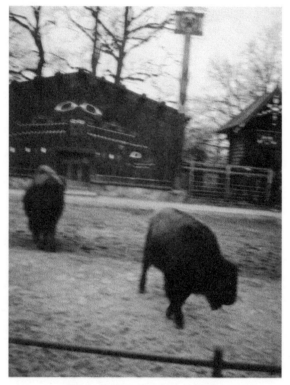

Bison, Zoologischer Garten, Berlin

Animal Crackers

I WAS LATE getting to Café 'Ino. My table in the corner was taken and a petulant possessiveness provoked me to go into the bathroom and wait it out. The bathroom was narrow and candlelit with a few fresh flowers in a small vase resting atop the toilet tank. Like a tiny Mexican chapel, one that you could piss in without feeling blasphemous. I left the door unlocked in case someone was in genuine need, waited for about ten minutes, and exited just as my table was freed. I wiped off the surface and ordered black coffee, brown toast, and olive oil. I wrote some notes on paper napkins for my forthcoming talk, then sat daydreaming about the angels in *Wings of Desire*. How wonderful it would be to meet an angel, I mused, but then I immediately realized I already had. Not an archangel like Saint Michael, but my human angel from Detroit, wearing an overcoat and no hat, with lank brown hair and eyes the color of water.

My travel to Germany was uneventful save that a security agent at the Newark Liberty Airport did not recognize my

1967 Polaroid as a camera and several minutes were wasted swiping it for explosive traces and sniffing the mute air within its bellows. A generic female voice repeated the same monotone instructions throughout the airport. *Report suspicious behavior. Report suspicious behavior.* As I approached the gate another woman's voice superimposed over hers.

—We are a nation of spies, she cried, all spying on one another. We used to help one another! We used to be kind!

She was carrying a faded tapestry duffel bag. She had a dusty appearance, as if she had emerged from the bowels of a foundry. When she set down her bag and walked away, passersby seemed visibly disturbed.

On the plane I watched consecutive episodes of the Danish crime drama *Forbrydelsen,* the blueprint for the American series *The Killing.* Detective Sarah Lund is the Danish prototype of Detective Sarah Linden. Both are singular women, both wear Fair Isle ski sweaters. Lund's are formfitting. Linden's are dumpy, but she wears hers as a moral vest. Lund is driven by ambition. Linden's obsessional nature is kin to her humanity. I feel her devotion to each terrible mission, the complexity of her vows, her need for solitary runs through the high grass of marshy fields. I sleepily track Lund in subtitle but my subconscious mind seeks out Linden, for even as a character in a television series she is dearer to me than most people. I wait for her every week, quietly fearing the day when *The Killing* will come to a finish and I will never see her again.

I follow Sarah Lund yet dream of Sarah Linden. I awake as *Forbrydelsen* abruptly ends and stare blankly at the screen of my personal player before passing unconscious into an incident room where a stream of briefings stakeouts and strange arcs empty into the rude smoke of isolation.

MY BERLIN HOTEL was in a renovated Bauhaus structure in the Mitte district of the former East Berlin. It had everything I needed and was in close proximity to the Pasternak café, which I discovered on a walk during a previous visit, at the height of an obsession with Mikhail Bulgakov's *The Master and Margarita*. I dropped my bags in my room and went directly to the café. The proprietress greeted me warmly and I sat at my same table beneath a photograph of Bulgakov. As before, I was taken by the Pasternak's old-world charm. The faded blue walls were dressed in photographs of the beloved Russian poets Anna Akhmatova and Vladimir Mayakovsky.

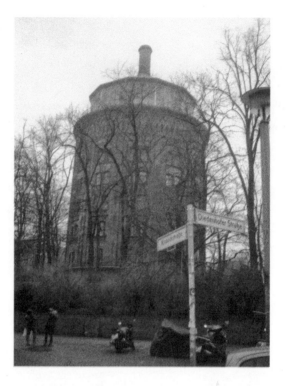

On the wide windowsill to my right sat an old Russian type-writer with its round Cyrillic keys, a perfect mate for my lonely Remington. I ordered the Happy Tsar—black sturgeon caviar served with a small shot of vodka and a glass of black coffee. Contented, I sat for quite a while mapping my talk on paper napkins, and then strolled the small park with the city's oldest water tower rising from its center.

On the morning of my lecture I rose early and had coffee, watermelon juice, and brown toast in my room. I hadn't wholly mapped out my talk, leaving a section open for improvisation and the whims of fate. I crossed the wide thoroughfare to the left of the hotel and passed through an ivy-covered gate, hoping to meditate on the coming event in the small church of St. Marien and St. Nikolai. The church was locked, but I found a secluded enclave with a statue of a boy reaching for a rose at the foot of the Madonna. Both possessed an enviable expressiveness, their marble skin worn by time and weather. I took several photographs of the boy and then returned to my room, curling up in a dark velvet armchair, drifting into a small patch of dreamless sleep.

At six I was spirited to a small lecture hall in a nearby location, like Holly Martins in *The Third Man*. There was nothing to distinguish our postwar meeting hall from others scattered around the former East Berlin. All twenty-seven CDC members were in attendance and the room vibrated with an air of expectancy. The proceedings opened with our theme song, a light, melancholic melody played on accordion by its composer, Number Seven, a gravedigger from the Umbrian town of Gubbio, where Saint Francis tamed the wolves. Number Seven was neither scholar nor trained musician but had the enviable distinction of being a distant relative of one of Wegener's original team.

Our moderator delivered his opening remarks, quoting from Friedrich Schiller's *The Favor of the Moment: Once more, then, we meet / In the circles of yore.*

He spoke at length concerning issues under current watch by the Alfred Wegener Institute, particularly the troubling decline of the breadth of the arctic ice sheets. After a while I felt my mind wandering and enviously glanced sidelong at my fellow members, most of whom appeared positively riveted.

As he droned on I predictably drifted, weaving a tragic tale: a girl in a sealskin coat watches helplessly as the surface of the ice cracks and cruelly separates her from her Prince Charming. She falls to her knees as he floats away. The compromised ice sheet tilts and he sinks into the Arctic Sea on the back of his faltering white Icelandic pony.

Our secretary presented the minutes of our last gathering in Jena, then cheerily announced the forthcoming AWI species of the month: *Sargassum muticum*—a brown Japanese seaweed distinguished by the way it drifts with the ocean currents. She also noted that our request to partner with the AWI and develop their species of the month into a full-color calendar was denied, which elicited a collective groan from the calendar enthusiasts. Next we were treated with a brief slide show of Number Nine's color landscape photography of the sites last visited by the CDC in eastern Germany, which sparked a proposal of using such images for a whole different calendar. I noticed my palms were sweating and without thinking wiped them dry with my napkin notes.

Finally, after a meandering introduction, I was invited to the podium. My talk was unfortunately introduced as *The Lost Moments of Alfred Wegener.* I explained that the title was actually the last, not the lost, moments, which led to a flurry of semantic bloodletting. I stood there facing the brethren with my limp stack of napkins as they laid out all the reasons why it should be one title as opposed to the other. Mercifully our moderator called them to order.

A hush fell over the room. I looked over toward the stoic portrait of Alfred Wegener for a bit of strength. I recounted the events leading to his last days: With a heavy heart but scientific resolve the great polar researcher left his beloved home in the spring of 1930 to lead a grueling, unprecedented scientific expedition into Greenland. His mission was to collect the necessary scientific data to prove his revolutionary hypothesis that the continents as we know them were formerly one great landmass that had broken apart and drifted to their present location. His theory was not only dismissed by the scientific community but ridiculed. And it was to be the research from this historic but ill-fated expedition that would eventually redeem him.

The weather was exceedingly harsh in late October of 1930. Hoarfrost formed like starry ferns on the cavern ceiling of their outpost. Alfred Wegener stepped out into the black night. He examined his conscience, assessing the situation in which his loyal colleagues had been drawn. Counting himself and a loyal Inuit guide named Rasmus Villumsen, there were five men, and the Eismitte station was low on food and supplies. Fritz Loewe, whom he deemed his equal in knowledge and leadership, had several frostbitten toes and could no longer stand. It was a 250-mile walk to the next supply station. Wegener reasoned that Villumsen and he were the sturdiest among them and most likely to survive the long trek and decided to leave on All Saints' Day.

At dawn on November 1, his fiftieth birthday, he placed his precious notebook inside his coat and optimistically set forth with his team of dogs and Inuit guide. He felt his own strength and the righteousness of his mission. But before long the clear weather shifted as the pair moved through a blistering whirlwind. Snowdrifts followed one another in waves. It was a spectacular vortex of swirling light. White way, white sea, white sky. What could be fairer than such a sight? The face of his wife framed in an immaculate oval of ice? He had given his heart twice, first to her and then to science. Alfred Wegener dropped to his knees. What did he then see? What images might he have projected upon God's arctic canvas?

My dramatic sense of unity with Wegener was such that I failed to notice a burgeoning disruption. An argument suddenly broke out concerning the validity of my premise.

—He didn't stumble in the snow.

—He died in his sleep.

—There's no real proof of that.

—His guide laid him to rest.

—That is conjecture.

—It's all conjecture.

—It's not a premise but a prognosis.

—You can't project such a thing.

—This isn't science, it's poetry!

I thought for a moment. What is mathematic and scientific theory but projection? I felt like a straw sinking in Berlin's River Spree.

What a disaster. Possibly the most antagonistic CDC talk to date.

—Here, here, said our moderator, I think it's time to call an intermission; perhaps a drink is in order.

—But shouldn't we hear the end of Twenty-three's talk? It was the compassionate gravedigger speaking.

I noticed some of the members were already gravitating

toward the refreshments and I quickly gained my composure. In measured tones to stake their attention:

—I suppose, I said, that we could let it stand that the last moments of Alfred Wegener have been lost.

Their hearty laughter far surpassed any private hopes of entertaining this endearingly stodgy bunch. All stood as I hastily crammed my scrawled napkins into my pocket and we adjourned to a large drawing room. Each of us had a glass of sherry while our moderator made some closing remarks. Then, as customary, our minister issued a prayer, ending in a moment of silent remembrance.

There were three vans to shuttle the members to their various hotels. As everyone left, the secretary asked me to sign the register.

—Could you give me a copy of your lecture so that I may at least attach it to the minutes? The opening remarks were lovely.

—There actually isn't anything written, I said.

—But your words, where were they to come from?

— I was sure to pluck them from the air.

She looked at me quite hard and said, Well, then, you must dip back into the air and retrieve something that I can insert into the minutes.

—Well, I do have some notes, I said, feeling for the napkins.

I had never had much conversation with our secretary. She was a widow from Liverpool, consistently dressed in a gray gabardine suit and flowered blouse. Her coat was of brown boiled wool, topped with a matching brown felt hat with an actual hatpin.

—I have an idea, I said. Come with me to the Pasternak café. We can sit at my favorite table beneath a photograph of Mikhail Bulgakov. Then I can tell you what I might have said and you can write it down.

—Bulgakov! Splendid! The vodkas are on me.

—You know, she added, standing before a large photograph of Wegener that was set on an easel, there is a resemblance between these two men.

—Maybe Bulgakov was a bit more handsome.

—And what a writer!

—A master.

—Yes, a master.

I stayed in Berlin a few more days, revisiting places where I had already been, taking pictures I had already shot. I had breakfast at the Café Zoo in the old train station. I was the

only customer and sat watching a worker scrape the familiar black silhouette of a camel off the heavy glass door, which
aroused my suspicion. Renovation? Closing? I paid my check
as if in farewell and crossed the road to the Zoological Garden, entering through the Elephant Gate. I stood before them,
somewhat comforted by their solid presence. Two elephants,
skillfully carved from Elbe sandstone toward the end of the
nineteenth century, kneeling peacefully, supporting two great
columns joined by a brightly painted curved roof. A bit of
India, a bit of Chinatown, welcoming the astonished visitor.

The zoo was also empty, absent of tourists or the usual
schoolchildren. My breath materialized before me and I buttoned my coat. There were some animals about and large
birds with tagged wings. A sudden haze drifted over the area.
I could just make out giraffes necking between the bare trees,
flamingos mating in the snow. Appearing from an unexpected American mist were log cabins, totem poles, bison in
Berlin. Wisent immobile shapes like the toys of a child giant.
Toys to deftly pluck up like animal crackers and deposit safely
into a crate decorated with friezes of bright circus trains carrying aardvarks, dodos, swift dromedaries, baby elephants, and
plastic dinosaurs. A box of mixed metaphors.

I asked around if Café Zoo was closing. No one seemed
aware that it still existed. The new central train station down-
graded the once important Zoo Station, now a regional railway station. Conversations switched to progress. Somewhere
in the back of my mind was the whereabouts of an old Café
Zoo receipt with the image of the black camel. I was tired.
I had a light dinner at my hotel. There was an episode of

Law & Order: Criminal Intent dubbed in German on the television. I turned down the sound and fell asleep with my coat on.

On my last morning I walked to the Dorotheenstadt Cemetery, with its block-long bullet-riddled walls, a bleak souvenir of World War II. Passing through the portal of angels, one can easily locate where Bertolt Brecht is buried. I noticed that some of the bullet holes had been filled in with white plaster since my last visit. The temperature was dropping and a light snow was falling. I sat before Brecht's grave and hummed the lullaby Mother Courage sings over the body of her daughter. I sat as the snow fell, imagining Brecht writing his play. Man gives us war. A mother profits from it and pays with her children; they fall one by one like wooden pins at the end of a bowling alley.

As I was leaving I took a photograph of one of the guardian angels. The bellows of my camera were wet with snow and somewhat crushed on the left side, which resulted in a black crescent blotting a portion of the wing. I took another of the wing in close-up. I envisioned printing it much larger on matte paper, and then I would write the words of the lullaby on its white curve. I wondered if these words caused Brecht to weep as he wrung the heart of the mother who was not as heartless as she would lead us to believe. I slipped the photographs into my pocket. My mother was real and her son was real. When he died she buried him. Now she is dead. Mother Courage and her children, my mother and her son. They are all stories now.

•

Guardian angel, Dorotheenstadt Cemetery

THOUGH RELUCTANT to go home I packed my things and flew to London to make my connection. My flight back to New York was delayed, which I took as a sign. I stood before the departure board and a further delay was posted. Impulsively I rebooked my ticket, took the Heathrow Express to Paddington Station, and from there I took a cab to Covent Garden and checked into a small favored hotel to watch detective shows.

My room was bright and cozy with a small terrace overlooking the London rooftops. I ordered tea and opened my journal, then immediately closed it. I am not here to work, I told myself, but to watch ITV3 mystery dramas, one after another late into the night. I had done this a few years before in the same hotel while ill; delirious nights dominated by a procession of clinically depressed, bad-tempered, heavy-drinking, opera-loving detective inspectors.

To warm up for the evening I watched a vintage episode of *The Saint,* delighted to follow Simon Templar in his white Volvo, tooling the dark recesses of London and as usual saving the world from imminent disaster. This time with a naïve platinum blonde in a pale cardigan and straight skirt, searching for her uncle—a brilliant professor of biochemistry—who has been kidnapped and is in the clutches of an equally brilliant though malevolent nuclear scientist. It was still early so after a second episode of *The Saint,* with an entirely different blonde in distress, I walked over to Charing Cross Road and roamed the bookstores. I bought a first edition of Sylvia Plath's *Winter Trees* and a copy of Ibsen's plays. I wound up reading *The Master Builder* until late afternoon before the fireplace in the hotel library. It was a bit warm and I was nodding off when a man in a tweed overcoat tapped my shoulder, asking if I might be the journalist he was supposed to be meeting.

—No, sorry.

—Reading Ibsen?

—Yes, *The Master Builder.*

—Hmmm, lovely play but fraught with symbolism.

—I hadn't noticed, I said.

He stood before the fire for a moment then shook his head and left. Personally, I'm not much for symbolism. I never get it. Why can't things be just as they are? I never thought to psychoanalyze Seymour Glass or sought to break down "Desolation Row." I just wanted to get lost, become one with somewhere else, slip a wreath on a steeple top solely because I wished it.

Returning to my room, I bundled up and had tea on the balcony. Then I settled in, giving myself over to the likes of Morse, Lewis, Frost, Wycliffe, and Whitechapel—detective inspectors whose moodiness and obsessive natures mirrored my own. When they had a chop, I ordered same from room service. If they had a drink, I consulted the minibar. I adopted their manner whether entirely engrossed or dispassionately disconnected.

In between shows were upcoming scenes from the highly anticipated *Cracker* marathon, to be aired on ITV3 the following Tuesday. Though *Cracker* wasn't the standard detective show it stands among my favorites. Robbie Coltrane portrays Fitz, the foul-mouthed, chain-smoking, and brilliantly erratic, overweight criminal psychologist. The show was discontinued some time ago, akin to the character's hard luck, and as it's rarely aired, the opportunity of twenty-four hours of *Cracker* was pretty tempting. I deliberated on staying a few more days, but how crazy would that be? No crazier than coming here in the first place, my conscience pipes. I content myself with the generous clips, so relentlessly promoted that I am actually able to piece together a projection of an entire episode.

During a break between *Detective Frost* and *Whitechapel,* I decided to have a farewell glass of port in the honesty bar adjacent to the library. Standing by the elevator I suddenly felt a presence beside me. We turned at the same moment and stared at one another. I was stunned to find Robbie Coltrane, as if I'd willed him, some days ahead of the *Cracker* marathon.

—I've been waiting for you all week, I said impetuously.

—Here I am, he laughed.

I was so taken aback that I failed to join him in the elevator and promptly returned to my room, which seemed subtly yet utterly transformed, as if I had been drawn into the parallel quarters of a proper tea-drinking genie.

—Can you imagine the odds of such an encounter? I say to my floral bedspread.

—All things considered, odds-on favorite. But you really should have conjured John Barrymore.

A worthy suggestion but I had no desire to encourage a continuing dialogue. Unlike a channel changer it's literally impossible to turn off a floral bedspread.

I consulted the minibar and settled on elderberry water and sweet-and-salty popcorn. I hesitated to turn the television back on, as I was certain I would be met with a close-up of

Fitz's face in a dark alcoholic stupor. I wondered if Robbie Coltrane was hitting the honesty bar. I actually thought of going down and peeking but instead rearranged my belongings that were haphazardly stuffed in my small suitcase. In my haste I pricked my finger and was astonished to find the pearl-studded hatpin of the secretary of the CDC lodged between my tee shirts and sweaters. It was the color of iridescent ash and misshapen—more teardrop than pearl. I turned it in the lamplight then wrapped it in a small linen handkerchief embroidered with forget-me-nots, a present from my daughter.

I went over our last exchange outside the Pasternak. We'd had a few shots of vodka. I couldn't remember anything about a hatpin.

—Where do you think the compass points for our next meeting? I asked.

She seemed evasive and I thought it best not to press. She rummaged through her purse and gave me a hand-colored photograph of the club's namesake. It was the size and shape of a holy card.

—Why do you think we gather in remembrance of Mr. Wegener? I asked.

—Why, for Mrs. Wegener, she answered without hesitation.

As if it had followed me from Berlin a heavy mist descended on Monmouth Street. From my small terrace I caught the moment when drapes of cloud dropped upon the ground. I had never seen such a thing and lamented I was without film for my camera. On the other hand I was able to experience the moment completely unburdened. I put on my overcoat and turned and said good-bye to my room. Downstairs I had black coffee, kippers, and brown toast in the breakfast room. My car was waiting. My driver was wearing sunglasses.

The mist grew heavier, a full-blown fog, enveloping all we passed. What if it suddenly lifted and everything was gone? The column of Lord Nelson, the Kensington Gardens, the looming Ferris wheel by the river, and the forest on the heath. All disappearing into the silvered atmosphere of an interminable fairy tale. The journey to the airport seemed endless. The outlines of bare trees faintly visible like an illustration from an English storybook. Their naked arms drew across other landscapes: Pennsylvania, Tennessee, and the avenue of plane trees on Jesus Green. The Zentralfriedhof in Vienna where Harry Lime was interred and the Montparnasse cemetery where penciled trees line the paths from grave to grave. Plane trees with pom-poms, dried brown seedpods, swinging ghosts of Christmas ornaments. One could well imagine a former century when a young Scotsman dwelled in such an atmosphere of dropping clouds and shimmering mists and gave it the name of Neverland.

My driver let out a deep sigh. I wondered if my flight would be delayed, but it didn't matter. No one knew where I was. No one was expecting me. I didn't mind slowly crawling through the fog in an English cab, black as my coat, flanked by the shivering outline of trees, as if hastily sketched by the posthumous hand of Arthur Rackham.

The Flea Draws Blood

B Y T H E T I M E I got back to New York I had forgotten why I'd left. I attempted to resume my daily routine but was waylaid by an unusually oppressive bout of jet lag. A thick torpor coupled with a surprisingly internal luminosity gave me the impression I had been overcome with a numinous malady transmitted by the Berlin and London fog. My dreams were like outtakes from *Spellbound:* liquefying columns, straining saplings, and irreducible theorems turning in a swirl of heart-stopping weather. Recognizing the poetic possibilities of this temporary affliction I attempt to rein something in, treading my internal haze in search of elemental creatures or the hare of a wild religion. Instead I am greeted with shuffling face cards with no faces mouthing nothing worth preserving and certainly no cowpoke spinning loopholes. No luck at all. My hands are as empty as the pages of my journal. *It's not so easy writing about nothing.* Words caught from a voice-over in a dream more compelling than life. *It's not so easy writing about nothing:* I scratch them over and over onto a white wall with a chunk of red chalk.

Sundown, I feed the cats their evening meal, slide on my coat, and wait at the corner for the light to change. Streets are empty, a few cars: red, blue, and a yellow taxi, primary colors saturated by the last of the cold-filtered light. Phrases swoop in on me as if skywritten by tiny biplanes. *Replenish your marrow. Have your pockets ready. Wait for the slow burn.* Gumshoe phrases bringing to mind the low side-mouthed tones of William Burroughs. Crossing over I wonder how William would decipher the language of my current disposition. There was a time when I could simply pick up the phone and ask him, but now I must summon him in other ways.

'Ino is empty, as I am ahead of the evening rush. It's not my usual hour but I sit at my same table and have white bean soup and black coffee. Thinking to write something of William I open my notebook, but a pageant of scenes and the faces that inhabited them is quietly paralyzing; couriers of wisdom I was privileged to break bread with. Gone Beats that once ushered my generation into a cultural revolution, though it is William's distinctive voice that speaks to me now. I can hear him elucidating on the Central Intelligence Agency's insidious pervasion of our daily life or the perfect bait for catching walleyed pike in Minnesota.

I last saw him in Lawrence, Kansas. He lived in a modest house, with his cats, his books, a shotgun, and a portable wooden medicine cabinet locked away. He sat at his typewriter; the one with the ribbon so used up that sometimes only impressions of words made it to the page. He had a miniature pond with darting red fish and tin cans set up in his backyard. He enjoyed a little target practice and was still a great shot. I purposely left my camera in its sack and stood quietly observing as he took aim. He was somewhat dried and bent, yet he was beautiful. I looked at the bed where he slept and watched the curtains on his window move ever so slightly. Before I said good-bye we stood together before a print of William Blake's miniature of *The Ghost of a Flea*. It was an image of a reptilian being with a curved yet powerful spine enhanced with scales of gold.

—That's how I feel, he said.

I was buttoning my coat. I wanted to ask why but I didn't say anything.

The ghost of a flea. What was William telling me? My coffee cold, I gesture for another, sketching possible answers then abruptly crossing them out. Instead I opt to follow William's shadow snaking a winding medina bathed in flickering images of freestanding arthropods. William the exterminator, drawn to a singular insect whose consciousness is so highly concentrated that it conquers his own.

The flea draws blood, depositing it as well. But this is no ordinary blood. What the pathologist calls blood is also a substance of release. A pathologist examines it in a scientific way, but what of the writer, the visualization detective, who sees not only blood but the spattering of words? Oh, the activity in that blood, and the observations lost to God. But what would God do with them? Would they be filed away in some hallowed library? Volumes illustrated with obscure shots taken with a dusty box camera. A revolving system of stills indistinct yet familiar projecting in all directions: a fading drummer boy in white costume, sepia stations, starched shirts, bits of whimsy, rolls of faded scarlet, close-ups of doughboys laid out on the damp earth curling like phosphorescent leaves around the stem of a Chinese pipe.

The boy in white costume. Where did he come from? I didn't make him up but referenced something. Forgoing a third coffee I close my notes on William, leave some money on the table, and head back home. The answer is in a book somewhere, in my own blessed library. Still in my coat I revisit my book piles, trying not to be sidetracked nor lured into another dimension. I pretend not to notice *After-Dinner Declarations* by Nicanor Parra or Auden's *Letters from Iceland.* I momentarily open Jim Carroll's *The Petting Zoo,* essential to anyone in search of concrete delirium, then immediately close it. Sorry, I tell them all, I can't revisit you now, it's time to reel myself in.

As I unearth *After Nature* by W. G. Sebald it occurs to me that the image of the boy in white is on the cover of his *Austerlitz.* Uniquely haunting, it drew me to the book and thus introduced me to Sebald. Mystery solved, I abandon my search and eagerly open *After Nature.* At one time the three lengthy poems in this slim volume had such a profound effect on me that I could hardly bear to read them. Scarcely would I enter their world before I'd be transported to a myriad of other worlds. Evidences of such transports are crammed onto the endpapers as well as a declaration I once had the hubris to scrawl in a margin—*I may not know what is in your mind, but I know how your mind works.*

Max Sebald! He squats on the damp earth and examines a curved stick. An old man's staff or a humble branch turned with the saliva of a faithful dog? He sees, not with eyes, and yet he sees. He recognizes voices within silence, history within negative space. He conjures ancestors who are not ancestors, with such precision that the gilded threads of an embroidered sleeve are as familiar as his own dusty trousers.

Images hang to dry on a line that stretches around an enormous globe: the reverse of the Ghent altarpiece, a single leaf torn from a wondrous book illustrating an extinct yet glorious fern, a goatskin map of the Gotthard Pass, the coat of a slaughtered fox. He lays out the world in 1527. He gives us a man—the painter Matthias Grünewald. The son, the sacrifice, the great works. We believe it will go on forever, then an abrupt tearing of time, the death of everything. The painter, the son, the strokes all recede, without music, without fanfare, only a sudden and distinct absence of color.

What a drug this little book is; to imbibe it is to find oneself presuming his process. I read and feel that same compulsion; the desire to possess what he has written, which can only be subdued by writing something myself. It is not mere envy but a delusional quickening in the blood. Soon abstracted, the book slips off my lap and I am off, diverted by the calloused heels of a young lad delivering loaves.

He bows his head. As an apprentice to his father, his destiny is decided and there is nothing to do but follow. He bakes bread but dreams of music. One night he rises as his father sleeps. He wraps a loaf and throws it in a sack and steals his father's boots.

Ecstatically he distances himself from his village. He crosses the wide plains, winds through Hindu forests, and scales the white peaks. He journeys until he collapses half starved in a square where a benevolent widow of a famed violinist rescues him. She tends to him and slowly he regains his health. In gratitude he makes himself useful. One evening the young man watches her as she sleeps. He senses her husband's priceless violin buried in the pit of her memory. Deeply coveting it he picks the lock of her dreams with her own hairpin. He finds the concealed case and triumphantly holds the glowing instrument in his two hands.

I place *After Nature* back on the shelf, safely among the many portals of the world. They float through these pages often without explanation. Writers and their process. Writers and their books. I cannot assume the reader will be familiar with them all, but in the end is the reader familiar with me? Does the reader wish to be so? I can only hope, as I offer my world on a platter filled with allusions. As one held by the stuffed bear in Tolstoy's house, an oval platter that was once overflowing with the names of callers, infamous and obscure, small *cartes de visite,* many among the many.

Tolstoy's bear, Moscow

Hill of Beans

I N MICHIGAN I became a solitary drinker, as Fred never touched coffee. My mother had given me a pot that was a smaller version of hers. How many times had I watched her scoop the grounds from the red Eight O'Clock Coffee tin into the metal basket of the percolator, waiting patiently by the stove as it brewed? My mother, sitting at the kitchen table, the steam rising from her cup entwining with the smoke curling from her cigarette resting on an invariably chipped ashtray. My mother in her blue flowered housecoat, no slippers on her long bare feet identical to my own.

I made my coffee in her pot and sat and wrote at a card table in the kitchen by the screen door. A photograph of Albert Camus hung next to the light switch. It was a classic shot of Camus in a heavy overcoat with a cigarette between his lips, like a young Bogart, in a clay frame made by my son, Jackson. It had a green glaze and the inner edge had pointed teeth like the open mouth of an aggressive robot. There was no glass in the frame and the image discolored through the years.

My son, seeing him every day, got the idea that Camus was an uncle who lived far away. I would glance up at him from time to time as I was writing. I wrote about a traveler who didn't travel. I wrote about a girl on the lam whose namesake was Saint Lucy, symbolized by the image of two eyes upon a plate. Every time I fried two eggs sunny-side up I thought of her.

We lived in an old stone country house on a canal that emptied into the Saint Clair River. There were no cafés within walking distance. My one respite was the coffee machine at 7-Eleven. On Saturday morning I would rise early and walk a quarter mile to 7-Eleven and get a large black coffee and a glazed donut. Then I would stop at the lot behind the fish-and-tackle store, a simple, whitewashed cement outpost. To me it looked like Tangier, though I had never been there. I sat on the ground in the corner surrounded by low white walls, shelving real time, free to rove the smooth bridge connecting past and present. My Morocco. I followed whatever train I wanted. I wrote without writing—of genies and hustlers and mythic travelers, my *vagabondia*. Then I would walk back home, happily satisfied, and resume my daily tasks. Even now, having at last been to Tangier, my spot behind the bait store seems the true Morocco in my memory.

Michigan. Those were mystical times. An era of small pleasures. When a pear appeared on the branch of a tree and fell before my feet and sustained me. Now I have no trees, there is no crib nor clothesline. There are drafts of manuscripts spread over the floor where they slipped off the edge of the bed in the night. There is the unfinished canvas tacked to the wall and the scent of eucalyptus failing to mask the sickening smell of used turpentine and linseed oil. There are telltale drips of cadmium red staining the bathroom sink—along the edge of the baseboard—or splotches on the wall where the brush got away. One step into a living space and one can sense the centrality of work in a life. Half-empty paper coffee cups. Half-eaten deli sandwiches. An encrusted soup bowl. Here is joy and neglect. A little mescal. A little jacking off, but mostly just work.

—This is how I live, I am thinking.

I knew the moon would eventually rise above my skylight, but I couldn't wait for it. I remember a comforting darkness, as when a night maid enters a hotel room and turns down the bedding and closes the drapes. I surrendered to waves of sleep, sampling the offerings, layer by layer, of a mysterious box of chocolates. I awoke somewhat startled with a radiating pain that moved through my arms. A band tightening, but I remained calm. Lightning struck near my skylight, followed by heavy thunder and punishing rain. It's only the storm, I said half aloud. I had been dreaming of the dead. But which dead? Blood leaves covered them. Pale blossoms fell and covered the red leaves. I leaned over and checked the digital clock on the VCR I rarely use, never able to remember the necessary chain of commands to get it going: 5:00 A.M. I had a sudden recall of the lengthy taxi scene in the movie *Eyes Wide Shut*. An uncomfortable Tom Cruise caught in the flow of real time.

What was Kubrick thinking? He was thinking that real-time cinema is the only hope for art. He was thinking about how Orson Welles had Rita Hayworth cut and bleach her famous red tresses for *The Lady from Shanghai.*

Cairo was hacking a hairball. I got up and drank some water and she hopped onto the bed and went to sleep beside me. My dreams shifted. Trials of a person I didn't know lost in a labyrinth of aisles formed by the immense filing cabinets of *Brazil*—the movie, not the country. I awoke out of sorts, felt under the bed for socks but found only a lost slipper. After wiping up traces of kitty vomit I went downstairs barefoot, stepping on a rotting rubber frog, then spent a disproportionate amount of time preparing the cats' breakfast. The Abyssinian runt circling, the oldest and most intelligent eyeing the treat jar, and a huge tomcat, there by default, riveted by my every move. I rinsed the water bowls, filled them with filtered water, handpicked personality-appropriate saucers from a mismatched stack, and carefully measured their food. They seemed more suspicious than grateful.

The café was empty, but the cook was unscrewing the outlet plate above my seat. I took my book into the bathroom and read while he finished. When I emerged, the cook was gone and a woman was ready to sit in my seat.

— Excuse me, this is my table.

—Did you reserve it?

—Well, no, but it's my table.

—Did you actually sit here? There's nothing on the table and you have your coat on.

I stood there mutely. If this were an episode of *Midsomer*

Murders she would surely be found strangled in a wild ravine behind an abandoned vicarage. I shrugged and sat at another table, hoping to wait her out. She spoke loudly, asking for eggs Benedict and iced coffee with skim milk, neither offered on the menu.

She'll leave, I thought. But she didn't. She plopped her oversized red lizard bag on my table and made numerous calls on her cell phone. There was no way to escape her odious conversation, fixed on a tracking number for some missing FedEx package. I sat and stared at the heavy white coffee mug. If this were an episode of *Luther,* she would be found faceup in the snow with the objects from her purse arranged about her: a bodily corona like Our Lady of Guadalupe.

—*Such dark thoughts for the sake of a corner table.* My inner Jiminy Cricket spoke up. Oh, all right, I said. May the world's small things fill her with delight.

— Good, good, spoke the cricket.

—And may she purchase a lottery ticket and possess the winning number.

—Unnecessary, but fine.

—And may she order a thousand such bags, each one more splendid than the last, delivered and dumped by FedEx, and may she be trapped by a storeroom's worth, without food, water, or cell phone.

— I'm leaving, said my conscience.

— Me too, I said, and I went back out onto the street.

Delivery trucks were gridlocked on little Bedford Street. The water department in search of a mainline was jackhammering near Father Demo Square. I crossed over to Broadway

and walked north to Twenty-fifth Street to the Serbian Ortho-
dox Cathedral dedicated to Saint Sava, the patron saint of the
Serbs. I stopped, as I had many times before, to visit the bust
of Nikola Tesla, the patron saint of alternating current, placed
outside the church like a lone sentinel. I stood as a Con Edison
truck parked within eyeshot. No respect, I thought.

—And you think you have problems, he said to me.

—All currents lead to you, Mr. Tesla.

—*Hvala!* How can I serve you?

—Oh, I'm just having trouble writing. I move back and
forth from lethargy to agitation.

—A pity. Perhaps you should step inside and light a candle
to Saint Sava. He calms the sea for ships.

—Yeah, maybe. I'm off balance, not sure what's wrong.

—You have misplaced joy, he said without hesitation.
Without joy, we are as dead.

—How do I find it again?

—Find those who have it and bathe in their perfection.

—Thank you, Mr. Tesla. Is there something I can do for
you?

—Yes, he said, could you move a bit toward the left? You're
standing in my light.

Roaming around for a few hours looking for landmarks no
longer there. Pawnshops, diners, flophouses gone. Some
changes around the Flatiron Building but it is still there. I
stood in awe just as I had done in 1963, saluting its creator,
Daniel Burnham. It took just a year to build his masterpiece

with its triangular ground plan. Walking home I stopped for a slice of pizza. I wondered if the triangular shape of the Flatiron Building had triggered my desire for it. I got a coffee to go, which spilled over the front of my coat, as the lid wasn't secured.

When I entered Washington Square Park some kid tapped me on the shoulder. I turned around and he grinned and handed me a sock. I recognized it immediately. A pale brown cotton lisle sock with a gilded bee embroidered by its edge. I have several pairs of such socks, but where did this one come from? I noticed his companions—two girls around twelve or thirteen—in a fit of laughter. It was undoubtedly yesterday's sock caught up in my pantleg that shimmied down and slid to the ground. Thanks, I mumbled, and stuffed it into my pocket.

Approaching the Caffè Dante I could see the murals of Florence through the wide window. I wasn't ready to go home so I went inside and ordered Egyptian chamomile tea. It arrived in a glass pot and bits of golden flowers were floating at the bottom. Blossoms covering the dead where they lie, like a line from an old murder ballad. I finally placed where the images in my morning dream might have come from—the Battle of Shiloh in the Civil War. Thousands of young soldiers lay dead on the battleground in a peach orchard in full bloom. It was said that the blossoms fell upon them, covering them like a thin layer of fragrant snow. I wondered why I had dreamed that, but then again, why do we dream about anything?

I sat there for a long time drinking tea and listening to the radio. Happily there seemed to be an actual human choosing songs with abandoned disconnect. A version of "White Wedding" by a Serbian hardcore punk band, then Neil Young singing, *No one wins; it's a war of man.* Neil is right, no one wins anything; winning is an illusion, that's for sure. The sun was going down. Where did the day go? Suddenly I remembered how Fred once found a small portable record player in the closet of a cabin we'd rented in northern Michigan. When he opened it up there was a single of "Radar Love" on the turntable. A telepathic love song by Golden Earring that seemed to speak of our long-distance courtship and the electric thread that drew us together. It was the only record there and we turned it up and played it over and over.

A local and statewide newsbreak, then a weather alert announced another hard rain coming. I could already feel it in my bones. The song "Your Protector" by Fleet Foxes followed. Its melancholic menace filled my heart with strange adrenaline. Time to go. I put some money down on the table and bent down to tie my bootlace, which had been dragging as I crossed through some puddles in Washington Square. Sorry, I told my lace, wiping off traces of mud with my napkin. I noticed there was a funnel of words written on it and I shoved it into my pocket. I would decipher it later. While I was retying my boots, the song "What a Wonderful World" came on. When I sat up, tears were welling. I leaned back in my chair and closed my eyes, trying not to listen.

—If you don't have one, then everyone is your valentine.

The morning's Hallmark greeting, courtesy of that darned cowpoke. I felt around for my spectacles. They were wrapped in the sheets along with a beat-up paperback of *The Laughing Policeman* and a chain with an Ethiopian cross. How does he keep reappearing and how did he know it was Valentine's Day? I slipped into my moccasins, shuffled into the bathroom, somewhat surly. Salt clung to my lashes and the lenses of my specs were cloudy with fingerprints. I pressed a hot washcloth against my lids and glanced at the low wood bench that once served as a daybed for a young villager on the Ivory Coast. There was a small pile of white dress shirts, tattered tee shirts worn thin through the years, and Fred's old flannel shirts washed into weightlessness. I was thinking that when Fred's clothes needed mending I did it myself. I chose one with red-and-black buffalo checks; it seemed a good choice. I picked my dungarees off the floor and shook out the socks.

Yeah, I had no valentine, so the cowpoke was probably right. When you don't have one, everyone is potentially your valentine. A notion I decided to keep to myself lest I be obliged to spend the day pasting hearts of lace on red construction paper to send out into the whole of the world.

The world is everything that is the case. There's a positively elegant wisecrack courtesy of Wittgenstein's *Tractatus Logico,* easy to grasp yet impossible to break down. I could print it in the center of a paper doily and deposit it into the pocket of a passing stranger. Or maybe Wittgenstein could be my valentine. We could live in a little red house in cantankerous silence on the side of a mountain in Norway.

On the way to 'Ino I noticed the lining of my left-hand pocket was torn and made a mental note to mend it. My mood suddenly lifted. The day was crisp and bright, the atmosphere quivering with life, like the translucent strands of a rare aquatic species with long, flowing tentacles, lappets flowing vertically from a jellyfish's bell. Would that human energy could materialize in such a way. I imagine such strands waving horizontally from the edges of my black coat.

There were red rosebuds in a small vase in the bathroom at 'Ino. I draped my coat over the empty chair across from me, and then spent much of the next hour drinking coffee and filling pages of my notebook with drawings of single-celled animals and various species of plankton. It was strangely comforting, for I remembered copying such things from a heavy textbook that sat on the shelf above my father's desk. He had all kinds of books rescued from dustbins and deserted houses and bought for pennies at church bazaars. The range of subjects from ufology to Plato to the planarian reflected his ever-curious mind. I would pore over this particular book for hours, contemplating its mysterious world. The dense text was impossible to penetrate but somehow the monochromic renderings of living organisms suggested many colors, like flashing minnows in a fluorescent pond. This obscure and nameless book, with its paramecia, algae, and amoebas, floats alive in memory. Such things that disappear in time that we find ourselves longing to see again. We search for them in close-up, as we search for our hands in a dream.

My father claimed that he never remembered his dreams, but I could easily recount mine. He also told me that seeing one's own hands within a dream was exceedingly rare. I was sure I could if I set my mind to it, a notion that resulted in a plethora of failed experiments. My father questioned the usefulness of such a pursuit, but nevertheless invading my own dreams topped my list of impossible things one must one day accomplish.

In grade school I was often scolded for not paying attention. I suppose I was busy thinking about such things or attempting to untangle the mystery of an expanding network of seemingly unanswerable questions. The hill-of-beans equation, for example, occupied a fair portion of second grade. I was contemplating a problematic phrase in *The Story of Davy Crockett* by Enid Meadowcroft. I wasn't supposed to be reading it as it was in the bookcase for third graders. But drawn to it I slipped it into my schoolbag and read it in secret. I instantly identified with young Davy, who was tall and gangly, telling equally tall tales, getting into scrapes, and forgetting his chores. His pa reckoned that Davy wouldn't amount to a hill of beans. I was only seven and these words stopped me in my tracks. What could his pa have meant by that? I lay awake at night thinking about it. What was a hill of beans worth? Would a hill of anything be worth a boy like Davy Crockett?

I followed my mother around the A&P pushing the shopping cart.

—Mommy, how much would a hill of beans cost?

—Oh, Patricia, I don't know. Ask your father. I'll take the cart and you go pick out your cereal and don't lag behind.

I quickly did as I was told, grabbing a box of shredded wheat. Then I was off to the dry-goods aisle to check the price of beans, confronted with a new dilemma. What kind of beans? Black beans kidney beans fava beans lima beans green beans navy beans all kinds of beans. To say nothing of baked beans, magic beans, and coffee beans.

In the end I figured Davy Crockett was far beyond measuring, even by his pa. Despite any shortcomings he labored hard to be of use and paid off all of his father's debts. I read and reread the forbidden book, following him down paths that set my mind in unanticipated directions. If I got lost along the way I had a compass that I had found embedded in a pile of wet leaves I was kicking my way through. The compass was old and rusted but it still worked, connecting the earth and stars. It told me where I was standing and which way was west but not where I was going and nothing of my worth.

Clock with No Hands

In the beginning was real time. A woman enters a garden that is bursting with color. She has no memory, only a burgeoning curiosity. She approaches the man. He is not curious. He stands before a tree. Within the tree is a word that becomes a name. He receives the name of every living thing. At one with the present he has neither ambition nor dream. The woman reaches toward him, gripped by the mystery of sensation.

I closed my notebook and sat in the café thinking about real time. Is it time uninterrupted? Only the present comprehended? Are our thoughts nothing but passing trains, no stops, devoid of dimension, whizzing by massive posters with repeating images? Catching a fragment from a window seat, yet another fragment from the next identical frame? If I write in the present yet digress, is that still real time? Real time, I reasoned, cannot be divided into sections like numbers on the face of a clock. If I write about the past as I simultaneously dwell in the present, am I still in real time? Perhaps there is

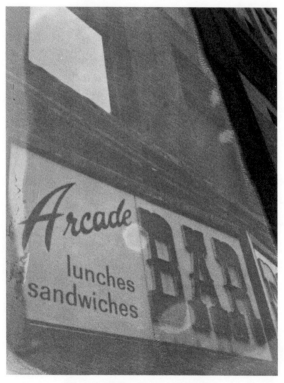

The Arcade Bar, Detroit, Michigan

no past or future, only the perpetual present that contains this trinity of memory. I looked out into the street and noticed the light changing. Perhaps the sun had slipped behind a cloud. Perhaps time had slipped away.

Fred and I had no specific time frame. In 1979 we lived at the Book Cadillac Hotel in downtown Detroit. We lived around the clock, moving through the days and nights with little regard for time. We would stay up until dawn talking then sleep until nightfall. When we awoke we'd search for twenty-four-hour diners or stop and mill around Art Van's furniture outlet that opened at midnight and served free coffee and powdered donuts. Sometimes we'd just drive aimlessly and stop before the sun rose at some motel in a place like Port Huron or Saginaw and sleep all day.

Fred loved the Arcade Bar that was close to our hotel. It opened in the morning, a thirties-style bar with a few booths, a grill, and a large railway clock with no hands. There was no time real or otherwise at the Arcade and we could sit for hours with a handful of stragglers, spinning words or content within commiserating silence. Fred would have a few beers and I would drink black coffee. One such morning at the Arcade Bar as he gazed at the great wall clock Fred suddenly got an idea for a TV show. These were the early days of cable, and he envisioned broadcasting on WGPR, Detroit's pioneering black independent television station. Fred's segment, *Drunk in the Afternoon,* fell in the realm of the clock with no hands, unfettered by time and social expectations. It would feature one guest who would join him at the table beneath the clock just drinking and talking. They could go as far as their mutual intoxication would take them. Fred could communicate well on any subject from Tom Watson's golf swing to the Chicago Riots to the decline of the railroad. Fred made a list of possible guests from all walks of life. On the top of his list was Cliff Robertson, a somewhat troubled B actor who shared Fred's enthusiasm for aviation, a man close to his heart.

Depending on how it was going, at unspecified intervals I would have a fifteen-minute segment called *Coffee Break*. The idea being that Nescafé would sponsor my segment. I would not have guests but would invite viewers to have a cup of Nescafé with me. On the other hand, Fred and his guest would not be obligated to communicate with the viewer, only with each other. I went as far as to find and purchase the perfect uniform for my segment—a gray-and-white pin-striped linen dress that buttoned down the front with cap sleeves and two pockets. French-penitentiary style. Fred decided he would wear his khaki shirt with a dark brown tie. On *Coffee Break* I planned to discuss prison literature, highlighting writers like Jean Genet and Albertine Sarrazin. On *Drunk in the Afternoon* Fred might offer his guest some extremely fine cognac from a brown paper bag.

Not all dreams need to be realized. That was what Fred used to say. We accomplished things that no one would ever know. Unexpectedly, when we returned from French Guiana, he decided to learn to fly. In 1981 we drove to the Outer Banks of North Carolina to salute America's first airfield at the Wright Brothers Memorial, taking US Highway 158 to Kill Devil Hills. We then made our way along the Southern coastline, moving from flight school to flight school. We journeyed through the Carolinas to Jacksonville, Florida, and on to Fernandina Beach, American Beach, Daytona Beach, then circled back to Saint Augustine. There we stayed in a motel by the sea with a small kitchenette. Fred flew and drank Coca-Cola. I wrote and drank coffee. We bought miniature vials of the water discovered by Ponce de León—a hole in the ground gushing the supposed water of youth. Let's never drink it, he said, and the vials became part of our trove of improbable treasure. For a time we considered buying an abandoned lighthouse or a shrimp trawler. But when I found I was pregnant we headed back home to Detroit, trading one set of dreams for another.

Fred finally achieved his pilot's license but couldn't afford to fly a plane. I wrote incessantly but published nothing. Through it all we held fast to the concept of the clock with no hands. Tasks were completed, sump pumps manned, sandbags piled, trees planted, shirts ironed, hems stitched, and yet we reserved the right to ignore the hands that kept on turning. Looking back, long after his death, our way of living seems a miracle, one that could only be achieved by the silent synchronization of the jewels and gears of a common mind.

Germantown, Pennsylvania, spring 1954

The Well

❧ ⚎ ☙

IT SNOWED on Saint Patrick's Day, causing a snag in the annual parade. I lay in bed and watched the snow swirl above the skylight. Saint Paddy's Day—my namesake day, as my father always said. I could hear the tones of his sonorous voice melding with the snowflakes, coaxing me to rise from my sickbed.

—Come, Patricia, it's your day. The fever's passed.

I had spent the first months of 1954 cosseted in the atmosphere of the child convalescent. I was the only child registered in the Philadelphia area with full-blown scarlet fever. My younger siblings held somber vigilance behind my door draped in quarantine yellow. Often I would open my eyes and see the edges of their little brown shoes. Winter was passing and I as their leader had not been able to go out and supervise the building of snow forts or strategize maneuvers over the homemade maps of our child wars.

—Today is your day. We're going outside.

It was a sunny day with mild winds. My mother laid out

my clothes. Some of my hair had fallen out due to a string of high fevers and I'd lost weight from my already lanky frame. I remember a navy-blue watch cap, like the kind fishermen wore, and orange socks in respect for our Protestant grandfather.

My father crouched down several feet away encouraging me to walk.

My siblings willed me on as I plodded unsteadily toward him. Initially weak, my strength and speed returned and I was soon racing ahead of the neighborhood children, long-legged and free.

My brother and sister and I were born in consecutive years after the end of World War II. I was the eldest, and I scripted our play, creating scenarios that they entered wholeheartedly. My brother, Todd, was our faithful knight. My sister Linda served as our confidante and nurse, wrapping our wounds with strips of old linens. Our cardboard shields were covered in aluminum foil and embellished with the cross of Malta, our missions blessed by angels.

We were good children, but our natural curiosity often got us into scrapes. If we were caught tangling with a rival gang or crossing a forbidden thoroughfare, our mother would place us together in one small bedroom, cautioning us not to make a single sound. We appeared to dutifully accept our sentence, but as soon as the door closed we quickly regrouped in perfect silence. There were two small beds and a wide oak bureau with double drawers adorned with carved acorns and large knobs. We would sit in a row before the bureau and I would whisper a code word, signaling our course. Solemnly we would turn the knobs, entering our three-way portal to

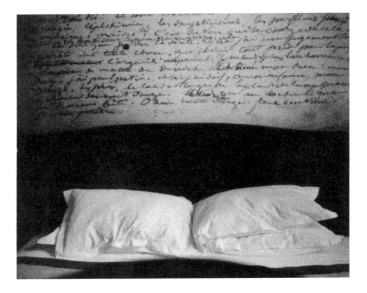

adventure. I held the lantern high and we scurried aboard our ship, our untroubled world, as children will. Charting new splendors, we played our Game of Knobs, braving new enemies or revisiting moonlit forests opening onto hallowed ground with burnished fountains and remains of castles we had come to know. We played in rapt silence until our mother released us and sent us off to sleep.

It was still snowing; I had to will myself to rise. Perhaps my present malaise is akin to that childhood convalescence, which drew me to bed where I slowly recuperated, read my books, scribbled my first little stories. My malaise. It was time to draw my paper sword, time to cut it to the ground. If my brother were still alive he would surely press me into action.

I went downstairs, eyeing rows of books, despairing of

what to choose. A prima donna in the bowels of a wardrobe dripping with dresses, but with nothing to wear. How could I have nothing to read? Perhaps it wasn't a lack of a book but a lack of obsession. I placed my hand on a familiar spine of green cloth with the gilt title *The Little Lame Prince,* a favorite of mine as a child—Miss Mulock's tale of a beautiful young prince whose legs were paralyzed as an infant from a neglectful accident. He is heartlessly locked away in a solitary tower until his true fairy godmother brings him a marvelous traveling cloak that can take him anywhere he wishes. It was a difficult book to find and I never had a copy of my own, and so I read and reread a deteriorating library copy. Then, in the winter of 1993, I received an early birthday gift from my mother along with some Christmas packages. It was to be a difficult winter. Fred was ill and I was plagued with a vague sense of trepidation. I woke up and it was 4 a.m. Everyone was sleeping. I tiptoed down the stairs and unwrapped the package. It was a bright 1909 edition of *The Little Lame Prince.* She had written *we don't need words* on the title page in her then-shaky hand.

I slipped it from the shelf, opening to her inscription. Her familiar writing filled me with longing that was also comforting. Mommy, I said aloud, and I thought of her suddenly stopping what she was doing, often in the center of the kitchen, and invoking her own mother whom she lost when she was eleven years old. How is it that we never completely comprehend our love for someone until they're gone? I took the book upstairs into my room and placed it with the books that had been hers: *Anne of Green Gables. Daddy-Long-Legs. A Girl of the Limberlost.* Oh, to be reborn within the pages of a book.

The snow continued to fall. On impulse I bundled up and went out to greet it. I walked east to St. Mark's Bookshop, where I roamed the aisles, randomly selecting, feeling papers, and examining fonts, praying for a perfect opening line. Dispirited I went to the M section, hoping that Henning Mankell had furthered the adventures of my favorite detective, Kurt Wallander. Sadly I had read them all, but in lingering in the M section I was fortuitously drawn into the interdimensional world of Haruki Murakami.

I had never read Murakami. I had spent the past two years reading and deconstructing Bolaño's *2666*—swept back to front and from every angle. Before *2666, The Master and Margarita* had eclipsed all else, and before reading all of Bulgakov there was an exhausting romance with everything Wittgenstein, including fitful attempts to break down his equation. I can't say I ever succeeded, but the process led me to a possible answer to the Mad Hatter's riddle: *Why is a raven like a writing desk?* I pictured the classroom in my country school in Germantown, Pennsylvania. We still had penmanship classes with real ink bottles and wooden dip pens with metal nibs. The raven and the writing desk? It was the ink. I am sure of it.

I opened a book called *A Wild Sheep Chase,* chosen for its intriguing title. A phrase caught my eye—*a maze of narrow streets and drainage canals*. I bought it immediately, a sheep-shaped cracker to dunk in my cocoa. Then I walked

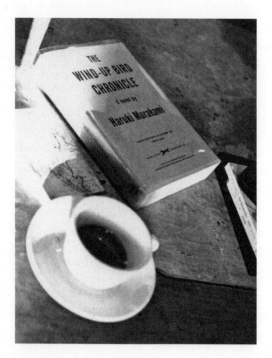

to nearby Soba-ya and ordered cold buckwheat noodles with yam and began to read. I was so taken by *Sheep Chase* that I stayed for over two hours, reading over a cup of sake. I could feel my blue-Jell-O funk melting at the edges.

In the weeks to come I would sit at my corner table reading nothing but Murakami. I'd come up for air just long enough to go to the bathroom or order another coffee. *Dance Dance Dance* and *Kafka on the Shore* swiftly followed *Sheep Chase*. And then, fatally, I began *The Wind-Up Bird Chronicle*. That was the one that did me in, setting in motion an unstoppable trajectory, like a meteor hurtling toward a barren and entirely innocent sector of earth.

There are two kinds of masterpieces. There are the classic works monstrous and divine like *Moby-Dick* or *Wuthering Heights* or *Frankenstein: A Modern Prometheus*. And then there is the type wherein the writer seems to infuse living energy into words as the reader is spun, wrung, and hung out to dry. Devastating books. Like *2666* or *The Master and Margarita*. *The Wind-Up Bird Chronicle* is such a book. I finished it and was immediately obliged to reread it. For one thing I did not wish to exit its atmosphere. But also, the ghost of a phrase was eating at me. Something that untied a neat knot and let the frayed edges brush against my cheek as I slept. It had to do with the fate of a certain property described by Murakami in the opening chapter.

The narrator is searching for his lost cat near his apartment in the Setagaya ward of the Tokyo prefecture. He makes his way through a narrow alley, winding up at the so-called Miyawaki place—an abandoned house on an overgrown lot, with a paltry bird sculpture and an obsolescent well. There is no indication that he is about to become so wrapped up that it will eclipse all else, and discover within the well an entrance into a parallel world. He is just looking for his cat, but as he is drawn into the murky atmosphere of the Miyawaki place, I was as well. So much so that I could think of little else and would have gladly bribed Murakami to write me a lengthy subchapter exclusively devoted to it. Of course it was impossible to be appeased by writing my own such chapter; it would be mere speculative fiction. Only Murakami could accurately describe every blade of grass in that wretched place. My preoccupation with the property had so completely taken me over that I became possessed with the idea to see it for myself.

I carefully sifted through the last chapters for the passage. Had the phrase indicated that the property would be sold? I finally located the answer in chapter 37. Several phrases beginning with the chilling words: *We'll be getting rid of this place soon.* It would indeed be sold and the well filled and sealed. I had somehow skimmed past this fact and would have missed it entirely had it not been for a sense of something wriggling in my memory like a twist of animated string. I was somewhat shaken, for I had projected that the narrator would make it his home, becoming guardian of the well and its portal. I had already reconciled myself to the surreptitious removal of the anonymous bird sculpture that I had grown attached to. It was suddenly gone without explanation and nothing mentioned anywhere of its whereabouts.

I have always hated loose ends. Dangling phrases, unopened packages, or a character that inexplicably disappears, like a lone sheet on a clothesline before a vague storm, left to flap in the wind until that same wind carries it away to become the skin of a ghost or a child's tent. If I read a book or see a film and some seemingly insignificant thing is left unresolved, I can get remarkably unsettled, going back and forth and looking for clues or wishing I had a number to call or that I could write someone a letter. Not to complain, but just to request clarification or to answer a few questions, so I can concentrate on other things.

There were pigeons moving around above the skylight. I wondered what the wind-up bird looked like. I could picture the bird sculpture, stone indistinctive, poised to fly, but I had no clue about the wind-up bird. Did it possess a tiny bird heart? A hidden spring composed of an unknown alloy? I paced about. Images of other automated birds such as the Die Zwitscher-Maschine of Paul Klee and the mechanical nightingale of the emperor of China came to mind but posed no insight into comprehending the key to the wind-up bird. Normally this would have been the detail of the book that would have intrigued me, but it was overshadowed by my irrational obsession with the ill-fated Miyawaki place, so I stored away that particular rumination for another time.

I sat in my bed watching back-to-back episodes of *CSI: Miami* led by the stoical Horatio Caine. I momentarily nodded off, not quite asleep, neither here nor there, sliding into that mystically nauseating area in between. Perhaps I could worm my way to the outpost of the cowpoke. If I did I would suspend sarcasm and just listen as if in answer. I saw his boots. I crouched down to see what kind of spurs he had. If they were golden I could be sure he'd traveled far, maybe as far as China. He was swatting an extremely large horsefly. He was about to say something, I could tell. I was squatting low and saw his spurs were nickel with a series of numbers engraved on the outer curve, which I thought may be a possible sequence for a winning lottery ticket. He yawned and stretched out his legs.

—There are actually three kinds of masterpieces, was all he said.

I jumped up, grabbed my black coat and copy of *Wind-Up Bird,* and headed to Café 'Ino. It was later than usual, happily empty, but a handwritten sign saying Out of Order was taped to the coffee machine. A small blow, but I stayed anyway. I played a game of randomly opening the book, hoping to come across some allusion to *the property,* like choosing a card from a tarot deck that reflects your current state of mind. Then I amused myself by making lists on its blank endpapers. Two kinds of masterpieces, then I started on the third kind—as dictated by the know-it-all cowpoke. I wrote lists of possibilities, adding, subtracting, and relocating masterpieces like a mad clerk in a subterranean reading room.

Lists. Small anchors in the swirl of transmitted waves, reverie, and saxophone solos. A laundry list of lists actually retrieved in the laundry. Another in the family Bible dated 1955—the best books I ever read: *A Dog of Flanders. The Prince and the Pauper. The Blue Bird. Five Little Peppers and How They Grew.* And what about *Little Women* or *A Tree Grows in Brooklyn*? And what about *Through the Looking-Glass* or *The Glass Bead Game*? Which of them qualify for a slot in masterpiece column one, two, or three? Which are merely beloved? And should classics be in their own column?

—Don't forget *Lolita,* the cowpoke whispered emphatically.

He was now emerging out of dreamtime, a left-handed version of a numinous voice. In any event I added *Lolita.* An American classic penned by a Russian, right up there with *The Scarlet Letter.*

The new girl suddenly appeared at my table.

—Someone is coming to fix the machine.

—That's good.

—Sorry there is no coffee.

—That's okay. I have my table.

—And no people!

—Yeah! No people.

—What are you writing?

I looked up at her, somewhat surprised. I had absolutely no idea.

On the way home I stopped at the deli and got a medium black coffee and a slice of hermetically sealed cornbread. It was chilly but I didn't feel like going inside. I sat on my stoop and held my coffee in both hands until they were warm, then spent several minutes trying to unwind the Saran wrap; easier to strip Lazarus. It suddenly came to me that I failed to enter *An Episode in the Life of a Landscape Painter* by César Aira in the list of masterpieces. And what about a sublist of digressional masterworks such as René Daumal's *A Night of Serious Drinking*? It was getting all too out of hand. So much easier to write a list of what to pack for a forthcoming journey.

The truth is that there is only one kind of masterpiece: a masterpiece. I shoved my lists into my pocket, got up, and went inside, leaving a trail of cornmeal from stoop to door. My thought processes had the destination futility of a child's locomotive. Inside, chores needed to be done. I tied up a stack of cardboard for recycling, washed the cats' water bowls, swept up their scattered dry food, then ate a tin of sardines while standing at the sink, brooding over Murakami's well.

The well had gone dry, but due to the miraculous opening

of the portal by the narrator it consequently brimmed with pure, sweet water. Were they really going to fill it? It was too sacred to fill up solely because it was deemed so through a single sentence in a book. In truth the well seemed so appealing that I wanted to procure it myself, and sit like a Samaritan in hope that the Messiah might return and stop for a drink. There would be absolutely no time frame involved, for armed with such a hope one could be induced to wait forever. Unlike the narrator, I had no desire to actually enter it and go down like Alice into Murakami's wonderland. I could never conquer my aversion for enclosure, or being underwater. I merely wanted to be in its proximity and be free to drink from it. For like some mad conquistador I craved it.

But how to find the Miyawaki place? Truthfully I wasn't daunted. We are guided by roses, the scent of a page. Hadn't I traveled all the way to King's College after reading of the infamous scuffle between Karl Popper and Ludwig Wittgenstein in the book *Wittgenstein's Poker*? So enthralled that with a mere slip of paper scribbled with an enigmatic H-3, I successfully routed out the whereabouts of the Cambridge Moral Sciences Club, where the contentious battle between the two great philosophers occurred. Found, gained entrance, and took several oblique photographs relatively useless to anyone save myself. I can say that it was no easy task. Some additional sleuthing sent me past a concealed farmhouse at the end of a long dirt road to the unkempt grave of Wittgenstein, whose name was all but obliterated by a stippled network of mildew, algae, and lichen, appearing as if strange equations from his own hand.

·

I suppose it could seem ludicrous to be fixated on a property some twelve thousand miles away; even more problematic the attempt to locate a place that may or may not exist save in the mind of Murakami. I could see if I could channel his channel or just dive into the animate mental pool and call out, *Hey, where's the bird sculpture?* or *What's the number of the real estate agent selling the Miyawaki place?* Or I could simply ask Murakami himself. I could find his address or write him through his publisher. This was a unique opportunity— a living writer! So much easier than attempting to channel a nineteenth-century poet or an eleventh-century icon painter. Yet wouldn't that be an act of out-and-out chicanery? Imagine Sherlock Holmes going to Conan Doyle for the answer to a difficult riddle instead of working it out himself. He would never deign to ask Doyle, even if a life depended on it, especially his own. No, I would not ask Murakami. Though I could attempt an aerial CAT scan of his subconscious network or just innocently meet him for coffee where portals connect.

What would the portal look like? I wondered.

Several voices rang out, their answers crisscrossing one another.

—Like a vacant terminal at the Berlin Tempelhof airport.

—Like the open circle in the roof of the Pantheon.

—Like the oval table in the garden of Schiller.

This was interesting. Unrelated portals. Red herring or clue? I went through some boxes, certain that I had taken a few shots of the old Berlin terminal. I had no luck but did find two pictures of the oval table in a small book of poems by Friedrich Schiller. I removed them from their glassine envelope, identical save for the sun blotting more of one shot than the other, taken from an obscure angle to emphasize its resemblance to the mouth of a baptismal font.

In 2009 a few members of the CDC met in the city of Jena, in the east of Thuringia, within the wide valley of the Saale River. It was not an official meeting, more a poetic mission, at the Friedrich Schiller summerhouse, in the garden where he wrote *Wallenstein*. We were celebrating the oft-forgotten Fritz Loewe, Alfred Wegener's right-hand man.

Loewe was a tall, sensitive man with slightly protruding teeth and an awkward gait. A classic scientist with meditative fortitude, he joined Wegener for the expedition to Greenland to assist in glaciological work. In 1930 he accompanied Wegener on the grueling journey from Western Station to

Eismitte where two scientists, Ernst Sorge and Johannes Georgi, were camped. Loewe suffered severe frostbite and could go no farther than the Eismitte camp and Wegener continued on without him. Toes on both of Loewe's feet were crudely amputated on-site without anesthesia, leaving him prone in his sleeping bag for the coming months. Unaware their leader had perished, Loewe and his fellow scientists waited from November to May for his return. On Sunday evenings Loewe would read them poems of Goethe and Schiller, filling their ice crypt with the warmth of immortality.

We sat together in the grass by the oval table where Schiller and Goethe once spent hours conversing. We read a passage from Sorge's essay, "Winter at Eismitte," that spoke of Loewe's stoicism and endurance, and then from a selection of the poems he had read during their terrible isolation. It was late May and flowers were in bloom. From the distance we could hear a lilting melody played on a concertina that we affectionately called "Loewe's Song." We said our farewells and I continued on, boarding a train to Weimar, in search of the house where Nietzsche had lived under the care of his younger sister.

I taped one of the photographs of the stone table above my desk. Despite its simplicity I thought it innately powerful, a conduit transporting me back to Jena. The table was indeed a valuable element for comprehending the concept of portal-hopping. I was certain that if two friends laid their hands upon it, like a Ouija board, it would be possible for them to be enveloped in the atmosphere of Schiller at his twilight, and Goethe in his prime.

All doors are open to the believer. It is the lesson of the Samaritan woman at the well. In my sleepy state it occurred to me that if the well was a portal out, there must also be a portal in. There must be a thousand and one ways to find it. I should be happy with the one. It might be possible to pass through the orphic mirror like the drunken poet Cègeste in Cocteau's *Orphée*. But I did not wish to pass through mirrors, nor quantum tunnel walls, or bore my way into the mind of the writer.

In the end it was Murakami himself who provided me with an unobtrusive solution. The narrator in *Wind-Up Bird* accomplished moving through the well into the hallway of an indefinable hotel by visualizing himself swimming, akin to his happiest moments. As Peter Pan instructed Wendy and her brothers in order to fly: *Think happy thoughts.*

I scoured the niches of former joys, halting at a moment of secret exaltation. Though it would take some time, I knew just how to do it. First I would close my eyes and concentrate on the hands of a ten-year-old girl fingering a skate key on a cherished lace from the shoe of a twelve-year-old boy. Think happy thoughts. I would simply roller skate through the portal.

Frida Kahlo's bed, Casa Azul, Coyoacán

Wheel of Fortune

—•— ⟨•⟩ —•—

For a time I did not dream. My ball bearings somewhat rusted, I went round in waking circles, then on horizontal treks, one touchstone after another, nothing actually to touch. Not getting anywhere, I reverted to an old game, one invented long ago as an insomnia counterattack but also useful on long bus rides as a distraction from carsickness. An interior hopscotch played in the mind, not on foot. The playing field amounted to a kind of a road, a seemingly limitless but actually finite alignment of pyrite squares one must succeed in advancing in order to reach a destination of mythic resonance, say, the Alexandria Serapeum with its entrance card attached to a tasseled velvet rope swaying from above. One proceeds by uttering an uninterrupted stream of words beginning with a chosen letter, say, the letter M. Madrigal minuet master monster maestro mayhem mercy mother marshmallow merengue mastiff mischief marigold mind, on and on without stopping, advancing word by word, square by square. How many times have I played this game, always falling short of the swinging tassel, but at the worst winding up in a dream somewhere? And so I played again. I closed my eyes, let my wrist go limp, my hand circling above the keyboard of my Air, then stopped and my finger pointed the way. V. Venus Verdi Violet Vanessa villain vector valor vitamin vestige vortex vault vine virus vial vermin vellum venom veil, suddenly parting as easily as a vaporous curtain signaling the beginning of a dream.

I was standing in the middle of the same café in its recurring dreamscape. No waitress, no coffee. I was obliged to go to the back and grind some beans and brew them myself. No one was around save the cowpoke. I noticed he had a scar like a small snake moving down his collarbone. I poured us both a steaming mug but avoided his eyes.

—Greek legends don't tell us anything, he was saying. Legends are stories. People interpret them or attach morals to them. Medea or the Crucifixion, you can't break them down. The rain and the sun came simultaneously and begat a rainbow. Medea found Jason's eyes and she sacrificed their children. These things happen, that's all, the undeniable domino effect of being alive.

He went to relieve himself while I contemplated the Golden Fleece according to Pasolini. I stood at the door and looked out into the horizon. The dusty scape was interrupted by rocky hills devoid of vegetation. I wondered if Medea climbed such rocks after her rage was satiated. I wondered who the cowpoke was. A kind of Homeric drifter, I supposed. I waited for him to exit the john but he was taking too long. There were signs that things were about to shift: an erratic timepiece, the spinning barstool, and an ailing bee levitating above the surface of a small table coated with cream-colored enamel. I thought to save it but there was nothing I could do. I was about to leave without paying for my coffee, then thinking better of it, dropped a few coins on the table next to the expiring bee. Enough for the coffee and a modest matchbox burial.

I shook myself out of my dream, got out of bed, washed my face, braided my hair, found my watch cap and notebook, and headed out still thinking of the cowpoke spewing on about Euripides and Apollonius. Initially he had rubbed me the wrong way, but I had to admit his recurring presence was a comfort. Someone I could find, if need be, in that same scape on the edge of sleep.

As I crossed Sixth Avenue *Callas is Medea is Callas* looped in rhythm with my boot heels hitting the surface of the street. Pier Paolo Pasolini peers into his casting ball and chooses Maria Callas, one of the most expressive voices of all time, for an epic role with little dialogue and absolutely no singing. Medea does not sing lullabies; she slaughters her children. Maria was not a perfect singer; she drew from the depths of her infinite well and conquered the worlds of her world. But all the heartbreak of her heroines had not prepared her for her own. Betrayed, forsaken, she was left without love, voice, or child, condemned to live out her life in solitude. I preferred to imagine Maria free of the heavy vestments of Medea, the burned queen in a pale yellow sheath. She is wearing pearls. The light floods her Paris apartment as she reaches for a small leather casket. Love is the most precious jewel of all, she whispers, unclasping the pearls that drop from her throat, scales of sorrow that soar and diminish.

Café 'Ino was open but empty; the cook was there alone roasting garlic. I walked over to a nearby bakery, bought a coffee and a piece of crumb cake, and sat on a bench in Father Demo Square. I watched a boy lift his younger sister so she could drink from a water fountain. When she was done he drank his fill. Pigeons were already congregating. As I unwrapped the cake I projected a shambolic crime scene involving frenzied pigeons, brown sugar, and armies of extremely motivated ants. I looked down at the bits of grass protruding through cracked cement. Where are all the ants? And the bees and the little white butterflies we used to see everywhere? And what about the jellyfish and the shooting stars? Opening my journal I glanced at a few drawings. An ant made its way across a page devoted to a Chilean wine palm found in the Orto Botanico in Pisa. There was a small sketch of its trunk but not the leaves. There was a small sketch of heaven but not the earth.

A letter arrived. It was from the director of Casa Azul, home and resting place of Frida Kahlo, requesting I give a talk centering on the artist's revolutionary life and work. In return I would be granted permission to photograph her belongings, the talismans of her life. Time to travel, to acquiesce to fate. For although I craved solitude, I decided I could not pass on an opportunity to speak in the same garden that I had longed to enter as a young girl. I would enter the house inhabited by

Frida and Diego Rivera, and walk through rooms I had only seen in books. I would be back in Mexico.

My introduction to Casa Azul was *The Fabulous Life of Diego Rivera*—a gift from my mother for my sixteenth birthday. It was a seductive book, nourishing a growing desire to immerse myself in Art. I dreamed of traveling to Mexico, to taste their revolution, tread upon their earth, and pray before trees inhabited by their mysterious saints.

I reread the letter with a growing enthusiasm. I thought about the task ahead, and my young self traveling there in the spring of 1971. I was in my early twenties. I saved my money and bought a ticket to Mexico City. I had to make a connection in Los Angeles. I remember seeing a billboard with an image of a woman crucified on a telegraph pole—*L.A. Woman*. The Doors single "Riders on the Storm" was on the radio. Then, I had no such letter, no real-world plan, but I had a mission and that was good enough for me. I wanted to write a book called *Java Head*. William Burroughs had told me the best coffee in the world was grown in the mountains surrounding Veracruz, and I was determined to find it.

I arrived in Mexico City and went immediately to the train station where I bought a round-trip ticket. The overnight sleeper was leaving in seven hours. I shoved a notebook, a Bic pen, an ink-stained copy of Artaud's *Anthology,* and a small Minox camera into a linen knapsack and left the rest of my stuff in a locker. After changing some money I wandered into the cafeteria down the street from the now-defunct Hotel Ortega and ordered a bowl of codfish stew. I can still see the fish bones swimming in the saffron-colored stock, and a long spine lodged in my throat. I sat there alone, choking. Finally I succeeded in pulling it out with my thumb and forefinger without gagging or drawing attention to myself. I wrapped the bone in a napkin, pocketed it, summoned the waiter, and paid up.

I regained my composure and boarded a bus to Coyoacán in the southwest section of the city, the address for Casa Azul in my pocket. It was a beautiful day and I was filled with anticipation. But I arrived only to find it closed for extensive renovation. I stood numbly before the great blue walls. There was nothing I could do, no one to petition. I was not to enter Casa Azul that day. I walked a few blocks to the house where Trotsky was murdered; through such an intimate act of betrayal Genet would have elevated the assassin to sainthood. I lit a candle at the Church of the Baptist and I sat in a pew with my hands folded, periodically assessing the minor damage to my bone-bruised throat. Back at the train station a porter allowed me to board early. I had a small sleeping compartment. There was a wooden seat that folded down that I draped with a multicolored striped scarf, propping my Artaud book against the peeling mirror. I was really happy. I was on my way to Veracruz, an important center of the coffee trade in Mexico. It was there that I imagined I would write a post-Beat meditation on my substance of choice.

The train ride was uneventful, with no Alfred Hitchcock special effects. I reviewed my plan. I desired no major experience save to find fair lodgings and the perfect cup of joe. I could drink fourteen cups without compromising my sleep.

The first hotel I hit was all I could wish for. Hotel Internacional. I was given a whitewashed room with a sink, an overhead fan, and a window that overlooked the town square. I tore an image of Artaud in Mexico from my book and set it on the plaster mantel behind a votive candle. He had loved Mexico and I reasoned he would like being back. After a brief rest I counted out my money, took what I needed, and stuffed the rest in a handwoven cotton sock with a tiny rose embroidered on the ankle.

I hit the street and chose a well-situated bench as to clock the area. I watched as men periodically emerged from one of two hotels and headed down the same street. At midmorning I discreetly tailed one through a winding side street to a café that, despite its modest appearance, seemed the heart of the coffee action. It was not a real café, but it was a real coffee dealer. There was no door. The black-and-white chessboard floor was covered in sawdust. Burlap sacks heavy with coffee beans lined the walls. There were a few small tables, but everyone was standing. There were no women inside. There were no women anywhere. So I just kept walking.

On the second day of my beat, I sauntered in as if I belonged, shuffling through the sawdust. I wore my Wayfarers, acquired at the tobacco shop on Sheridan Square, and a raincoat I had bought secondhand on the Bowery. It was a high-class job, paper-thin though slightly frayed. My cover was journalist for *Coffee Trader Magazine*. I sat at one of the small round tables and lifted two fingers. I wasn't sure what this meant, but the men all did it with happy results. I wrote incessantly in my notebook. No one seemed to mind. The next slow-moving hours could only be described as sublime. I noticed a calendar tacked over a sack of overflowing beans marked Chiapas. It was February 14 and I was about to give my heart to a perfect cup of coffee. It was presented to me somewhat ceremoniously. The proprietor stood over me in wait. I offered him a bright, grateful smile. *Hermosa,* I said, and he smiled broadly in return. Coffee distilled from beans highland grown, entwined with wild orchids and dusted with their pollen; an elixir marrying nature's extremes.

The rest of the morning I sat watching the men come and go sampling coffee and sniffing out the various beans. Shaking them, holding them to their ears like shells, and rolling them on a flat table with their small, thick hands, as if divining a fortune. Then they would place an order. In those hours, the proprietor and I shared not a word, but the coffee kept coming. Sometimes in a cup, sometimes in a glass. At lunch hour everyone departed, including the proprietor. I rose and inspected the sacks, pocketing a few choice beans as souvenirs.

This regimen was repeated for the next few days. I finally admitted that I was not writing for a magazine but for posterity. I want to write an aria to coffee, I explained without apology, something enduring like the *Coffee Cantata* of Bach. The proprietor stood before me with his arms folded. How would he respond to such hubris? Then he left, gesturing that I stay put. I had no idea whether Bach's *Coffee Cantata* was a work of genius, but his mania for coffee, at a time when it was frowned upon as a drug, is well known. A habit Glenn Gould certainly adopted when he fused with the *Goldberg Variations* and cried out somewhat maniacally from the piano,

I am Bach! Well, I wasn't anybody. I worked in a bookstore and took leave to write a book I never really wrote.

Soon he reappeared with two plates of black beans, roasted corn, tortillas with sugar, and sliced cactus. We ate together, and then he brought me one last cup. I settled my bill and showed him my notebook. He bade me follow him to his worktable. He took his official seal as a coffee trader and solemnly stamped a blank page. We shook hands knowing most likely we would never meet again, nor would I find coffee as transporting as his.

I packed swiftly, tossing *Wind-Up Bird* on top of my small metal suitcase. Everything on my list: passport black jacket dungarees underwear 4 tee shirts 6 pairs of bee socks Polaroid film packs Land 250 Camera black watch cap tin of arnica graph paper Moleskine Ethiopian cross. I took my tarot deck out of its worn chamois pouch and drew a card, a little habit before traveling. It was the card of destiny. I sat and sleepily stared at the great revolving wheel. Okay, I thought, that will do.

I awoke dreaming of Pat Sajak. Actually, I couldn't be sure that it was really Pat Sajak, as I only saw male hands turning oversized cards to reveal particular letters. The peculiar thing is I felt I was revisiting a former dream. The hands would turn over several letters, enough for me to guess a word, but I would come up empty. In my sleep I strained to see the perimeter of the dream. It was all in close-up. There was no way to see any more than I was seeing. In fact the outer edges were slightly distorted, making the material of his fine gabardine suit seem warped, like a nubby raw silk. He also appeared to have a manicure, neat and trim. He was wearing a gold signet ring on his pinky. I should have examined it more closely, as it may have revealed whether it was stamped with his initials.

Later I remembered that Pat Sajak doesn't turn the letters over in real life. Though it's debatable whether a game show counts as real life. Everyone knows that Vanna White, not Pat, turns the letters. But I had forgotten and even worse, could not, for the life of me, conjure an image of her face. I was able to summon a parade of shiny sheath dresses but not her face, a fact that bothered me, producing the same uneasiness one might experience if questioned by the authorities about one's whereabouts on a specific day and having no substantial alibi. I was home, I would have answered feebly, watching Pat Sajak turning letters that formed words I could not make out.

My car arrived. I locked my suitcase, pocketed my passport, and got into the backseat. There was a lot of traffic, and we sat there waiting for a slot outside the Holland Tunnel. I got to thinking about Pat Sajak's hands. There is a theory that it is good luck to see one's own hands in a dream. A portent to aspire to, but one's own hands—not the hands of Pat in close-up doing Vanna's thing. Then I dozed off and had an entirely different dream. I was in a forest and the trees were laden with sacred ornaments that glittered in the sun. They were too high to reach so I shook them down with a long, wooden staff that was conveniently lying in the grass. When I poked at the leafy branches scores of tiny silver hands rained down and landed by my shoes. They were scuffed-up brown oxfords like I wore in grade school and when I reached down to scoop up the hands I saw a black caterpillar crawling up my sock.

I was disoriented when the car pulled up at Terminal A. Is this where I'm going? I asked. The driver muttered something and I got out, making sure I didn't leave my watch cap behind, and headed into the terminal. I was dropped off at the wrong end and had to snake through hundreds of people going who knows where to find the right ticket counter. The girl behind the counter insisted I use the kiosk. I don't know where I've been for the last decade, but when did the concept of a kiosk make its way into airline terminals? I want a person to give me my boarding pass, but she insisted I type my information on a screen using the damn kiosk. I had to rummage through my bag to find my reading glasses, and then after answering questions and scanning my passport it suggested I triple my mileage for $108. I pressed NO and the screen froze. I had to tell the girl. She said keep pressing it. Then she suggested I try another kiosk. I was getting agitated, the boarding pass jammed, and the girl was forced to fork around with a friendly-skies pen to dislodge it. Triumphantly she handed it to me in a crinkled, dead-lettuce kind of state. I trekked to Security, took my computer out of its case, removed my cap, watch, and boots, and placed them in a bin with my plastic baggie containing toothpaste, rose cream, and bottle of Power-immune, and went through the metal detector, then rounded up my stuff again and boarded the plane to Mexico City.

We sat on the runway for about an hour, the song "Shrimp Boats" looping in my head. I started questioning myself. Why did I get so steamed up at check-in? Why did I want the girl to give me a boarding pass? Why couldn't I just get into the swing of things and get my own? It's the twenty-first century;

they do things differently now. We were about to take off. I was reprimanded for not buckling my seat belt. I forgot to hide the fact by throwing my coat over my lap. I hate being confined, especially when it's for my own good.

I arrived in Mexico City and got a ride to my district. I checked into my hotel and set up camp in a room on the second floor overlooking a small park. There was a big window in the bathroom and I noticed that the same people I was looking down upon were looking up at me. I had a late lunch, looking forward to Mexican food, but the hotel menu was dominated by Japanese fare. This confused yet strangely wedded me to my sense of place: reading Murakami in a Mexican hotel that specializes in sushi. I settled on shrimp tacos with wasabi dressing and a small shot of tequila. Afterwards I stepped out onto the street and noticed I was on Veracruz Avenue, which gave me hope that I might find good coffee. Roaming around I passed a window filled with flesh-colored plaster hands. I figured I must be where I was supposed to be, though things seemed slightly offset, like an image of Mandrake the Magician in the Sunday comics.

Twilight was approaching. I walked up and down the shaded streets and passed rows of taco trucks and newsstands that sold wrestling magazines, flowers, and lottery tickets. I was tired but stopped in the park across Veracruz Avenue. A medium-size yellow mutt broke away from his master, fairly leaping upon me. I felt my being entered by his deep brown eyes. His master quickly retrieved him but the dog kept straining to keep me in his sights. How easy it is, I mused, to fall in love with an animal. I was suddenly very tired. I had been awake since five in the morning. I returned to my room, which had been tended to in my absence. My clothes were neatly folded and my dirty socks were soaking in the sink. I plopped on the bed still fully dressed. I pictured the yellow dog and wondered if I would see him again. I shut my eyes and slowly faded. The sound of someone speaking through a distorted megaphone brought me back. Disembodied words carried by the wind and landing on my windowsill like a deranged homing pigeon. It was after midnight, a strange hour to be speaking through a megaphone.

I awoke late and had to hustle as I had been invited to the American Embassy. We drank tepid coffee and engaged in a semi-successful cultural conversation. But what struck me was something an intern said a moment before my car drove away. Two journalists, a cameraman, and a child were found murdered in Veracruz the night before. The woman and child were strangled and the two men disemboweled. A disconcerting image of the cameraman thrown in a shallow grave passed through my sights; he sat up in the dark and noticed the blanket on his bed was made of sod.

I was hungry. I had what may be loosely termed huevos rancheros for lunch in a place called Café Bohemia. A bowl of soggy tortilla chips, fried eggs, and green salsa, but I ate it anyway. The coffee was lukewarm with a chocolate aftertaste. I struggled with my few Spanish words and managed to piece together *más caliente*. The young waiter grinned and made me another, a perfect hot cup of coffee.

That evening I sat in the park, drinking watermelon juice from a conical paper cup bought from a street vendor. Every child laughing made me think of the slain child. Every dog that barked was yellow in my eyes. Back in my room I could hear all the action below. I sang little songs to the birds on my windowsill. I sang for the journalists and the cameraman and the woman and child slain in Veracruz. I sang for those left to rot in ditches, landfills, and junkyards, like fodder for a Bolaño story he had already considered. The moon was nature's spotlight on the bright faces of the people who gathered in the park below. Their laughter rose with the breeze, and for a brief moment there was no sorrow, no suffering, only unity.

Wind-Up Bird was on the bed next to me but I didn't open it. Instead I thought about the photographs I was going to take in Coyoacán. I fell asleep and was dreaming I had perfect coordination and swift reflexes. Suddenly I awoke unable to move. My bowels exploding, vomit shooting across my bedding, coupled with a crippling migraine. Incapable of rising I just lay there. Instinctively I felt for my glasses. They were blessedly unscathed.

In the first light I was able to grip the telephone and tell the front desk I was very sick and needed help. A maid came into my room and called down for medicine. She helped me undress and wash, scrubbing my bathroom, changing my sheets. My gratitude to this woman was overflowing. She sang as she rinsed out my soiled clothes, hanging them over the window ledge. My head was still pounding. I held on to her hand. As her smiling face hovered over mine I was pulled into a deep sleep.

I opened my eyes and imagined I saw the maid sitting in a

chair by the bed, in a fit of hysterical laughter. She was waving several pages of the manuscript I had slipped under my pillow. I was immediately put off. Not only was she reading my pages, but also they were written in Spanish, seemingly in my own hand, yet incomprehensible to me. I thought about what I had written and could not imagine what had propelled her uproarious state.

—What's so damn funny? I demanded, though I felt a mounting desire to join in, as her laugh was so appealing.

—It's a poem, she answered, a poem completely devoid of poetry.

I was taken aback. Was that a good thing or not? She let my pages slide to the floor. I got up and followed her to the window. She pulled on a slim rope tied to a net sack that contained a struggling pigeon.

—Dinner! she cried triumphantly, throwing it over her shoulder.

As she walked toward the door she seemed to grow smaller and smaller, stepping from her dress, no more than a child. I ran to the window and watched her race across Veracruz Avenue. I stood there transfixed. The air was perfect, like milk from the breast of the great mother. Milk that could be suckled by all her children—the babes of Juárez, Harlem, Belfast, Bangladesh. I could still hear the maid laughing, bubbly little sounds that materialized as transparent wisps, like wishes from another world.

In the morning I assessed how I felt. The worst seemed over, but I felt weak and dehydrated and the headache had migrated to the base of my skull. As my car arrived to take me to Casa

Azul I hoped that it would stay at bay so I could perform my tasks. When the director welcomed me I thought of my young self, standing before the blue door that did not open.

Although Casa Azul is now a museum it maintains the living atmosphere of the two great artists. In the workroom everything was made ready for me. Frida Kahlo's dresses and leather corsets were laid out on white tissue. Her medicine bottles on a table, her crutches against the wall. I suddenly felt unsteady and nauseous, but I was able to take a few photographs. I shot quickly in the low light, slipping the unpeeled Polaroids into my pocket.

I was led to Frida's bedroom. Above her pillow were mounted butterflies so she could look at them as she lay in bed. They were a gift from the sculptor Isamu Noguchi so that she could have something beautiful to view after she lost her leg. I took a photograph of the bed where she had suffered much.

I could no longer hide how sick I felt. The director gave me a glass of water. I sat in the garden with my head in my hands. I felt faint. After conferring with her colleagues she insisted that I rest in Diego's bedroom. I wanted to protest, but I was unable to speak. It was a modest wooden bed with a white coverlet. I set my camera and the small stack of images onto the floor. Two women tacked a long muslin cloth over the entrance to his room. I leaned over and unpeeled the pictures but could not look at them. I lay thinking of Frida. I could feel her proximity, sense her resilient suffering coupled with her revolutionary enthusiasm. She and Diego were my secret guides at sixteen. I braided my hair like Frida, wore a straw hat like Diego, and now I had touched her dresses and was lying in Diego's bed.

One of the women came in and covered me with a shawl. The room was naturally dark, and thankfully I went to sleep.

The director woke me gently with a concerned expression.

—The people will be arriving soon.

—Don't worry, I said, I am fine now. But I will need a chair.

I got up and put on my boots and gathered my pictures: the outline of Frida's crutches, her bed, and the ghost of a stairwell. The atmosphere of sickness glowed within them. That evening I sat before nearly two hundred guests in the garden. I scarcely could say what I talked about, but in the end I sang to them, as I had sung to the birds on my windowsill. It was a song that came to me while I lay in Diego's bed. It was about the butterflies that Noguchi had given to Frida. I saw tears streaming down the faces of the director and the women who had administered to me with such tender care. Faces I no longer remember.

Late that night there was a party in the park across from my hotel. My headache was completely gone. I packed, then looked out the window. The trees were strung with tiny Christmas lights though it was only the seventh of May. I went down to the bar and had a shot of a very young tequila. The bar was empty, as nearly everyone was in the park. I sat for a long time. The bartender refilled my glass. The tequila was light, like flower juice. I closed my eyes and saw a green train with an M in a circle; a faded green like the back of a praying mantis.

Frida Kahlo's crutches, Casa Azul

Dress, Casa Azul

How I Lost the Wind-Up Bird

— ·· ·– ≖◆≣ –· ·· —

I GOT A MESSAGE from Zak. His beach café was open. All the free coffee I wanted. I was happy for him but hesitated to go anywhere, as it was Memorial Day weekend. The city was deserted, just the way I like it, and there was a new episode of *The Killing* on Sunday. I decided to visit Zak's café on Monday and spend the weekend in the city with Detectives Linden and Holder. My room was in a state of complete disarray and I was more unkempt than usual, ready to be comrade to their mute misery, swilling cold coffee in a battered car during a bleak stakeout coming out equally cold. I filled my thermos at the Korean deli, deposited it next to my bed for later, chose a book, and walked over to Bedford Street.

Café 'Ino was empty, so I happily sat and read *The Confusions of Young Törless,* a novel by Robert Musil. I reflected on the opening line: *It was a small station on the long railroad to Russia,* fascinated by the power of an ordinary sentence that leads the reader unwittingly through interminable fields of wheat opening onto a path leading to the lair of a sadistic predator contemplating the murder of an unblemished boy.

I read through the afternoon, on the whole doing nothing. The cook was roasting garlic and singing a song in Spanish.

—What is the song about? I asked.

—Death, he answered with a laugh. But don't worry, nobody dies, it is the death of love.

On Memorial Day I woke early, straightened my room, and filled a sack with what I needed—dark glasses, alkaline water, a bran muffin, and my *Wind-Up Bird.* At the West Fourth Street Station I got the A train to Broad Channel and made my connection; it took fifty-five minutes. Zak's was the only café in the lone concession area on the long stretch of boardwalk along Rockaway Beach. Zak was glad to see me and introduced me to everyone. Then as promised he served me coffee free of charge. I stood drinking it, black, watching the people. There was a happy, relaxed atmosphere with an amiable mix of laid-back surfers and working-class families. I was surprised to see my friend Klaus coming toward me on a bicycle. He was wearing a shirt and tie.

—I was in Berlin visiting my father, he said. I just came from the airport.

—Yeah, JFK is very close, I laughed, watching a low-flying plane coming in for a landing.

We sat on a bench watching small children negotiate the waves.

—The main surfer beach is just five blocks down by the jetty.

—You seem to know this area pretty well.

Klaus was suddenly serious.

—You won't believe this, but I have just bought an old Victorian house here, by the bay. It has a very big yard and I'm planting a huge garden. Something I never could do in Berlin or Manhattan.

We walked across the boardwalk and Klaus got coffee.

—Do you know Zak?

—Everybody knows everybody, he said. It's a real community.

We said our good-byes and I promised to come see his house and garden soon. In truth I was swiftly falling for this area myself, with its endless boardwalk and brick projects overlooking the sea. I removed my boots and walked along the shore. I have always loved the ocean but never learned to swim. Possibly the sole time I was submerged in water was during the involuntary throes of baptism. Nearly a decade later the polio epidemic was in full swing. A sickly child, I wasn't allowed to go in shallow lakes or pools with other kids as the virus was thought to be waterborne. My one respite was the sea, for I was allowed to walk and frolic by its edge. In time I developed a self-protective fear of the water, which expanded into fear of immersion.

Fred didn't swim either. He said that Indians didn't swim. But he loved boats.

We spent a lot of time looking at old tugboats, houseboats, and shrimp trawlers. He especially liked old wooden boats, and on one of our excursions in Saginaw, Michigan, we found one for sale: a late-fifties Chris Craft Constellation, not guaranteed to be seaworthy. We bought it quite cheaply, hauled it back home, and parked it in our yard facing the canal that led to Lake Saint Clair. I had no interest in boating but worked side by side with Fred stripping the hull, scouring the cabin, waxing and polishing the wood, and sewing small curtains for the windows. Summer nights with my thermos of black coffee and a six-pack of Budweiser for Fred, we'd sit in the cabin and listen to Tigers games. I knew little about sports but Fred's devotion to his Detroit team obliged me to know the basic rules, our team members, and our rivals. Fred had been scouted as a young man for a shortstop position on the Tigers farm team. He had a great arm but chose to use it as a guitarist, yet his love of the sport never diminished.

It turned out that our wooden boat had a broken axle, and we didn't have the resources to have it repaired. We were advised to scrap it but we didn't. To the amusement of our neighbors we decided to keep her right where she was, in the better part of our yard. We deliberated on her name and finally chose *Nawader,* an Arabic word for rare thing, taken from a passage in Gérard de Nerval's *Women of Cairo.* In the winter we covered her with a heavy tarp and when baseball season opened again we removed it and listened to Tigers games on a shortwave radio. If the game was delayed we would sit and listen to cassettes on a boom box. Nothing with words, usually something of Coltrane's, like *Olé* or *Live at Birdland.* On the rare occasion of a rainout we would switch over to Beethoven, whom Fred particularly admired. First a piano sonata, and then with the rain steadily falling, we'd listen to Beethoven's *Pastoral* Symphony, following the great composer on an epic walk into the countryside listening to the songs of the birds in the Vienna Woods.

Toward the end of the baseball season Fred surprised me with the official orange-and-blue Detroit Tigers jacket. It was early fall, a bit chilly. Fred fell asleep on the couch and I slipped on the jacket and went out into the yard. I picked up a pear that had fallen from our tree, wiped it off on my sleeve, and sat on a wooden lawn chair in the moonlight. Zipping up my new jacket, I felt the satisfaction of a young athlete receiving his varsity letter. Taking a bite of the pear I imagined being a young pitcher, coming out of nowhere, delivering the Chicago Cubs from their long championship drought by winning thirty-two games in a row. One game more than Denny McClain.

One Indian-summer afternoon the sky turned a distinct

chartreuse. I opened our balcony window to get a closer look; I had never seen such a thing. Suddenly the sky went dark; a massive thunderbolt filled our bedroom with a blinding light. For a moment everything went completely silent, followed by a deafening sound. The lightning had struck our immense weeping willow and it had toppled. It was the oldest willow in Saint Clair Shores and its length stretched from the edge of the canal to clear across the street. As it fell, its massive weight crushed our *Nawader.* Fred was standing at the screen door and I at the window. We watched it happen at the same moment, electrically bound as one consciousness.

I picked up my boots and was admiring the stretch of boardwalk, an infinity of teak, when Zak suddenly appeared with a large coffee to go. We stood there looking out at the water. The sun was going down and the sky turned a pale rose.

—See you soon, I said. Maybe sooner.

—Yeah, this place gets into your blood.

I checked out the surfers and walked up and down the streets between the ocean and the elevated train. As I walked back toward the station I was drawn to a small lot surrounded by a high, weatherbeaten stockade fence. It resembled the kind that secured the Alamo-style forts that my brother and I built as kids. The remains of a cyclone fence propped up the wood palings and a hand-drawn For Sale by Owner sign was tied to the fence with white string. The fence was too high to see what lay behind it, so I stood on my toes and stole a glimpse through a broken slat, like peering into the peephole

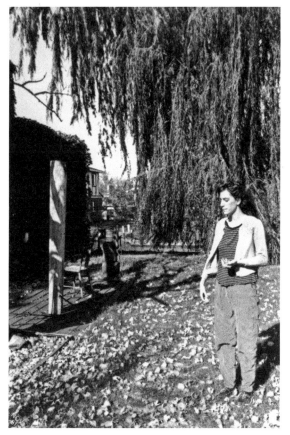

Willows, Saint Clair Shores

in the wall of a museum to view *Étant donnés*—Marcel Du-champ's last stand.

The lot was about twenty-five feet wide and less than a hundred feet deep, the standard size allotted for workers constructing the amusement park in the early twentieth century. Some built makeshift dwelling places, few surviving. I located another weak spot in the fence and got a closer look. The small yard was overgrown, liberally strewn with rusting debris, stacks of tires, and a fishing boat on a bent-up trailer nearly obscuring the bungalow. On the train I tried to read but couldn't concentrate, I was so taken by Rockaway Beach and the ramshackle bungalow behind the derelict wooden fence that I could think of nothing else.

A few days later I was walking aimlessly and found myself in Chinatown. I suppose I had been daydreaming, for I was sur-prised as I passed a window display of duck carcasses hanging to dry. I badly needed coffee, so I entered a small café and took a seat. Unfortunately the Silver Moon Café was not a café at all, but once entered, it was nearly impossible to leave. The wood tables and floors were wiped down with tea and its mild fragrance hung in the air. There was a clock with the hour hand missing and a faded picture of an astronaut in a baby blue plastic frame. There was no menu except a lami-nated card showing four dishes of similar-looking steamed buns, each with a small, raised red, blue, or silver square in the center, like stamps of faded sealing wax. As to the filling it seemed to be a crapshoot.

I was disappointed as I was dying for a cup of coffee, yet I could not get up. The scent of oolong seemed to have the dozy effect of the poppy fields of Oz. An old woman poked me in the shoulder and I blurted: Combo. She mumbled something in Chinese, then left. A small dog sat dutifully beneath a table watching the movements of an elderly man with a yo-yo. He repeatedly tried to lure the dog with his yo-yo skills, but the dog turned his head. I tried not to watch the motion of the yo-yo, up and down and then sideways on the string.

I must have nodded off, for when I opened my eyes a glass of oolong tea and three buns on a narrow bamboo tray had been set before me. The middle bun had a faded blue stamp. I hadn't a clue as to what that meant but I decided to save it for last. The ones on either side were savory. But the filling in the middle one was a revelation—an elegantly textured red-bean paste that lingered on my breath. I paid the check and the old woman reversed the Open sign as soon as I closed the door, although there were still customers inside as well as the dog and the yo-yo. I had the distinct impression that if I doubled back there would be no trace of the Silver Moon.

Still in need of coffee I stopped at the Atlas Café then walked over to Canal Street to get the subway. I bought a MetroCard from a machine, knowing I would eventually lose it. I much prefer tokens, but those days are gone. I waited for about ten minutes, then boarded the express train to the Rockaways, feeling oddly exhilarated. My brain was fast-forwarding at a speed that could not be translated into mere language. The train was pretty empty, which was good, since I spent much of the ride interrogating myself. By the time it reached Broad Channel, just two stops from Rockaway Beach, I knew what I was going to do.

I stood in front of the fence on tiptoe and peered through the broken slat. All kinds of indistinct memories collided. Vacant lots skinned knees train yards mystical hobos forbidden yet wondrous dwellings of mythical junkyard angels. I had lately been seduced by a piece of abandoned property described in the pages of a book, but this was real. The For Sale by Owner sign seemed to radiate like the electric sign Steppenwolf comes across while on a solitary night walk: *Magic Theater. Entrance Not for Everybody. For Madmen Only!* Somehow the two signs seemed equivalent. I scribbled the seller's phone number on a scrap of paper and walked across the road to Zak's café and got a large black coffee. I sat on a bench on the boardwalk for a long time, looking out at the sea.

This area had thoroughly bewitched me, casting a spell that originated much further back than I could remember. I thought of the mysterious wind-up bird. Have you led me here? I wondered. Close to the sea, though I cannot swim. Close to the train, as I cannot drive. The boardwalk echoed a youth spent in South Jersey with its boardwalks—Wildwood, Atlantic City, Ocean City—more active perhaps but not as beautiful. It seemed the perfect place, with no billboards and few signs of encroaching commerce. And the hidden bungalow! How quickly it had charmed me. I imagined it transformed. A place to think, make spaghetti, brew coffee, a place to write.

Back home I looked at the number I'd written on the scrap of paper but could not bring myself to dial it. I placed it on my night table before my little television set, a strange talisman. Finally I called my friend Klaus and asked him to make the call for me. I suppose a part of me was afraid it was not really for sale or that someone else had already gotten it.

—Of course, he said. I will talk to the owner and find out the details. It would be wonderful if we were neighbors. I'm already renovating my house and it's only ten blocks from the bungalow.

Klaus dreamed of a garden and found his land. I believed I dreamed of this exact place without knowing it. The wind-up bird had awakened an old yet recurring desire—a dream as old as my café dream—to live by the sea with a ragged garden of my own.

A few days later the seller's daugher-in-law, a good-natured young woman with two small boys, met me in front of the old blockade fence. We could not enter through the gate, as the owner padlocked it as a safety precaution. Klaus had given me all the information I needed. Because of its condition and some tax liens it was not a bank-friendly property, so the buyer would be obliged to produce cash. Other prospective buyers, seeking a bargain, had grossly underbid. We discussed a fair amount. I told her I would need three months to raise the money, and after some discussion with the owner, all agreed.

—I'm working all summer. When I come back in September I will have the sum I need. I suppose we will have to trust one another, I said.

We shook hands. She removed the For Sale by Owner sign

and waved good-bye. Although I was unable to see inside the house I had no doubt that I had made the right decision. Whatever I found to be good I would preserve, and transform what was not.

—I already love you, I told the house.

I sat at my corner table and dreamed of the bungalow. By my calculations I would have the sum I needed to acquire the property by Labor Day. I already had a busy workload and took every other available job I could get from the middle of

June through August. I had quite a diverse itinerary of readings, performances, concerts, and lectures. I placed my manuscript into a folder, my pile of scribbled napkins into a large plastic baggie, wrapped my camera in linen, and then locked it all away. I packed my small metal suitcase and flew to London for a night of room service and ITV3 detectives and then I was off to Brighton, Leeds, Glasgow, Edinburgh, Amsterdam, Vienna, Berlin, Lausanne, Barcelona, Brussels, Bilbao, and Bologna. Afterwards I flew to Gothenburg and embarked on a small concert tour of Scandinavia. I plunged happily into work, carefully measuring myself in the heat wave that doggedly pursued me. At night, unable to sleep, I completed an introduction for *Astragal,* a monograph on William Blake, and meditations on Yves Klein and Francesca Woodman. Every so often I returned to my Bolaño poem, still languishing between 96 and 104 lines. It became something of a hobby, a deeply wrenching one that produced no finished result. How much easier if I had simply assembled small airplane models, applying minute decals and touches of enamel paint.

In early September I returned somewhat exhausted but well satisfied. I had accomplished my mission, losing only one pair of glasses. I had yet one last commitment in Monterrey, Mexico, and then could take a long-needed break. I was among a handful of speakers at a forum of women for women, serious activists whose travails I could barely comprehend. I felt humbled in their presence and wondered how I could possibly serve them. I read poems, sang them songs, and made them laugh.

In the morning a few of us went through two police checkpoints to La Huasteca to a roped-off canyon at the foot of a

steep mountain cliff. It was a breathtaking though danger-
ous place, but we felt nothing but awe. I said a prayer to the
lime-dusted mountain, then was drawn to a small rectangular
light some twenty feet away. It was a white stone. Actually
more tablet than stone, the color of foolscap, as if waiting for
another commandment to be etched on its polished surface. I
walked over and without hesitation picked it up and put it in
my coat pocket as if it were written to do so.

I had thought to bring the strength of the mountain to my
little house. I felt an instantaneous affection for it and kept
my hand in my pocket in order to touch it, a missal of stone. It
was not until later at the airport, as a customs inspector confis-
cated it, that I realized I had not asked the mountain whether
or not I could have it. Hubris, I mourned, sheer hubris. The
inspector firmly explained it could be deemed a weapon. It's
a holy stone, I told him, and begged him not to toss it away,
which he did without flinching. It bothered me deeply. I had
taken a beautiful object, formed by nature, out of its habitat to
be thrown into a sack of security rubble.

When I disembarked to change planes in Houston, I went to
the bathroom. I was still carrying *The Wind-Up Bird Chronicle*
along with a copy of *Dwell* magazine. There was a stainless-steel
ledge on the right side of the toilet. I placed them there noting what a nice element it was, but as I boarded my connecting
plane I realized my hands were empty. I felt quite sad. A heavily marked-up paperback stained with coffee and olive oil, my
traveling companion and the mascot of my resurging energy.

The stone and the book: what did it mean? I took the stone
from the mountain and it was taken from me. A kind of moral

balance, I well understood. But the loss of the book seemed different, more capricious. Quite by accident I had let go of the string attached to Murakami's well, the abandoned lot, and the bird sculpture. Perhaps because I had found a place of my own and now the Miyawaki place could spin in reverse, happily back to the interconnected world of Murakami. The wind-up bird's work was done.

September was ending and already cold. I was heading up Sixth Avenue and stopped to buy a new watch cap from a street vendor. As I pulled it on an old man approached me. His blue eyes burned and his hair was white as snow. I noticed that his wool gloves were unraveling and his left hand was bandaged.

—Give me the money you have in your pocket, he said.

Either I am being tested, I thought, or I have wandered into the opening of a modern fairy tale. I had a twenty and three singles, which I placed in his hand.

—Good, he said after a moment, and then returned the twenty.

I thanked him and continued on, more buoyant than before.

There were a lot of people in a hurry on the street, as if last-minute shoppers on Christmas Eve. I hadn't noticed at first and it seemed they were steadily multiplying. A young woman brushed past me with an armful of flowers. A dizzying perfume lingered, then dispelled, replaced by a vertiginous refrain. I felt conscious of everything: a beating heart, the scent of a song wafting in a conflict of breezes, and the human current heading home.

Three dollars short, richer longer love.

The signs were good. Closing date was October 4. My real estate lawyer attempted to sway me against buying the bungalow due to its ramshackle state and questionable resale value. He failed to comprehend that these were positive qualities in my book. A few days later I paid the sum that I had amassed and was given the key and the deed for an uninhabitable little house on a withered lot, steps away from the train to the right and the sea to the left.

The transformation of the heart is a wondrous thing, no matter how you land there. I heated up some beans and ate quickly, walked to the West Fourth Street Station, and got the A train to the Rockaways. I thought of my brother, our hours on rainy mornings assembling Lincoln Log forts and cabins. We were devoted to Fess Parker, our Davy Crockett. *Be sure you're right, then go ahead* was his maxim that soon became ours. He was a good man amounting to much more than a hill of beans. We walked with him as I walk with Detective Linden.

I got off at Broad Channel and boarded the shuttle. It was a mild October day. I loved this short walk from the train up the quiet street, each step closer to the sea. I no longer had to peer longingly at the bungalow through a broken slat. I ignored the No Trespassing sign and for the first time I stepped inside my house. It was empty save a child's acoustic guitar with broken strings and a black rubber horseshoe. Nothing but good. Small rooms rusted sink vaulted ceiling century-old smells mingling with musty animal smells. I couldn't stay very long, for the mold and a prevailing dampness ignited my cough yet did not dampen my enthusiasm. I knew exactly what to do:

one great room, one turning fan, skylights, a country sink, a desk, some books, a daybed, Mexican-tile floor, and a stove. I sat on my lopsided porch and gazed with girlish happiness at my yard dotted with resilient dandelions. A wind picked up and I could feel the sea within it. I locked my door and closed the gate as a stray cat squeezed through an open slat. Sorry, no milk today, only joy. I stood before the battered blockade fence. My Alamo, I said, and from that moment on my house had a name.

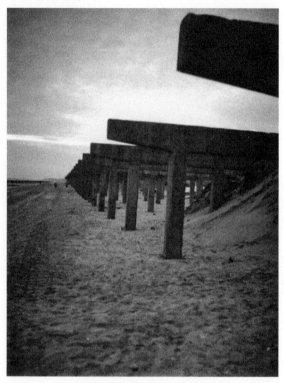

Aftermath, Rockaway Beach

Her Name Was Sandy

THERE WERE PUMPKINS on sale outside the Korean deli. Halloween. I got some coffee and stood looking at the sky. A distant storm was brewing; I could feel it in my bones. The light was already low and silvery and I had a sudden impulse to go to Rockaway to take some pictures of my house. As I gathered some things, providence brought my friend Jem to my door. Every now and then he pops by unannounced and I am always glad of that. Jem, a filmmaker, was carrying his Bolex 16-mm camera and a portable tripod.

—I was shooting nearby, he said. Want some coffee?

—I just had some, but come to Rockaway Beach with me. You can see my house and the most beautiful boardwalk in America.

Jem was game so I grabbed my Polaroid camera. We hopped the A train, catching up with things on the way, mining the troubles of the world. We made the connection at Broad Channel, ascended the long metal stairs of the elevated train, and walked to my house. I needed no portal to enter;

I had the key on an old rabbit's foot from my father's desk drawer.

—You are mine, I whispered, opening the door.

It was too dusty for me to stay inside very long, but I happily sketched out my plans for future renovation as Jem shot some film. I took a few pictures of my own and then we walked over to the beach.

The cold light over the sea was swiftly fading. I went by the water's edge and stood with some gulls who seemed undaunted by my presence. Jem had set up his tripod and was hunched over, filming. I took his picture and several of the empty boardwalk, then sat on a bench as Jem packed up. Halfway back I realized that I'd left my camera on the bench, but I still had the pictures as I'd slid them into my pocket. It wasn't my only camera but it was my favorite, for it had blue bellows, and had served me well. It was unsettling to imagine it alone on the bench without film, unable to record its own passage into the hands of a stranger.

Jem and I said our good-byes as the train pulled into his stop. There's a storm coming, he said, as the doors closed. The sky was already dark when I arrived at the West Fourth Street Station. I stopped at Mamoun's and got a falafel to go. The atmosphere was heavy and I noticed my breathing was shallow. When I got home I put some dry food out for the cats, switched on *CSI: Miami,* turned down the volume, and fell asleep with my coat on.

I awoke late, feeling apprehensive, an uneasiness that I willed myself to shake. I told myself it was just the coming storm. But in my heart I knew it was also something else, the time of year, one of emotional duality. A happy time for children, marking Fred's passing.

I was fidgety at 'Ino. I had some bean soup for lunch, hardly touching my coffee. I wondered if it was a bad omen leaving my camera on the boardwalk. I thought to go back, irrationally hoping to find it still sitting on the bench. It was an outmoded object not worth much to most people. I decided to return to Rockaway, and walked home quickly trying to avoid mounting images of Fred's last days. I threw a few things in a sack, and then stopped back at the deli for a corn muffin to take on the train.

The human mood was frenetic. People were crowding the normally laid-back deli, piling up supplies, preparing for an impending storm that had in the last hours dissipated, then strengthened to a category 1 hurricane, and was now heading our way. I was several beats behind and felt suddenly hemmed in. A coastal emergency plan was being issued, and we stood listening to the small shortwave radio perched atop the cash register. Planes were grounded, subways were closing, and a mass evacuation of the beach-lying areas was already set in motion. There was no getting to Rockaway Beach today; there was no getting anywhere.

Back home I checked supplies—plenty of cat food, spaghetti, a few cans of sardines, peanut butter, and bottled water. Computer charged, candles, matches, a few flashlights, and an inbred cockiness that would eventually be challenged. By nightfall the city had turned off our gas and electric. No light, no heat. Temperatures were dropping and I sat on the bed wrapped in a down comforter with all three cats. They know, I thought, like the birds of Iraq before *shock and awe* on the first day of spring. It was said that the sparrows and songbirds stopped singing, their silence heralding the dropping of bombs.

Since I was a child I have been extremely storm sensitive, I can usually feel when one is coming and its magnitude by the amount of pain in my limbs. The most powerful storm I could remember was Hurricane Hazel, which blew into the East Coast in 1954. My father had night work and my mother, sister, and brother were huddled together beneath the kitchen table. I had a migraine and lay on the couch. My mother was terrified by storms, but they excited me, for when a storm broke, my discomfort was replaced with a kind of euphoria. But this one felt different; the air was remarkably charged and I felt nauseous and somewhat breathless.

The enormous full moon dropped its milky light through the skylight like a rope ladder that spread across my Chinese rug and the edge of my quilt. Everything was still. I read with the aid of a battery-powered lantern that projected a white rainbow across the objects arranged on the bookcase not six feet from my bed. The rain was hammering the skylight. I felt the trepidation of October's end, magnified by the waxing moon and a commemoration of storms assembling in the sea.

A multitude of converging forces seemed to bring these memories entirely present. Halloween. All Saints' Day. All Souls' Day. Fred's passing day.

Racing through Detroit on Mischief Morning with Fred in the back of an ambulance to the same hospital where our children were born. Returning home alone after midnight in a raging thunderstorm. Fred was not born in a hospital. He was born during an electrical storm at his grandparents' home in West Virginia. Lightning streaked the purple sky and the midwife did not make it, so his grandfather saw to the birth, delivering him in the kitchen. Fred believed that if he ever entered a hospital he would never leave. His Indian blood felt such inexplicable things.

Flash floods, high winds, the canal overflowing. Jackson and I piling sandbags before the door leading to the flooding basement, metal trash cans and twisted bicycles littering the rain-sodden streets. Fred, fighting for his life, could be felt in the howling wind. A great branch from our oak tree fell across the driveway, a message from him, my quiet man.

On Halloween, resilient children with raincoats over their costumes ran through the black rain-soaked streets with sacks of candy. Our little daughter slept in her costume, believing her father would see it when he came home.

I turned off the lantern and sat listening to high vocal winds and the pounding rain. The storm's energy drew out every memory of these days, a dark autumn journey. I could feel Fred closer than ever. His rage and sorrow for being torn away. The skylight was leaking badly. It was a time of the tearing. I rose in the dark and moved my books and got a bucket. The moon was now obscured but I could feel it, massive and full, drawing out the tides and melding powerful natural forces that were to transform our coastline into a twisted version of itself.

Her name was Sandy. I had felt her coming yet never could

have predicted her awesome power and the terrible destruction left in her wake. The following days after the storm I still walked over to 'Ino, full knowing it would be closed, as was our quadrant of the city. No gas or electricity, so no coffee, but a comforting habit I did not wish to break.

On All Saints' Day, I remembered that it was Alfred Wegener's birthday. I tried to devote a measure of my thoughts to him, but I was really with Rockaway. Bit by bit I received news. The boardwalk was gone. Zak's café was gone. The train line crippled and its sad bowels ripped apart, thousands of salt-coated wires, the gone intestines of motion. Roads were closed indefinitely. No power, gas, or electricity. November winds were strong. Hundreds of homes were burned to the ground and thousands flooded.

But my little house, built one hundred years ago, scoffed at by realtors, condemned by inspectors, and denied insurance, had apparently stood through it. Though severely damaged my Alamo had survived the first great storm of the twenty-first century.

In mid-November I flew to Madrid, escaping the suffocating aspects of Sandy's aftermath, to visit friends with problems of their own. I brought along *The Thief's Journal,* Genet's hymn to Spain, and traveled by bus from Madrid to Valencia. In Cartagena we made a pit stop at a restaurant called Juanita, across a wide highway from another restaurant, also called Juanita, each a mirror of the other, except the one across the highway had a small loading dock and diesel trucks in the back lot. I was sitting at the bar, having lukewarm coffee and a bowl of marinated beans warmed in possibly the first microwave ever made, when I realized some guy had sidled up to me. He opened a well-worn oxblood wallet to reveal a solitary lottery ticket with the number 46172. I didn't get the feeling it was a winning number, but in the end I paid six euros for it, which was a lot for a lottery ticket. Then he sat down next to me, ordered a beer and a plate of cold meatballs, and paid for them with my euros. We ate together in silence. Then he got up, looked me straight in the face, and grinned, saying *buena suerte*. I smiled back and wished him luck as well.

It occurred to me that my ticket may be worthless, but I didn't care. I was willingly drawn into the whole scene, like a random character in a B. Traven novel. Lucky or not, I went along with the part I was targeted to play: the pigeon who gets off a bus at a pit stop on the road to Cartagena, hit on to invest in a suspiciously limp lottery ticket. The way I look at it is that fate touches me and some rumpled straggler has a repast of meatballs and warm beer. He is happy, I feel at one with the world—a good trade.

When I got back on the bus a few passengers told me I paid too much for my ticket. I told them it didn't matter and if I won I would give the money to the dogs of the region. I'll give the prize money to the dogs, I said too loudly, or maybe the gulls. I decided the winnings were for the birds, even as the people were discussing how the dogs would righteously spend it.

Later at my hotel I heard gulls screaming and watched as

two of them plunged toward the recesses of the tilted crown of the great roof outside my terrace. I believe they were conjugating or whatever bird fucking is called, but after a while they were silent, so either they were satisfied or had died trying. I was plagued by a vicious mosquito and finally slept, only to wake again at 5 a.m. I went out on the terrace and looked at the tilted crown as a light mist rolled in. There were gull feathers everywhere, enough for an elaborate headdress.

The winning lottery number was in the morning paper. Nothing for the dogs or the birds.

—Do you think you paid too much for your ticket? I was asked over breakfast.

I poured some more black coffee, reached for some dark bread, and dipped it into a small dish of olive oil.

—You never can pay too much for peace of mind, I answered.

We piled on the bus and drove to Valencia. Several of the passengers were taking part in a strike against the projected demolition of the neighborhood of El Cabanyal. Old multicolored tiled houses, fishermen's shacks, and bungalows such as my own. Fragile structures that can never be replaced, only mourned. Like butterflies that will one day just disappear. Joining them I felt their proud fury mingled with degrees of helplessness. David and Goliath in Valencia. I was coughing again, time to go home. But which home? I had begun to think of the Alamo as my home. But it would be a long time before it could be made livable. Dogged by projections of the battered coastline, the boardwalk swept away, a majestic roller coaster bobbing in the waves like the skeleton of a whale, more woeful than the carcass of Moby Dick, containing the joyrides of generations of risk takers. All is present tense on such a ride, physically impossible to look back.

I was plagued by an inventory of floating objects, leaping sheep to sleep. But I was past anything as commonplace as sleep. Open your eyes, said a voice, shake yourself from your torpor. Time once moved in concentric circles. Wake up and call out, like the fishmonger from the streets of the Bastille. I got up and opened the window. The sweetest of breezes greeted me. Which is it going to be, revolution or slumber? I wrapped a banner proclaiming *Salvem el Cabanyal* around my pillow, curled up, and went inside myself, seeking consolation that was mine for the asking.

I arrived home some days before Thanksgiving. I had yet to face the changes in Rockaway. I drove out with Klaus for a local gathering beneath a generator-heated tent. My future neighbors: families, surfers, local officials, maverick bee-keepers. I took a walk on the beach where cement pylons stretched as far as the eye could see. They had once supported the boardwalk. Roman ruins in New York, something never imagined save by the mind of J. G. Ballard. An old black dog approached me. He stopped and I petted his back, and as if it was the most natural thing in the world we stood and faced the sea, watching the waves approach and retreat.

It was a perfect Thanksgiving. The weather was milder than usual and Klaus and I walked over to the Alamo. My neighbors had boarded up the shattered windows, placed a padlock over the broken door, and hung a large American flag across the front of it.

—Why did they do that?

—To protect it from looters. To show it's under protection of the people.

Klaus had the combination and opened the door. The odor of mildew was so overwhelming I felt faint. There was a four-foot waterline and the wet floors were rotted. I noticed the porch was tilting and my yard was now a small patch of desert.

—You are still standing, I said proudly.

I felt something warm and grainy. Cairo had thrown up on the edge of my pillow. I sat up completely awake trying to remember. I looked at the clock. It was earlier than usual, not quite six. Ah, yes, my birthday, drifting in and out of sleep.

I finally arose out of sorts. There was a small misshapen cat toy in my boot. I looked at myself in the mirror. I cut the ends of my braids because they felt like straw, depositing the dried-out wisps into a brown envelope, definite DNA evidence.

As always, I quietly thanked my parents for my life, then went down and fed the cats. I could not believe another year was ending. It seemed like I had only just shot the silver balloon heralding its beginning.

I was surprised when the doorbell rang. Klaus was at my door with his friend James. They were armed with flowers and a car and insisted we go to the ocean.

—Happy birthday! Come to Rockaway with us, they said.

—I can't go anywhere, I protested.

Yet the prospect of being by the sea on my birthday was impossible to decline. I grabbed my coat and watch cap and we drove to Rockaway Beach. It was bitter cold but we stopped by my house to say hello. The door was nailed shut and the flag was still intact. A neighbor stopped us.

—Does it need to be torn down?

— No, don't worry. I will save it.

I took a picture and promised I would soon return. But I knew it was to be a long winter of waiting, the destruction was so vast. We walked along the street where Klaus lived. Styrofoam snowmen and waterlogged sofas were draped in tinsel. His massive garden was ravaged; only a few resilient trees survived. We bought powdered donuts and coffee from the only deli still open, and they sang "Happy Birthday." Back in the car we passed high mounds of appliances from flooded basements. Like the Seven Hills of Rome: the hill of refrigerators, stoves, dishwashers, mattresses, looming above us, like a massive installation in memory of the twentieth century.

We continued on to Breezy Point, where more than two hundred homes had been burnt to the ground. Blackened trees. Paths once leading to the shore obscured by an industrial mesh of strange fibers, scattered limbs of dolls, shattered porcelain. Like a tiny Dresden, a small stage replaying the art of war. But there was no war, no enemy. Nature knows nothing of these things. She is one with the messengers.

I spent the balance of my birthday watching Elvis Presley in *Flaming Star,* reflecting on the premature end of certain men. Fred. Pollock. Coltrane. Todd. I have lived well past them. I wondered if one day they would seem like boys. I had no desire for sleep so I made coffee, slipped on a hoodie, and sat on the stoop. I considered what it meant to be sixty-six. The same number as the original American highway, the celebrated Mother Road that George Maharis, as Buz Murdock, took as he tooled across the country in his Corvette, working on oil rigs and trawlers, breaking hearts and freeing junkies. Sixty-six, I thought, what the hell. I could feel my chronology mounting, snow approaching. I could feel the moon, but I could not see it. The sky was veiled with a heavy mist illuminated by the perpetual city lights. When I was a girl the night sky was a great map of constellations, a cornucopia spilling the crystalline dust of the Milky Way across its ebony expanse, layers of stars that I would deftly unfold in my mind.

I noticed the threads on my dungarees straining across my

protruding knees. I'm still the same person, I thought, with all my flaws intact, same old bony knees, thanks be to God. Shivering, I got up; time to turn in. The phone was ringing, a birthday wish from an old friend reaching from far away. As I said good-bye I realized I missed that particular version of me, the one who was feverish, impious. She has flown, that's for sure. Before retiring I drew a card from my tarot—Ace of Swords—mental force and fortitude. Good. I didn't slip it back into the deck but left it faceup on my worktable so I would see it in the morning when I awoke.

Vecchia Zimarra

◦—◦—⟨◊⟩—◦—◦

A sudden gust of wind shakes the branches of trees scattering a swirl of leaves that shimmer eerily in the bright filtered light. Leaves as vowels, whispers of words like a breath of net. Leaves are vowels. I sweep them up hoping to find the combinations I am looking for. The language of the lesser gods. But what of God himself? What is his language? What is his pleasure? Does he meld with the lines of Wordsworth, the musical phrases of Mendelssohn, and experience nature as genius conceives it? The curtain rises. The human opera unfolds. And in the box reserved for kings, more throne than box, sits the Almighty.

He is greeted by the turning skirts of novices singing his praises as they recite the *Masnavi*. His own son is portrayed as the beloved lamb and then again as the shepherd in *Songs of Innocence*. Within an offering by Puccini from *La Bohème*, the impoverished philosopher Colline, resigned to pawn his only coat, sings the humble aria "Vecchia Zimarra." He bids his ragged but beloved coat farewell as he imagines it ascending the pious mountain, while he remains behind walking the bitter earth. The Almighty closes his eyes. He drinks from the well of man, quenching a thirst that none could comprehend.

I HAD A BLACK COAT. A poet gave it to me some years ago on my fifty-seventh birthday. It had been his—an ill-fitting, unlined Comme des Garçons overcoat that I secretly coveted. On the morning of my birthday he told me he had no gift for me.

—I don't need a gift, I said.

—But I want to give you something, whatever you wish for.

—Then I would like your black coat, I said.

And he smiled and gave it to me without hesitation or regret. Every time I put it on I felt like myself. The moths liked it as well and it was riddled with small holes along the hem, but I didn't mind. The pockets had come unstitched at the seam and I lost everything I absentmindedly slipped into their holy caves. Every morning I got up, put on my coat and watch cap, grabbed my pen and notebook, and headed across Sixth Avenue to my café. I loved my coat and the café and my morning routine. It was the clearest and simplest expression of my solitary identity. But in this current run of harsh weather, I favored another coat to keep me warm and protect me from the wind. My black coat, more suitable for spring and fall, fell from my consciousness, and in this relatively short span it disappeared.

•

My black coat gone, vanished like the precious league ring that disappeared from the finger of the faulty believer in Hermann Hesse's *The Journey to the East*. I continue to search everywhere in vain, hoping it will appear like dust motes illuminated by sudden light. Then, ashamedly, within my childish mourning, I think of Bruno Schulz, trapped in the Jewish ghetto in Poland, furtively handing over the one precious thing he had left to give to mankind: the manuscript of *The Messiah*. The last work of Bruno Schulz drawn into the swill of World War II, beyond all grasp. Lost things. They claw through the membranes, attempting to summon our attention through an indecipherable mayday. Words tumble in helpless disorder. The dead speak. We have forgotten how to listen. Have you seen my coat? It is black and absent of detail, with frayed sleeves and a tattered hem. Have you seen my coat? It is the dead speak coat.

Mu

(Nothingness)

━┅━━◆〓━┅━

A young man was tramping through the snow with a great bundle of branches tied to his back with a measure of vine. He was bent over from the weight yet I could hear him whistling. Occasionally a branch would slip from the bundle and I would pick it up. The branches were completely transparent, so I filled in their color and texture and added a few thorns. After a time I noticed there were no tracks in the snow. There was no sense of backwards or forwards, only blankness sprinkled here and there with minuscule red droplets.

I tried to map out the fragile spatters, but they kept rearranging themselves, and when I opened my eyes they dissipated completely. I felt around for the channel changer and switched on the TV, careful to avoid any last-year wrap-ups or New Year's projections. The warm drone of a *Law & Order* marathon was exactly what I needed. Detective Lennie Briscoe had obviously fallen off the wagon and was gazing at the bottom of a glass of cheap scotch. I got up and poured some mescal in a small water glass and sat at the edge of the bed drinking along with him, watching in stupefied silence, a rerun of a rerun. A New Year's shot toasting nothing.

I imagined my black coat tapping me on the shoulder.

—Sorry, old friend, I said. I tried to find you.

I called out but heard nothing; crisscrossing wavelengths obscured any hope of feeling out its whereabouts. That's the way it is sometimes with the calling and the hearing. Abraham heard the demanding call of the Lord. Jane Eyre heard the beseeching cries of Mr. Rochester. But I was deaf to my coat. Most likely it had been carelessly flung on a mound with wheels rolling far away toward the Valley of the Lost.

So foolish, lamenting a coat, such a small thing in the grand scheme. But it wasn't just the coat; it was an inescapable heaviness reigning over everything, one perhaps easily traceable to Sandy. I can no longer take a train to Rockaway Beach and get a coffee and walk the boardwalk, for there is no more a running train, café, nor boardwalk. Just six months ago I had scrawled *I love the boardwalk* on a page of my notebook with the effusive sincerity of a teenage girl. Gone is that infatuation, that untapped simplicity embraced. And I am left with a longing for the way things were.

I went down to feed the cats but got waylaid on the second floor. I mechanically took a sheet of drawing paper from my flat file and taped it to the wall. I ran my hand down the skin of its surface. It was nice paper from Florence with an angel watermarked in the center. Searching through my drawing materials I located a box of red Conté crayons and attempted to replicate the pattern that had slipped through my dreamscape into my waking one. It resembled an elongated island. I noticed the cats watching as I executed it. Then I went down to the kitchen, put out their food, adding a treat, and made myself a peanut butter sandwich.

I returned to my drawing but at certain angles it no longer resembled an island. Examining the watermark, more cherub than angel, I remembered another drawing from a few decades ago. On a large sheet of Arches I had stenciled *the angel is my watermark,* a phrase from Henry Miller's *Black Spring,* then drew an angel, crossed it out, and scrawled a message—*but Henry, the angel is not my watermark*—beneath it. Tapping it lightly, I went back upstairs. I had no idea what to do with myself. Café 'Ino was closed for the holiday. I sat at the edge of the bed eyeing the bottle of mescal. I should really clean up my room, I was thinking, but I knew I wouldn't.

At sundown I walked over to Omen, a Kyoto country-style restaurant and had a small bowl of red miso soup and complimentary spiced sake. I lingered for a while, ruminating on the coming year. It would be late spring before I could begin to rebuild my Alamo; I would first have to wait until work was under way for my more unfortunate neighbors. Dream must defer to life, I told myself, accidently spilling some of the sake. I was about to wipe the table with my sleeve when I noticed the droplets eerily formed the shape of an elongated island, perhaps a sign. Feeling a surge of investigative energy I paid my check, wished everyone a happy new year, and headed home.

I cleared my worktable, placed my atlas before me, and studied the maps of Asia. Then I opened my computer and searched for the best flights to Tokyo. Every once in a while I would look up at my drawing. I wrote the flights and hotel I wanted on a sheet of paper, the first journey of the year. I would spend some time alone, to write, in the Hotel Okura, a classic sixties hotel near the American Embassy. Afterwards, I'd improvise.

That evening I decided to write to my friend Ace, a modest and knowledgeable movie producer of such films as *Nezulla the Rat Monster* and *Janku Fudo*. He speaks little English, but his comrade and translator Dice is so adept at congenial and simultaneous translation that our conversations have always felt seamless. Ace knows where to find the best sake and soba noodles as well as the resting places of all the revered Japanese writers.

On my last visit to Japan we visited the grave of Yukio Mishima. We swept away dead leaves and ash, filled wooden water buckets and washed the headstone, placed fresh flowers and burned incense. Afterwards we stood in silence. I envisioned the pond that surrounds the golden temple in Kyoto. A large red carp darting beneath the surface joined with another that looked as if it was cloaked in a uniform of clay. Two elderly women in traditional dress approached carrying buckets and brooms. They seemed pleasantly surprised at the state of things, said a few words to Ace, bowed, and went their way.

—They seemed happy to see Mishima's grave tended to, I said.

—Not exactly, laughed Ace. They were friends of his wife, whose remains are also here. They didn't mention him at all.

I watched them, two hand-painted dolls receding in the

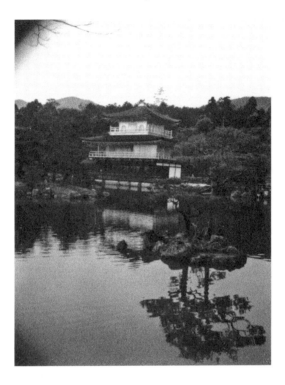

distance. As we were leaving I was given the straw broom I had used to sweep the grave of the man who wrote *The Temple of the Golden Pavilion*. It leans against the wall in a corner of my room next to an old butterfly net.

I wrote to Ace through Dice. *Greetings for the New Year. When I saw you last, it was spring. Now I am coming in the winter. I place myself in your hands.* Then a note to my Japanese publisher and translator, finally accepting a long-standing invitation. Lastly to my friend Yuki. Japan had suffered a catastrophic earthquake nearly two years before. The aftermath, still intensely present, eclipsed anything I had ever experienced. From afar I had supported her grassroots relief efforts centering on the needs of orphaned children. I promised to come soon.

I hoped to set aside my impatient woes, be of service, and possibly add a few images to adorn my Polaroid rosary. I was glad to be going somewhere else. All I needed for the mind was to be led to new stations. All I needed for the heart was to visit a place of greater storms. I overturned a card from my tarot deck, and then another, as casually as turning over a leaf. *Find the truth of your situation. Set out boldly.* I covered all three envelopes with leftover Christmas stamps and slipped them in the letterbox on the way to the deli. Then I bought a box of spaghetti, green onions, garlic, and a tin of anchovies, and made myself a meal.

Café 'Ino looked empty. There were tiny ice formations dripping along the edge of the orange awning. I sat at my table, had my brown toast with olive oil, and opened Camus's *The First Man*. I had read it some time ago but was so completely immersed that I retained nothing. This has been an intermittent, lifelong enigma. Through early adolescence I sat and read for hours in a small grove of weed trees near the railroad track in Germantown. Like Gumby I would enter a book wholeheartedly and sometimes venture so deeply it was as if I were living within it. I finished many books in such a manner there, closing the covers ecstatically yet having no memory of the content by the time I returned home. This disturbed me but I kept this strange affliction to myself. I look at the covers of such books and their contents remain a mystery that I cannot bring myself to solve. Certain books I loved and lived within yet cannot remember.

Perhaps in the case of *The First Man* I was transported more by language than by plot, beguiled by the hand of Camus. But either way, I couldn't recall a single thing. I was determined to remain present as I read, but was obliged to reread the second sentence of the first paragraph, a spiraling length of words journeying east on the tail of sinewy clouds. I became drowsy—a hypnotic drowsiness that even a cup of steaming black coffee could not compete with. I sat up, shifted to my pending travels, and made a list of things to pack for Tokyo. Jason, the manager of 'Ino, came over to say hello.

—Are you leaving again? he asked.

—Yes, how did you know?

—You're making lists, he laughed.

It was the same list I always make; yet I was still compelled to write it. Bee socks, underwear, hoodie, six Electric Lady Studio tee shirts, camera, dungarees, my Ethiopian cross, and balm for joint pain. My great quandary was what coat to wear and which books to bring.

That night I had a dream about Detective Holder. We were making our way through a mass grave of engines mattresses stripped laptops—another kind of crime scene. He climbed to the top of an appliance hill, scrutinizing the surrounding area. He had his rabbit twitch going and seemed even more restless than within the confines of *The Killing*. We climbed over the debris surrounding an abandoned airplane hangar that faced a canal where I had a small tugboat. It was about fourteen feet long, made of wood and hammered aluminum. We sat on some packing crates and watched rusting barges moving slowly in the distance. In my dream I knew it was a dream. The colors of the day were like a painting by Turner—rust, golden air, several shades of red. I could almost make out Holder's thoughts. We sat there in silence and after a time he got up.

—I have to go, he said.

I nodded. The canal seemed to widen as the barges drew closer.

—Strange proportions, he muttered.

—This is where I live, I said aloud.

I could hear Holder on his cell and his voice growing fainter.

—Tying up some loose ends, he was saying.

For the next few days I searched again for my black coat. A futile effort, though I did find a large canvas bag in the basement filled with old laundry from Michigan—some of Fred's flannel shirts, slightly musty. I took them upstairs and washed them in the sink. As I rinsed them out I found myself thinking of Katharine Hepburn. She had captivated me as Jo March in George Cukor's film adaptation of *Little Women*. Years later when working as a clerk at Scribner's Bookstore I gathered books for her. She sat at the reading table examining each volume carefully. She wore the late Spencer Tracy's leather cap, held in place by a green silk headscarf. I stood back and watched as she turned the pages, pondering aloud whether Spence would have liked it. I was a young girl then, not wholly comprehending her ways. I hung Fred's shirts to dry. In time we often become one with those we once failed to understand.

I had yet to settle on the books I would take. I went back into the basement and located a box of books labeled *J—1983,* my year of Japanese literature. I took them out one by one. Some were heavily notated; others contained lists of tasks on small slips of graph paper—household needs, packing lists for fishing trips, and a voided check with Fred's signature. I traced my son's scribbles on the endpapers of a library copy of *Yoshitsune,* and reread the first pages of Osamu Dazai's *The Setting Sun,* whose fragile cover was adorned with Transformer stickers.

I finally chose a few books by Dazai and Akutagawa. Both had inspired me to write and would serve as meaningful companionship for a fourteen-hour flight. But as it turned out I barely read on the plane. Instead, I watched the movie *Master and Commander.* Captain Jack Aubrey reminded me so much of Fred that I watched it twice. Midflight I began to weep. Just come back, I was thinking. You've been gone long enough. Just come back. I will stop traveling; I will wash your clothes. Mercifully, I fell asleep, and when I awoke snow was falling over Tokyo.

ENTERING THE MODERNIST LOBBY of the Hotel Okura, I had the sensation that my movements were somehow being monitored and that the viewers were hysterical with laughter. I decided to play along and reinforce their amusement by channeling my inner Mr. Magoo, prolonging registration, then shuffling beneath the string of high hexagonal lanterns straight toward the elevator. I went immediately to the Grand Comfort Floor. My room was unromantic but warmly

Ghost robe

efficient with the special addition of extra oxygen pumped into it. There was a stack of menus on the desk but all were in Japanese. I decided to explore the hotel and its array of restaurants, but I was unable to locate coffee, which was troubling. My body had no sense of time. *I didn't know if it was day or night.* Words to the song "Love Potion No. 9" looped as I staggered from floor to floor. I finally ate in a Chinese place that had booths. I had dumplings served in a bamboo box and a pot of jasmine tea. When I returned to my room I hardly had the energy to turn down my blanket. I looked at the small stack of books on the bed table. I reached out for *No Longer Human.* I vaguely remember sliding my fingers down its spine.

I followed the motion of my pen, dipping into an inkwell and scratching across the surface of the paper before me. In my dream I was focused and prolific, filling page after page in a room that was not my room in a small rented house in a whole other district. There was an engraved plaque by a sliding panel that opened onto a large closet with a rolled mat for sleeping. Though it was written in Japanese characters I was able to decipher most of it: *Please be silent for these are the preserved rooms of the esteemed writer Ryūnosuke Akutagawa.* I knelt down and examined the mat, careful not to draw attention to myself. The screens were open and I could hear the rain. When I rose I felt quite tall, as everything was set low to the ground. There was a shimmering wisp of a robe lying across a rattan chair. As I drew close I could see it was weaving itself. Silkworms were repairing small tears and elongating the wide sleeves. The sight of the spinning worms made me nauseous and, steadying myself, I accidently crushed two or three of them. I watched them struggling half alive in my hand as tiny strands of liquefied silk spread across my palm.

I awoke groping for the water tumbler, spilling its contents. I suppose I wanted to wash off the unfortunate wriggling half-worms. My fingers found my notebook and I sat up abruptly and searched for what I had written, but it seemed I had added nothing, not a single word. I got up and took a bottle of mineral water from the minibar and opened the drapes. Night snow. The sight of it provoked a deep sense of estrangement. Though from what was hard to tell. There was a kettle in my room, so I prepared tea and ate some biscuits I had pocketed in the airport lounge. Soon the sun would rise.

I sat at the portable metal desk before my open notebook, straining to get something down. On the whole I thought more than I wrote, wishing I could just transmit straightaway to the page. When I was young I had the notion to think and write simultaneously, but I could never keep up with myself. I gave up the pursuit and I wrote in my head as I sat with my dog by a secret stream incandescent with rainbows, a mix of sun and petrol, skimming the water like weightless Merbabies with iridescent wings.

The morning was still overcast but the snowfall had lightened. I wondered if extra oxygen was really being pumped into the air and whether it escaped whenever I opened the door. Down below crossing the parking lot was a procession of girls in elaborate kimonos with long swinging sleeves. It was Coming of Age Day, a scene of flurrying innocence. Poor little feet! I shivered as they trod through the snow in their zori sandals, yet their body language suggested squeals of laughter. Half-formed prayers like streamers found their mark and trailed the hems of their colorful kimonos. I watched until they disappeared around a bend into the arms of an enveloping mist.

I returned to my station and gazed at my notebook. I was determined to produce something despite an inescapable lassitude, no doubt due to the deeper effect of travel. I could not resist closing my eyes for just a moment and was instantaneously greeted with an expanding lattice that shook soundly, blanketing the edge of an impeccable maze with a torrent of petals. Horizontal clouds formed above a distant mountain: the floating lips of Lee Miller. Not now, I said half aloud, for I was not about to get lost in some surreal labyrinth. I was not thinking about mazes and muses. I was thinking about writers.

After our son was born Fred and I stayed close to home. We often went to the library, checked out stacks of books and read through the night. Fred was fixated on every aspect of aviation and I was immersed in Japanese literature. Rapt in the atmosphere of certain writers I converted the small storage room, adjacent to our bedroom, into my own. I bought yards of black felt and covered the floor and baseboards. I had an iron teapot and a hot plate and four orange crates for my books, that Fred painted black. I sat cross-legged on the black-felt-covered floor before a long, low table. On winter mornings the view outside the window seemed drained of color with slim trees bending in the white wind. I wrote in that room until our son came of age and then it became his room. After that I wrote in the kitchen.

Ryūnosuke Akutagawa and Osamu Dazai wrote the books that drove me to such wondrous distraction, the same books that are now on the bed table. I was thinking of them. They came to me in Michigan and I have brought them back to Japan. Both writers took their own lives. Akutagawa, fearing he had inherited his mother's madness, ingested a fatal dose of Veronal and then curled up in his mat next to his wife and son as they slept. The younger Dazai, a devoted acolyte, seemed to take on the hair shirt of the master, failing at multiple suicide attempts before drowning himself, along with a companion, in the muddied, rain-swollen Tamagawa Canal.

Akutagawa intrinsically damned and Dazai damning himself. At first I had it in mind to write something of them both. In my dream I had sat at the writing table of Akutagawa, but I hesitated to disturb his peace. Dazai was another story. His spirit seemed to be everywhere, like a haunted jumping bean. Unhappy man, I thought, and then chose him as my subject.

Deeply concentrating, I attempted to channel the writer. But I could not keep up with my thoughts, as they were swifter than my pencil and wrote nothing. Relax, I told myself, you have chosen your subject or your subject has chosen you, he will come. The atmosphere surrounding me was both animated and contained. I felt a growing impatience coupled with an underlying anxiety that I attributed to a lack of coffee. I looked over my shoulder as if expecting a visitor.

—What is nothing? I impetuously asked.

—It is what you can see of your eyes without a mirror, was the answer.

I was suddenly hungry but had no desire to leave my room. Nonetheless I went back down to the Chinese restaurant and pointed to a picture of what I wanted on the menu. I had shrimp balls and steamed cabbage dumplings wrapped in leaves in a bamboo basket. I drew a likeness of Dazai on the napkin, exaggerating his unruly hair atop a face at once handsome and comic. It occurred to me that both writers shared this charming characteristic, hair that stood on end. I paid my check and got back into the elevator. My sector of the hotel seemed inexplicably empty.

Sundown, dawn, full night, my body had no sense of time and I decided to accept it and proceed Fred's way. Following no hands. Within a week I would be in the time zone of Ace and Dice, but these days were entirely my own with no design other than the hope of filling a few pages with something of worth. I crawled under the covers to read but passed out in the middle of *Hell Screen* and missed the balance of the afternoon and sunset transitioning into evening. When I awoke it was too late to dine, so I grabbed some snacks from the minibar—a bag of fish-shaped crackers dusted with wasabi powder, an oversized Snickers bar, and a jar of blanched almonds. Dinner downed with ginger ale. I laid out some clothes and showered, then decided to go out, if only to walk around the parking lot. Covering my damp hair with a watch cap, I went out and followed the path the young girls had taken. There were steps carved into a small hill that seemed to lead nowhere.

Unconsciously I had already developed some semblance of routine. I read, sat before the metal desk, ate Chinese food, and retraced my own footsteps in the night snow. I attempted to quell any recurring agitation with a repetitive exercise: writing the name Osamu Dazai over and over, nearly a hundred times. Unfortunately, the page spelling out the name of the writer amounted to nothing. My regimen slipped into a pointless web of haphazard calligraphy.

Yet somehow I was drawing closer to my subject—Dazai the dazed one, a stumblebum, an aristocratic tramp. I could see the spikes of his unruly hair and feel the energy of his accursed remorse. I got up, boiled a pot of water, drank some powdered tea, and stepped into a cloud of well-being. Closing my journal I placed several sheets of hotel stationery before me. Taking long, slow breaths I emptied myself and began again.

The young leaves did not fall from the trees but clung desperately throughout winter. Even as the wind whistled, to the astonishment of everyone they had the audacity to remain green. The writer was unmoved. The elders regarded him with disgust, to them he is a wobbling poet on the brink. In turn he regarded them with contempt, imagining himself an elegant surfer riding the crest, never crashing.

The ruling class, he shouts, the ruling class.

He wakes in pools of sweat, his shirt stiff with salt. The tuberculosis he has carried since youth has calcified as tiny seeds— minute black sesame liberally seasoning his lung. A bout of drink sets him off: strange women, strange beds, a horrid cough spraying kaleidoscopic stains across foreign sheets.

I could not help it, he cries. The well begs for the lips of the drunkard. Drink me drink me, it calls. Insistent bells are tolling. A litany of He.

His sinewy arms tremble beneath billowing sleeves. He bends over his low table composing small suicide notes that somehow become something else entirely. Slowing his blood, the beating of his heart, with the forbearance of a fasting scribe he writes what has to be written, conscious of the movement of his wrist as words spread across the surface of the paper like an ancient magic spell. He savors his one joy, a cold pint of miruku that moves through his system like a transfusion of milky corpuscles.

The sudden brightness of dawn startles him. He staggers into the garden; bright blooms stick out their fiery tongues, sinister oleanders of the red queen. When did the flowers become so sinister? He tries to remember when it all went wrong. How the threads of his life unraveled like winding linen from the unbound feet of a fallen consort.

He is overcome with the disease of love, the drunkenness of generations past. When are we ourselves, he wonders, trudging through the snow-covered banks, his coat illuminated by moonlight. Long pelts, lined heavy silk the color of aged parchment, with the words Eat or Die written in his own distinct hand on the sleeves, vertically on the back and beneath the collar running down his left side over his heart. Eat or Die. Eat or Die. Eat or Die.

I paused, wishing I could hold such a coat in my hands, and realized the hotel phone was ringing. It was Dice calling on behalf of Ace.

—The phone rang many times. Have we disturbed you?

—No, no, I am happy to hear from you. I've been writing something for Osamu Dazai, I said.

—Then you will be happy with our itinerary.

—I am ready. What first?

—Ace has booked dinner at Mifune, then we can plan for tomorrow.

—I will meet you in the lobby in one hour.

I was delighted by the choice of Mifune, a sentimental favorite, themed on the life of the great Japanese actor Toshiro Mifune. Most likely, much sake would be consumed and perhaps a special soba dish prepared for me. My solitude could not have been severed in a more fortuitous way. I quickly straightened my things, slipped an aspirin into my pocket, and reunited with Ace and Dice. Just as I supposed, the sake flowed. Drenched in the atmosphere of a Kurosawa film, we immediately picked up the thread of a year ago—graves, temples, and forests in the snow.

The next morning, they picked me up in Ace's two-tone Fiat resembling a red-and-white saddle shoe. We drove around looking for coffee. I was so happy to finally have some that Ace had them fill a small thermos for later.

—Didn't you know, asked Dice, that in the renovated annex of the Okura they serve a full American breakfast?

—Oh no, I laughed. I bet I missed out on vats of coffee.

Ace is the one person I would accept an itinerary from, as his choices consistently correspond with my own desires. We drove to the Kōtoku-in, a Buddhist temple in Kamakura, and paid our respects to the Great Buddha that loomed above us like the Eiffel Tower. So mystically intimidating that I only took one shot. When I unpeeled the image it revealed that the emulsion was faulty and had not captured his head.

—Perhaps he is hiding his face, said Dice.

On the first day of our pilgrimage I barely used my camera. We laid flowers by the public marker for Akira Kurosawa. I thought of his great body of work from *Drunken Angel* to his masterpiece *Ran,* an epic that might have caused Shakespeare to shudder. I remember experiencing *Ran* in a local theater in the outskirts of Detroit. Fred took me for my fortieth

Kita-Kamakura Station, winter

birthday. The sun had not yet set and the sky was bright and clear. But in the course of the three-hour film, unbeknownst to us, a blizzard struck, and as we exited the theater a black sky whitewashed by a vortex of snow awaited us.

—We are still in the film, he said.

Ace consulted a printed map of Engaku-ji cemetery. As we passed the train station, I stopped to watch the people as they patiently waited, then crossed over the railway line. An old express rattled past, as if clattering hooves of past scenes galloped from brutal angles. Shivering, we searched for the grave of the filmmaker Ozu, a difficult undertaking, for it was isolated in a small enclave on higher ground. Several bottles of sake were placed before his headstone, a black granite cube containing only the character *mu*, signifying nothingness. Here a happy tramp could find shelter and drink himself into oblivion. Ozu loved his sake, said Ace; no one would dare to open his bottles. Snow covered everything. We mounted the stone steps and placed some incense and watched the smoke pour, then hover perfectly still, as if anticipating how it might feel to be frozen.

Scenes of films flickered through the atmosphere. The actress Setsuko Hara lying in the sun, her open clear expression, and her radiant smile. She had worked with both masters, first with Kurosawa and then six films with Ozu.

—Where is she resting? I asked, thinking to bring an armful of huge white chrysanthemums and lay them before her marker.

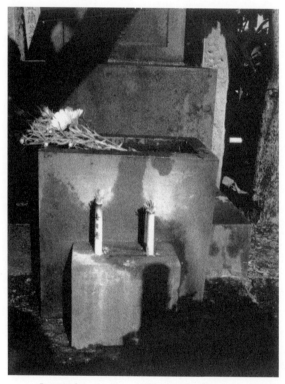

Incense burner, grave of Ryūnosuke Akutagawa

Departing gravesite

—She is still alive, Dice translated. Ninety-two years old.

—May she live to be one hundred, I said. Faithful to herself.

The next morning was overcast, the shadows oppressive. I swept the grave of Dazai and washed the headstone, as if it were his body. After rinsing the flower holders I placed a fresh bunch in each one. A red orchid to symbolize the blood of his tuberculosis and small branches of white forsythia. Their fruit contained many winged seeds. The forsythia gave off a faint almond scent. The tiny flowers that produce milk sugar represented the white milk that gave him pleasure through the worst of his debilitating consumption. I added bits of baby's breath—a cloud panicle of tiny white flowers—to refresh his tainted lungs. The flowers formed a small bridge, like hands touching. I picked up a few loose stones and slipped them into my pocket. Then I placed the incense in the circular holder, laying it flat. The sweet-smelling smoke enveloped his name. We were about to leave when the sun suddenly erupted, brightening everything. Perhaps the baby's breath had found its mark and with refreshed lung Dazai had blown away the clouds that had blocked the sun.

—I think he's happy, I said. Ace and Dice nodded in agreement.

Our final destination was the cemetery at Jigen-ji. As we approached the grave of Akutagawa, I recalled my dream and wondered how it would color my emotions. The dead regard us with curiosity. Ash, bits of bone, a handful of sand, the quiescence of organic material, waiting. We lay our flowers yet cannot sleep. We are wooed, then mocked, plagued like Amfortas, King of the Grail Knights, by a wound refusing to heal.

It was very cold and once again the sky grew dark. I felt strangely detached, numb, yet visually connected. Drawn to contrasting shadows I took four photographs of the incense burner. Though they were all similar I was pleased with them, envisioning them as panels on a dressing screen. Four panels one season. I bowed and thanked Akutagawa as Ace and Dice hurried to the car. As I followed after them, the capricious sun returned. I passed an ancient cherry tree bound in frayed burlap. The cold light deepened the texture of the binding and I framed my last shot: a comic mask whose ghostly tears seemed to streak the burlap's worn threads.

The following evening I mentally prepared to change hotels, already mourning my secluded repetitive routine. I had been encased in Hotel Okura's cocoon with two miserable moths, not wishing to emerge though not hiding their faces. Sitting at the metal desk I wrote a list of my coming duties including meetings with my publisher and translator. Then I would meet with Yuki and assist her with her continuing efforts on behalf of schoolchildren orphaned by the aftereffects of the 2011 Tohoku earthquake and tsunami. I packed my small suitcase in a haze of nostalgia for the present stream I was just about to divert, a handful of days in a world of my own making, fragile as a temple constructed with wooden matchsticks.

Comic mask

I went into the closet and removed a futon mat and buckwheat pillow. I unrolled the mat on the floor and wrapped my comforter around me. I was watching what appeared to be the end of a kind of soap opera set in the eighteenth century. It was slow-moving without subtitles or an ounce of happiness. Yet I was content. The comforter was like a cloud. I drifted, transient, following the brush of a maiden as she painted a scene of such sadness on the sails of a small wooden boat that she herself wept. Her robe made a swishing sound as she wandered barefoot from room to room. She exited through sliding panels that opened onto a snow-covered bank. There was no ice on the river and the boat sailed on without her. Do not cast your boat on a river of tears, cried the tearing wind. Small hands are still, be still. She knelt then lay on her side, clutching a key, accepting the kindness of endless sleep. The sleeve of her robe was adorned with the outlines of a lucent branch of delicate plum blossoms whose dark centers were a spattering of minuscule droplets. I closed my eyes as if to join the maiden as the droplets rearranged themselves, forming a pattern resembling an elongated island on the rim of an undisturbed blankness.

In the morning Ace drove me to a more central hotel chosen by my publisher, near the Shibuya train station. I had a room in a modern tower on the eighteenth floor with a view of Mt. Fuji. The hotel had a small café that served coffee in porcelain cups, all the coffee I wanted. The day was filled with duties, the lively atmosphere an unexpectedly welcome change. Late that night I sat before the window and looked at the great white-cloaked mountain that seemed to be watching over sleeping Japan.

In the morning I took the bullet train at Tokyo Station to Sendai where Yuki was waiting. Behind her smile I could see so many other things, a catastrophic sadness. I had assisted her from afar and now we would turn over the fruits of new efforts to the selfless guardians of the unfortunate children who suffered infinite loss, their family, their homes, and nature as they had known and trusted. Yuki spent time talking with the children's teachers. Before we left they presented us with a precious gift of a *Senbazuru,* a thousand paper cranes held together by string. Many small fingers worked diligently to present us with the ultimate sign of good health and good wishes.

Afterwards we visited the once bustling fisherman's port of Yuriage. The powerful tsunami, over one hundred feet high, had swept away nearly a thousand homes and all but a few battered ships. The rice fields, now unyielding, were covered with close to a million fish carcasses, a rotting stench that hung in the air for months. It was bitter cold and Yuki and I stood without words. I was prepared to see terrible damage but not for what I didn't see. There was a small Buddha in the snow near the water and a lone shrine overlooking what had once been a thriving community. We walked up the steps leading to the shrine, a humble slate monolith. It was so cold we could barely pray. Will you take a picture? she said. I looked down at the bleak panorama and shook my head. How could I take a picture of nothing?

Yuki gave me a package and we said our farewells. I

boarded the bullet train back to Tokyo. When I reached the station I found Ace and Dice waiting for me.

—I thought we said good-bye.

—We could not abandon you.

—Shall we go back to Mifune's?

—Yes, let's go. The sake is surely waiting.

Ace nodded and smiled. Time for sake, our last evening was drenched in it.

—What a nice cup and tokkuri, I noted. They were cerulean green with a small red stamp.

—That is the official sign of Kurosawa, said Dice.

Ace pulled on his beard, deep in thought. I roamed about the restaurant, admiring Kurosawa's bold and colorful renderings of the warriors of *Ran.* As we happily made our way back to his car he produced the tokkuri and cup from his worn leather sack.

—Friendship makes thieves of us all, I said.

Dice was going to translate but Ace stopped him with his hand.

—I understand, he said solemnly.

—I will miss you both, I said.

That night I set the cup and tokkuri on the table next to the bed. It still contained drops of sake that I did not rinse out.

I awoke with a mild hangover. I got a cold shower and made my way through a labyrinth of escalators that led me nowhere. What I really wanted was coffee. I searched and found an express coffee shop—nine hundred yen for coffee and miniature croissants. Sitting at the next table facing mine was a man in his thirties dressed in a suit, white shirt, and tie, working on his laptop. I noted a subtle stripe in his suit that was understated yet defiantly different. He had a demeanor above the average businessman's. He proceeded to change laptops, poured himself a coffee, then continued his work. I was touched by the serene yet complex concentration he manifested, the furrows of light on his smooth brow. He was handsome, in a certain way like a young Mishima, hinting at decorum, silent infidelities, and moral devotion. I watched the people passing. Time too was passing. I had thought to take a train to Kyoto for the day but preferred drinking coffee across from the quiet stranger.

In the end I did not go to Kyoto. I took one last walk, wondering what would happen if I bumped into Murakami on the street. But in truth I didn't feel Murakami at all in Tokyo, and I hadn't looked for the Miyawaki place, though its district was only a few miles away. So possessed with the dead I skipped contact with the fictional.

Murakami is not here anyway, I thought. He is most likely somewhere else, sealed in a space capsule in the center of a field of lavender, laboring over words.

That night I dined alone, an elegant meal of steaming abalone, green-tea soba noodles, and warm tea. I opened a gift from Yuki. It was a coral-colored box wrapped in heavy paper the color of sea foam. Inside the pale tissue were loops of soba from the Nagano prefecture. They lay in the oblong box like several strings of pearls. Lastly, I focused on my pictures. I spread them across the bed. Most of them went into a souvenir pile, but those of the incense burner at the grave of

Akutagawa had merit; I would not go home empty-handed. I got up for a moment and stood by the window, looking down at the lights of Shibuya and across to Mt. Fuji. Then I opened a small jar of sake.

—I salute you, Akutagawa, I salute you, Dazai, I said, draining my cup.

—Don't waste your time on us, they seemed to say, we are only bums.

I refilled the small cup and drank.

—All writers are bums, I murmured. May I be counted among you one day.

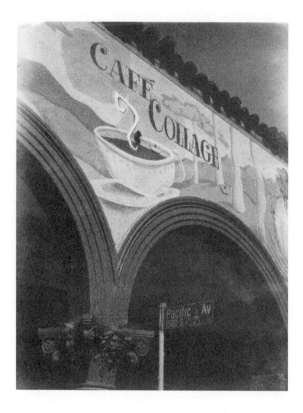

Tempest Air Demons

I TRAVELED HOME backwards through Los Angeles, stopping for a few days at Venice Beach, which is close to the airport. I sat on the rocks and stared at the sea, listening to crisscrossing music, discordant reggae with its revolutionary sense of harmonics drifting from various boom boxes. I ate fish tacos and drank coffee at the Café Collage, a block west from the Venice boardwalk. I never bothered to change my clothes. I rolled up my pant legs and walked in the water. It was cold but the salt felt good on my skin. I couldn't bring myself to open my suitcase or computer. I lived out of a black cotton sack. I slept to the sound of the waves and spent a lot of time reading discarded newspapers.

After a last coffee at the Collage I headed for the airport, where I discovered my bags had been left at the hotel. I boarded the plane with nothing but my passport, white pen, toothbrush, traveler tube of Weleda salt toothpaste, and midsize Moleskine. I had no books to read and there was no in-flight entertainment for the five-hour flight. I immediately felt trapped. I flipped through the airline magazine featuring the top-ten skiing resorts in the country, then occupied myself with circling the names of all the places I'd been on the double-spread map of Europe and Scandinavia.

There were about thirteen hundred yen and four photographs inside the inner flap of the Moleskine. I laid the pictures out on the tray table: an image of my daughter, Jesse, in front of Café Hugo in Place des Vosges, two outtakes of the incense burner at the grave of Akutagawa, and one of the poet Sylvia Plath's headstone in the snow. I tried to write something of Jesse but couldn't, as her face echoed her father's and the proud palace where the ghosts of our old life dwell. I slipped three of the pictures back into the pocket, then focused on Sylvia in the snow. It was not a good picture, the result of a kind of winter penitence. I decided to write of Sylvia. I wrote to give myself something to read.

It occurred to me that I was on a run of suicides. Akutagawa. Dazai. Plath. Death by water, barbiturates, and carbon monoxide poisoning; three fingers of oblivion, outplaying everything. Sylvia Plath took her life in the kitchen of her London flat on February 11, 1963. She was thirty years old. It was one of the coldest winters on record in England. It had been snowing since Boxing Day and the snow was piled high in the gutters. The River Thames was frozen and the sheep were starving on the fells. Her husband, the poet Ted Hughes, had left her. Their small children were safely tucked in their beds. Sylvia placed her head in the oven. One can only shudder at the existence of such overriding desolation. The timer ticking down. A few moments left, still a possibility to live, to turn off the gas. I wondered what passed through her mind in those moments: her children, the embryo of a poem, her philandering husband buttering toast with another woman. I wondered what happened to the oven. Perhaps the next tenant got an impeccably clean range, a massive reliquary for a poet's last reflection and a strand of light brown hair caught on a metal hinge.

The plane seemed insufferably hot, yet other passengers were asking for blankets. I felt the inklings of a dull but oppressive headache. I closed my eyes and searched for a stored image of my copy of *Ariel,* given to me when I was twenty. *Ariel* became the book of my life then, drawing me to a poet with hair worthy of a Breck commercial and the incisive observational powers of a female surgeon cutting out her own heart. With little effort I visualized my *Ariel* perfectly. Slim, with faded black cloth, that I opened in my mind, noting my youthful signature on the cream endpaper. I turned the pages, revisiting the shape of each poem.

As I fixed on the first lines, impish forces projected multiple images of a white envelope, flickering at the corners of my eyes, thwarting my efforts to read them.

This agitating visitation produced a pang, for I knew the envelope well. It had once held a handful of images I had taken of the grave of the poet in the autumnal light of northern Britain. I had traveled from London to Leeds, through Brontë country to Hebden Bridge to the ancient Yorkshire village of Heptonstall to take them. I brought no flowers; I was singularly driven to get my shot.

I had only one pack of Polaroid film with me but I had no

need of more. The light was exquisite and I shot with absolute assurance, seven to be exact. All were good, but five were perfect. I was so pleased that I asked a lone visitor, an affable Irishman, to take my picture in the grass beside her grave. I looked old in the photograph, but it contained the same scintillating light so I was content. In truth I felt an elation I hadn't experienced in quite a while—that of easily accomplishing a challenging goal. Yet I offered a mere preoccupied prayer and did not leave my pen in a bucket by her headstone, as countless others had. I only had my favorite pen, a small white Montblanc, and did not want to part with it. I somehow felt exempt from this ritual, a contrariness I thought she would understand but that I would regret.

On the long drive to the train station I looked at the photographs, then slipped them into an envelope. In the hours to come I looked at them several times. Then some days later in my travels the envelope and its contents disappeared. Heartsick, I went over my every move but never found them. They simply vanished. I mourned the loss, magnified by the memory of the joy I'd felt in the taking of them in a strangely joyless time.

In early February I again found myself in London. I took a train to Leeds, where I had arranged for a driver to take me back to Heptonstall. This time I brought a lot of film and had cleaned my 250 Land Camera and painstakingly straightened the interior of the semi-collapsed bellows. We drove up a winding hill and the driver parked in front of the moody ruins of Saint Thomas à Becket Churchyard. I walked to the west of the ruins to an adjacent field across Back Lane and quickly found her grave.

—I have come back, Sylvia, I whispered, as if she'd been waiting.

I hadn't factored in all the snow. It reflected the chalk sky already infused with murky smears. It would prove difficult for my simple camera, too much, then too little, available light. After half an hour my fingers were getting frostbitten and the wind was coming up, yet I stubbornly kept taking pictures. I hoped the sun would return and I irrationally shot, using all of my film. None of the pictures were good. I was numb with cold but couldn't bear to leave. It was such a desolate place in winter, so lonely. Why had her husband buried her here? I wondered. Why not New England by the sea, where she was born, where salt winds could spiral over the name PLATH etched in her native stone? I had an uncontrollable urge to urinate and imagined spilling a small stream, some part of me wanting her to feel that proximate human warmth.

Life, Sylvia. Life.

The bucket of pens was gone, perhaps retired for winter. I went through my pockets, extracting a small spiral notebook, a purple ribbon, and a cotton lisle sock with a bee embroidered near the top. I tied the ribbon around them and tucked them by her headstone. The last of the light faded as I trudged back to the heavy gate. It was only as I approached the car that the sun appeared and now with a vengeance. I turned just as a voice whispered:

—Don't look back, don't look back.

It was as if Lot's wife, a pillar of salt, had toppled on the snow-covered ground and spread a lengthening heat melting all in its path. The warmth drew life, drawing out tufts of green and a slow procession of souls. Sylvia, in a cream-colored sweater and straight skirt, shading her eyes from the mischievous sun, walking on into the great return.

In early spring I visited Sylvia Plath's grave for a third time, with my sister Linda. She longed to journey through Brontë country and so we did together. We traced the steps of the Brontë sisters and then traveled up the hill to trace mine. Linda delighted in the overgrown fields, the wildflowers, and the Gothic ruins. I sat quietly by the grave, conscious of a rare, suspended peace.

Spanish pilgrims travel on Camino de Santiago from

Grave of Sylvia Plath, winter

monastery to monastery, collecting small medals to attach to their rosary as proof of their steps. I have stacks of Polaroids, each marking my own, that I sometimes spread out like tarots or baseball cards of an imagined celestial team. There is now one of Sylvia in spring. It is very nice, but lacking the shimmering quality of the lost ones. Nothing can be truly replicated. Not a love, not a jewel, not a single line.

I awoke to the sound of church bells ringing from the tower of Our Lady of Pompeii. It was 8 a.m. At last some semblances of synchronicity. I was weary of having my morning coffee at night. Coming home through Los Angeles had twisted some inner mechanism, and like an errant cuckoo clock I was operating on time interrupted by itself. My reentry had spun out strangely. Victim of my own comedy of errors, my suitcase and computer stranded in Venice Beach, and then despite the fact I had only a black cotton sack to be mindful of, I left my notebook on the plane. Once home, in disbelief I dumped the meager contents of my sack onto my bed, examining them over and over as if the notebook would appear in the negative recesses between the other items. Cairo sat on the empty sack. I looked helplessly around my room. I have enough stuff, I told myself.

Days later an unmarked brown envelope appeared at my mail drop; I could see the outline of the black Moleskine. Grateful but perplexed I finally opened it. There was no note, no one to thank but the demon air. I extracted the photograph of Sylvia in the snow and examined it carefully. My penance for barely being present in the world, not the world between the pages of books, or the layered atmosphere of my own mind, but the world that is real to others. I then slipped it between the pages of *Ariel*. I sat reading the title poem, pausing at the lines *And I / Am the arrow,* a mantra that once emboldened a rather awkward but determined young girl. I had almost forgotten. Robert Lowell tells us in the introduction that Ariel does not refer to the chameleonlike sprite in Shakespeare's *Tempest,* but to her favorite horse. But perhaps the horse was named after the *Tempest* spirit. Ariel angel alters lion of God. All are good, but it is the horse that flies over the finish line with Sylvia's arms wrapped around his neck.

There was also a fair copy of a poem called "New Foal" that I placed in the book some time ago. It describes the birth and arrival of a foal, reminiscent of Superman as a babe, encrusted in a dark pod and hurled into space toward Earth. The foal lands, teeters, is smoothed by God and man to become horse. The poet who wrote it is one with the dust, but the new foal he created is lively, continually born and reborn.

I was glad to be home, sleeping in my own bed, with my little television and all my books. I had only been gone a few weeks but it somehow felt stretched into months. It was about time I salvaged a bit of my routine. It was too early to go to 'Ino, so I read. Rather, I looked at the pictures in *Nabokov's Butterflies* and read all the captions. Then I washed, put on clean versions of what I was already wearing, grabbed my notebook, and hurried downstairs, the cats trailing after me, finally recognizing my habits as their own.

March winds, both feet on the ground. The spell of jet lag broken, I was looking forward to sitting at my corner table and receiving my black coffee, brown toast, and olive oil without asking for it. There were twice as many pigeons than usual on Bedford Street, and a few daffodils had come up early. It didn't register at first, but then I realized that the blood-orange awning with 'Ino across it was missing. The door was locked, but I saw Jason inside and I tapped on the window.

—I'm glad you came by. Let me make you one last coffee.

I was too stunned to speak. He was closing up shop and that was it. I looked at my corner. I saw myself sitting there on countless mornings through countless years.

—Can I sit down? I asked.

—Sure, go ahead.

I sat there all morning. A young girl who frequented the café was going by carrying a Polaroid camera identical to my own. I waved and went out to greet her.

—Hello, Claire, do you have a moment?

— Of course, she said.

I asked her to take my picture. The first and last picture at my corner table in 'Ino. She was sad for me, having seen me through the window many times in passing. She took a few shots and laid one on the table—the picture of woebegone. I thanked her as she left. I sat there for a long time thinking of nothing, and then picked up my white pen. I wrote of the well and the face of Jean Reno. I wrote of the cowpoke and the crooked smile of my husband. I wrote of the bats of Austin, Texas, and the silver chairs in the interrogation room in

Criminal Intent. I wrote till I was spent, the last words written in Café 'Ino.

Before we parted, Jason and I stood and looked around the small café together. I didn't ask him why he was closing. I figured he had his reasons, and the answer wouldn't make any difference anyway.

I said good-bye to my corner.

—What will happen to the tables and chairs? I asked.

—You mean your table and chair?

—Yeah, mostly.

—They're yours, he said. I'll bring them over later.

That evening Jason carried them from Bedford Street

across Sixth Avenue, the same route I had taken for over a decade. My table and chair from the Café 'Ino. My portal to where.

I climbed the fourteen steps to my bedroom, turned off the light, and lay there awake. I was thinking about how New York City at night is like a stage set. I was thinking of how on a plane home from London I watched a pilot for a TV show I'd never heard of called *Person of Interest* and how two nights later there was a film crew on my street and they asked me to not pass while they were shooting and I spotted the main guy in *Person of Interest* being shot for a scene beneath the scaffolding about fifteen feet from the right of my door. I was thinking about how much I love this city.

I found the channel changer and watched the end of an episode of *Doctor Who*. The David Tennant configuration, the only Doctor Who for me.

—One may tolerate the demons for the sake of an angel, Madame Pompadour tells him before he transports into another dimension. I was thinking what a beautiful match they would have made. I was thinking of French time-traveling children with Scottish accents breaking the hearts of the future. Simultaneously, a blood-orange awning turned in my mind like a small twister. I wondered if it was possible to devise a new kind of thinking.

It was nearly dawn before I sank into sleep. I had another dream about the café in the desert. This time the cowpoke was standing at the door, gazing at the open plain. He reached over and lightly gripped my arm. I noticed that there was a crescent moon tattooed in the space between his thumb and forefinger. A writer's hand.

—How is it that we stray away from one another, then always come back?

—Do we really come back to one another, I answered, or just come here and lazily collide?

He didn't answer.

—There's nothing lonelier than the land, he said.

—Why lonely?

—Because it's so damn free.

And then he was gone. I walked over and stood where he had been standing and felt the warmth of his presence. The wind was picking up and unidentifiable bits of debris were circling in the air. Something was coming, I could feel it.

I stumbled out of bed, fully clothed. I was still thinking. Half asleep I slipped on my boots and dragged a carved Spanish chest from the back of the closet. It had the patina of a worn saddle, with a number of drawers filled with objects, some sacred and some whose origins were entirely forgotten. I found what I was looking for—a snapshot of an English greyhound with *Specter, 1971* written on the back. It was between the pages of a worn copy of *Hawk Moon* by Sam Shepard with his inscription, *If you've forgotten hunger your crazy.* I went to the bathroom to wash. A slightly waterlogged copy of *No Longer Human* was on the floor beneath the sink. I rinsed off my face, grabbed my notebook, and headed for Café 'Ino. Halfway across Sixth Avenue, I remembered.

I began to spend more time at the Dante but at irregular hours. In the mornings I just got deli coffee and sat on my stoop. I reflected on how my mornings at Café 'Ino had not only prolonged but also afforded my malaise with a small amount of grandeur. Thank you, I said. I have lived in my own book. One I never planned to write, recording time backwards and forwards. I have watched the snow fall onto the sea and traced the steps of a traveler long gone. I have relived moments that were perfect in their certainty. Fred buttoning the khaki shirt he wore for his flying lessons. Doves returning to nest on our balcony. Our daughter, Jesse, standing before me stretching out her arms.

—Oh, Mama, sometimes I feel like a new tree.

We want things we cannot have. We seek to reclaim a certain moment, sound, sensation. I want to hear my mother's voice. I want to see my children as children. Hands small, feet swift. Everything changes. Boy grown, father dead, daughter taller than me, weeping from a bad dream. Please stay forever, I say to the things I know. Don't go. Don't grow.

A Dream of Alfred Wegener

— ⊫◊⊨ —

Another restless night. I got up at dawn and worked, my eyes burned from deciphering scribbled envelopes, endpapers, and stained napkins, then transcribing the text to the computer with everything out of order, then trying to make sense of a subjective narrative with an asymmetrical timeline. I left the lot of it on my bed and went to Caffè Dante. I let my coffee run cold and thought about detectives. Partners depend on one another's eyes. The one says, tell me what you see. His partner must speak assuredly, not leaving anything out. But a writer has no partner. He has to step back and ask himself—tell me what you see. But since he is telling himself he doesn't have to be perfectly clear, because something inside holds any given missing part—the unclear or partially articulated. I wondered if I would have been a good detective. It kills me to say it, but I don't think so. I'm not the observant type. My eyes seem to roll within. I paid the check, marveling that the same murals of Dante and Beatrice have papered the café walls since at least my first visit in 1963. Then I left and went shopping. I bought a copy of a new translation of *The Divine Comedy* and laces for my boots. I noticed I felt optimistic.

I went to my mail drop and picked up the mail. A first edition of Anna Kavan's *A Scarcity of Love,* two royalty checks, a massive catalogue from Restoration Hardware, and an urgent missive from our CDC secretary. It was absent the customary seal, so I opened it quickly, with some trepidation. It contained a single watermarked sheet advising all members that the Continental Drift Club was formally disbanding. She suggested that we shred any official correspondence with the CDC letterhead or seal and wished us all good health and contentedness. At the bottom she had written *hope to meet again* in pencil. I immediately wrote her a brief note promising I would do as she asked, adding some verses I had written for the CDC theme song. As I addressed the envelope I could hear the plaintive sound of Number Seven's accordion.

> *Saints day in the snow, where did Wegener go*
> *Only Rasmus knows, and he is in God's hands*
> *Raise an iron cross, he's no longer lost*
> *Found within are notes, and they are in God's hands*

I removed a gray archival box from the top shelf of my closet and spread the contents on the bed—a dossier containing our objectives, printed reading lists, my official confirmation, and red card—Number Twenty-three. There was also a stack of notated napkins, a Polaroid of the chess table used by Bobby Fischer and Boris Spassky, and my sketch of Fritz

Loewe for the 2010 newsletter. I did not open the packet of official letters tied with blue string but instead built a small fire and watched them burn. I sighed and crumpled the paper napkins containing the notes for my somewhat ill-fated talk. My intention had been to channel the last moments in the life of Alfred Wegener, drawing from the members' unified mind, prodded by the query: what did he see? But the light chaos I had inadvertently ignited obstructed any possibility of realizing a vision akin to poetry.

He departed from Eismitte on All Saints' Day, seeking provisions for his friends waiting anxiously for his return. It was his fiftieth birthday. The white horizon beckoned. He detected an arc of color staining the snow. One soul breaking apart from another. He called out to his love, a drifting continent away. Dropping to his knees, he could see his guide, several yards before him, raising his arms.

I tossed the crumpled napkins into the flame, and each closed like a fist, slowly reopening like petals of small cabbage roses. Fascinated, I watched as they fused and formed one enormous rose. It ascended and hovered above the tent of the sleeping scientist. Its great thorns pierced the canvas, and its heavy fragrance rushed within, enveloping his sleep, becoming one with his breath, and penetrated the chambers of his exploding heart. I was blessed with a vision of his last moments, rising from the smoke of cherished mementos of the Continental Drift Club. An enthusiasm pulsed through me whose language I knew well. These are modern times, I told myself. But we are not trapped in them. We can go where we like,

Parsifal's robe, Neuhardenberg

communing with angels, to reprise a time in human history more science fiction than the future.

> *I have smoothed the hem of the robe of Parsifal.*
> *Watched Giotto's sheep wander from a fresco.*
> *Prayed before holy icons unveiled, surviving time.*
> *Held shavings swept from the hut of Geppetto.*
> *Unzipped a body bag and beheld the face of my brother.*
> *Witnessed the acolyte scatter petals over a dying poet.*
> *I saw the smoke of incense form the shape of my days.*
> *I saw my love return to God.*
> *I saw things as they are.*

Shard by shard we are released from the tyranny of so-called time. A curtain of purple wisteria partially conceals the entrance to a familiar garden. I take my seat at an oval table, Schiller's portal, and reach across to caress the wrist of the sad-eyed mathematician. The separating chasm closes. In a wink, a lifetime, we pass through the infinite movements of a silent overture. A lighthearted procession moves through the halls of an illustrious institution: Joseph Knecht, Évariste Galois, members of the Vienna Circle. I watch him as he rises, following at their heels, whistling softly.

The long vines sway ever so slightly. I picture Alfred Wegener and his wife, Else, having tea in a drawing room flooded with light. And then I begin to write. Not of science but of the human heart. I write fervently, as a student at her desk, bowed over her composition book, composing not as she is bid but as she desires.

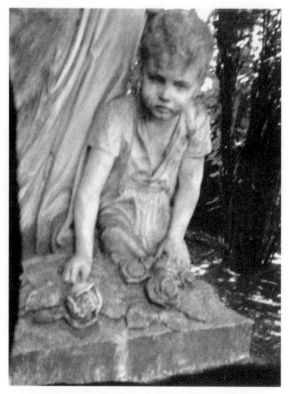

Statue detail, St. Marien and St. Nikolai Church

Road to Larache

✦ ⊠◆⊠ ✦

ON APRIL FOOL'S DAY, I reluctantly prepared for yet another journey. I was invited to participate in a conference of poets and musicians in Tangier to honor the Beat writers who had once made it their port of call. I much preferred to be in Rockaway Beach, drinking coffee with the workers and watching the slow but meaningful process of the salvation of my little house. On the other hand I would be joining good friends, and April 15 marked the passing day of Jean Genet. It seemed to be the right moment to deliver the stones from Saint-Laurent Prison to his grave in Larache, only sixty miles from the conference.

Paul Bowles once said that Tangier is a place where the past and present exist simultaneously in proportionate degree. There is something hidden in the fabric of this city, a weave that produces a sense of welcoming coupled with mistrust. I saw a bit of Tangier myself first through his work, then through his eyes.

I was first introduced to Bowles in a serendipitous way.

In the summer of 1967, shortly after I left home and went to New York City, I passed a large box of overturned books spilling out into the street. Several were scattered across the sidewalk, and a dated copy of *Who's Who in America* lay open before my feet. I bent down to look, as a photograph caught my eye above an entry for Paul Frederic Bowles. I had never heard of him but I noticed we shared the same birthday, the thirtieth of December. Believing it to be a sign, I tore out the page and later searched out his books, the first being *The Sheltering Sky*. I read everything he wrote as well as his translations, introducing me to the work of Mohammed Mrabet and Isabelle Eberhardt.

Three decades later, in 1997, I was asked by German *Vogue* to interview him in Tangier. I had mixed feelings about my assignment, for they mentioned he was ill. But I was assured that he had readily agreed and that I would not be disturbing him. Bowles lived in a three-room apartment on a quiet street in a straightforward fifties-modern building in a residential section. A high stack of well-traveled trunks and suitcases formed a column in the entranceway. There were books lining the walls and halls, books that I knew and books I wished to know. He sat propped up in bed, wearing a soft plaid robe, and appeared to brighten when I entered the room.

I crouched down trying to find a graceful position in the awkward air. We spoke of his late wife, Jane, whose spirit seemed to be everywhere. I sat there twisting my braids, speaking about love. I wondered if he was really listening.

—Are you writing? I asked.

—No, I am no longer writing.

—How do you feel now? I asked.

—Empty, he answered.

I left him to his thoughts and went upstairs to the patio on the roof. There were no camels in the courtyard. No burlap sack spilling over with kif. No sebsi cocked on the edge of a jar. There was a cement roof overlooking other roofs, and lengths of muslin hung on lines that crisscrossed the space opening onto the blue Tangier sky. I pressed my face against one of the damp sheets for a moment's respite from the stifling heat, yet immediately regretted doing so, for the impression marred its smooth perfection.

I returned to him. His robe lay at his feet, well-worn leather slippers by the side of his bed. A young Moroccan named Karim kindly served us tea. He lived across the hall and often came over to check on how Paul was faring.

Paul spoke of an island he owned that he no longer visited, music he no longer played, certain songbirds that were now extinct. I could see he was tiring.

—We share the same birthday, I told him.

He smiled wanly, his haloed eyes closing. We were approaching the end of our visit.

Everything pours forth. Photographs their history. Books their words. Walls their sounds. The spirits rose like an ether that spun an arabesque and touched down as gently as a benevolent mask.

—Paul, I have to go. I will come back to see you.

He opened his eyes and laid his long, lined hand upon mine.

Now he is gone.

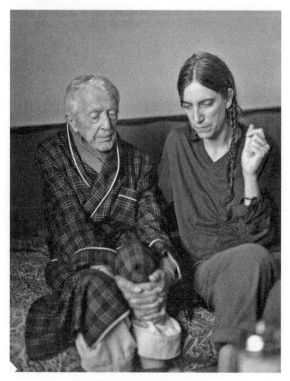

With Paul Bowles, Tangier, 1997

I raised the top of my desk and located the oversized Gitane matchbox still wrapped in Fred's handkerchief. I hadn't opened it for over two decades. The stones were safely there, with bits of prison earth clinging to them. The sight of them opened the wound of recognition. It was time to deliver them, though not in the way I had thought. I had already written Karim that I would be coming. When we had first met at Paul's apartment I told him the story of the stones and he promised that when the time came he would take me to Larache's Christian cemetery, where Genet was buried.

Karim swiftly answered, as if no time had passed.

—I am in the desert, but I will find you and we will find Genet.

I knew he would keep his word.

I cleaned my camera and wrapped a few packs of film in a bandanna and placed them between my shirts and dungarees. I was traveling even lighter than usual. I said good-bye to the cats, slipped the matchbox into my pocket, and left. My fellow compatriots Lenny Kaye and Tony Shanahan met me at the airport with their acoustic guitars—our first time together in Morocco. In the morning we were picked up in Casablanca but the conference van broke down halfway to Tangier. We sat on the side of the road sharing stories about William and Allen, Peter and Paul, our Beat apostles. Soon we boarded a lively bus with the radios blaring in French and Arabic, passing a disabled bicycle, a stumbling burro, and a child brushing small stones from an injured knee. One of the passengers, a woman weighted down by several shopping bags, was harassing the driver. He finally stopped the bus and some of the people got out and bought bottles of Coca-Cola at a convenience store. I happened to look out and saw the word Kiosque written in Kufic style above the door.

We checked into the Hôtel Rembrandt, a longtime haven for writers, from Tennessee Williams to Jane Bowles. We were given black notebooks with the words *Le Colloque à Tanger* stamped in green and our credentials—William Burroughs's face superimposed over the face of Brion Gysin— a third-mind laminate. It was the lobby of reunion. Poets Anne Waldman and John Giorno; Bachir Attar, leader of the Master Musicians of Jajouka; musicians Lenny Kaye and Tony Shanahan. Alain Lahana, of Le Rat des Villes, flew in from Paris, the filmmaker Frieder Schlaich from Berlin, and Karim drove in from the desert. For a moment we stood and looked at one another—the gone Beats' orphaned children.

We congregated in the early evenings for readings and panel discussions. As we read passages from the works of the writers we were saluting, a procession of overcoats worn by our great teachers entered and exited my sight line. Through the night, musicians improvised and dervishes whirled. Lenny and I fell into the familiar rhythms of our unconditional friendship. We had known each other for over forty years. Shared the same books, the same stages, the same birth month, the same year. We had long dreamed of working in Tangier and wandered aimlessly through the medina in contented silence. The snaking alleys were infused with a golden light that we religiously followed until we realized we were walking in circles.

After we performed our duties we spent the night at the

Palais Moulay Hafid listening to the Master Musicians of Jajouka followed by Dar Gnawa. Their high-spirited music drew me to dance; I danced surrounded by boys younger than my son. We moved in a similar style, but they displayed an inventiveness and flexibility that left me in awe. On my morning walk I saw some of the boys smoking cigarettes in front of an abandoned movie theater.

—You're up early, I said.

They laughed.

—We have not been to sleep yet.

On the last evening a small yet imposing figure dressed in a white djellaba stitched with gold thread entered our common area. It was Mohammed Mrabet, and we all rose. He had passed the sebsi with our beloved friends, and their tangible vibrations could be felt in the folds of his robe. As a youth he had sat at a table telling stories to Paul Bowles, who translated them for Black Sparrow Press. They formed a string of wonderful tales such as *The Beach Café* that I had read and reread sitting in the Caffè Dante while dreaming of having a café of my own.

—Do you want to go to the beach café tomorrow? asked Karim.

It never occurred to me that the café actually existed.

—It is a real café? I asked, taken aback.

—Yes, he laughed.

In the morning I met Lenny at the Gran Café de Paris on the Boulevard Pasteur. I had seen pictures of Genet having tea with the writer Mohamed Choukri there. Though it resembled an early-sixties cafeteria there was no fare offered, only tea and Nescafé. Carved wood-paneled walls brown leather-tufted benches wine-colored tablecloths heavy glass ashtrays. We sat in comfortable silence in a curved corner with wide windows so we could watch the comings and goings on the streets outside. My Nescafé was delivered in a soft tube with a glass of hot water. Lenny ordered tea. Several men had gathered to smoke cigars beneath a fading portrait of the king with a fishing pole and his impressive catch. On the green-marbled wall was a clock in the shape of a large pewter sun delivering time in a timeless realm.

Lenny and I drove along the coast to the beach café with Karim. It appeared closed and the beach deserted, an outpost on the other side of the cowpoke's mirror. Karim went into the café and found a man who reluctantly made us mint tea. He brought it outside on a table and went back inside. Down by the shore, hidden by a cliff, were the rooms described by Mrabet. I removed my shoes, rolled up my pants, and waded in the sea in a place I had come to know through the pages of his book.

I dried off in the sun and drank some of the tea, which was very sweet. There were many places to sit, but I was attracted to an ornate white plastic chair set against a bramble bush. I took two shots and then gave my camera to Lenny and he photographed me sitting in it. Back at the table not more than a few feet away I quickly unpeeled the Polaroids; I was dissatisfied with my framing of the chair and turned to take another but it was gone. Lenny and I were astonished. No one was around yet the chair had vanished within moments.

—This is crazy, said Lenny.

—This is Tangier, said Karim.

Karim went inside the café and I followed. The café was empty. I left my shot of the white chair in the center of the table.

—This is also Tangier, I said.

We drove along the coast to the sound of waves and the overriding song of crickets, then over a swirl of dusty roads and past whitewashed villages and bits of desert dotted with yellow flowers. Karim parked on the side of a road and we followed him to the house of Mrabet. We made our way down the hill as an unruly herd of goats was coming up. Much to our delight they parted, then surrounded us. The master was not in but his goats entertained us. As we headed back to Tangier we saw a shepherd guiding a camel with her calf. Rolling down the window, I called out:

—What is the little one's name?

—His name is Jimi Hendrix.

—Hooray, I wake from yesterday!

—Inshallah! he called out.

I rose early, slipped the matchbox into my pocket, and went for a last coffee at Café de Paris. Feeling strangely detached I wondered if I was about to engage in a meaningless ritual. Genet had passed away in the spring of 1986, before I was able to complete my mission, and the stones had remained in my desk for more than two decades. I ordered another Nescafé, remembering.

I was sitting at the small table in the kitchen beneath the picture of Camus when I heard the news. Fred placed his hand on my shoulder, then left me to my thoughts. I felt a sense of regret, of suspended gesture, but could do nothing but offer the words I would write.

In early April Genet had traveled with his companion Jacky Maglia from Morocco to Paris to correct the publisher's proofs of what would be his final book. He was turned away from his customary Paris residence, the Hôtel Rubens, because a night clerk failed to recognize him and was offended by his tramplike appearance. They walked in the pouring rain seeking shelter, ending at the Hôtel Jack, a then-dicey one-star near the Place d'Italie.

In a room no more than a cell, Genet labored over his pages. Although afflicted with terminal throat cancer he avoided painkillers, determined to remain unclouded. Having taken barbiturates throughout his life, he abstained just when he needed them most, for the desire to perfect his manuscript overrode all physical suffering.

On April 15, Jean Genet died alone on the floor of the bathroom of his tiny room in the transient hotel. Most likely he had tripped on the small step leading to the cubicle. On the night table was his legacy, his last work intact. On that same day the United States bombed Libya. There were rumors that Hana Gaddafi, the adopted child of Colonel Gaddafi, was killed in the raid. As I sat and wrote, I imagined the orphaned innocent leading the orphan thief into paradise.

My Nescafé had gone cold. I motioned for another. Lenny arrived and ordered tea. The morning was slow moving. We sat back and surveyed the room, conscious that the writers we so admired had spent many hours conversing in it together. They are all still here, we agreed, and walked back to the hotel.

Karim was called back to the desert but Frieder arranged for a driver to take us all to Larache. Five of us assembled—Lenny, Tony, Frieder, Alain, and I—all reaching for the hand of Genet. Surrounded by friends, I hadn't anticipated the deep loneliness I was to feel nor the resentful heartache I used all my strength to dispel. Genet was dead and belonged to no one. My knowledge of Fred, who had taken me all the way to Saint-Laurent-du-Maroni for a few small stones, belonged to me. I sought but could not feel his presence and sank back into the vestiges of memory until I found him. Dressed in khaki, his long hair shorn, standing alone in the undergrowth of tall grass and spreading palms. I saw his hand and wristwatch. I saw his wedding ring and his brown leather shoes.

As we approached the city of Larache the sense of sea was strong. It was an old fishing port not far from ancient Phoenician ruins. We parked near a fortress and made our way up a hill to the cemetery. An old woman and a small boy were there, as if in wait, and opened the gate for us. The cemetery had a Spanish feel and Genet's grave was facing east overlooking the sea. I cleared the debris from the gravesite, removing dead flowers, twigs, and bits of broken glass, and then washed the headstone with bottled water. The child watched me intently.

I said the words I wished to say, then poured water upon the ground and dug deep, inserting the stones. As we laid our flowers we could hear the distant sound of the muezzin calling the people to prayer. The boy quietly sat where I buried the stones and pulled petals off the flowers, sprinkling them on his trousers, staring at us with big black eyes. Before we left he handed me the remnants of a silk rosebud, faded pink, which I placed in the matchbox. We gave the old woman some money and she closed the gate. The boy seemed sad to see his strange playmates depart. The return was a sleepy one. Every so often I would look at my pictures. Eventually I would place the Polaroids of Genet's grave in a box with the graves of others. But in my heart I knew the miracle of the rose was not the stones, nor could be found in the photographs, but was within the cells of the child guardian, Genet's prisoner of love.

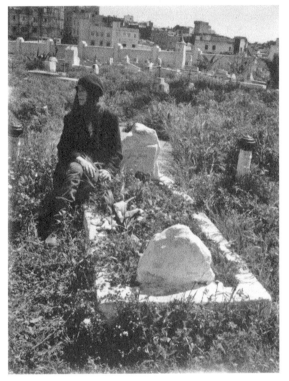

Genet's grave, Larache Christian Cemetery

Father's Day, Lake Ann, Michigan

Covered Ground

M EMORIAL DAY WAS fast approaching. I had a longing to see my little house, my Alamo, train or no train.
The great storm destroyed the Broad Channel rail bridge,
washing out more than fifteen hundred feet of track, completely flooding two stations on the A line, requiring massive
repairs, signals, switches, and wiring. There was no point in
being impatient. It remained a truly daunting task, like piec-
ing together the shattered mandolin of Bill Monroe.

I called my friend Winch, the overseer of its slow renovation, to hitch a ride to Rockaway Beach. It was sunny though
unseasonably cold, so I wore an old peacoat and my watch
cap. Having time to kill, I got a large deli coffee and waited
for him on my stoop. The sky was clear save for a few drifting clouds, and I followed them back to northern Michigan
on another Memorial Day in Traverse City. Fred was flying,
and our young son, Jackson, and I were walking along Lake

Michigan. The beach was littered with hundreds of feathers. I laid down an Indian blanket and got out my pen and notebook.

—I am going to write, I told him. What will you do?

He surveyed the area with his eyes, fixing on the sky.

—I'm going to think, he said.

—Well, thinking is a lot like writing.

—Yes, he said, only in your head.

He was approaching his fourth birthday and I marveled at his observation. I wrote, Jackson reflected, and Fred flew, somehow all connected through the blood of concentration. We had a happy day, and when the sun began to recede I gathered up our things along with a few feathers and Jack ran on ahead, anticipating his father's return.

Even now, his father dead for some twenty years, and Jackson a man anticipating the arrival of his own son, I can picture that afternoon. The strong waves of Lake Michigan lapping the shore littered with the feathers of molting gulls. Jackson's little blue shoes, his quiet ways, the steam rising from my thermos of black coffee, and the gathering clouds that Fred would be eyeing from the cockpit window of a Piper Cherokee.

—Do you think he can see us? Jack asked.

—He always sees us, my boy, I answered.

Images have their way of dissolving and then abruptly returning, pulling along the joy and pain attached to them like tin cans rattling from the back of an old-fashioned wedding vehicle. A black dog on a strip of beach, Fred standing in the shadows of mangy palms flanking the entrance to Saint-Laurent Prison, the blue-and-yellow Gitane matchbox wrapped in his handkerchief, and Jackson racing ahead, searching for his father in the pale sky.

I slid into the pickup truck with Winch. We didn't talk much, both of us lost in our own thoughts. There was little traffic and we made it in about forty minutes. We met with the four fellows who made up his crew. Hardworking men sensitive to their task. I noticed all my neighbors' trees were dead. They were the closest I had to trees of my own. The great storm surges that flooded the streets had killed most of the vegetation. I inspected all that there was to see. The mildewed pasteboard walls forming small rooms had been gutted, opening onto a large room with the century-old vaulted ceiling intact, and rotted floors were being removed. I could feel progress and left with a bit of optimism. I sat on the makeshift step of what would be my refurbished porch and envisioned a yard with wildflowers. Anxious for some permanency, I guess I needed to be reminded how temporal permanency is.

I walked across the road toward the sea. A newly stationed shore patrol shooed me away from the beach area. They were dredging where the boardwalk had been. The sand-colored outpost that had briefly housed Zak's café was under government renovation, repainted canary yellow and bright turquoise, expunging its Foreign Legion appeal. I could only hope the dramatically cheery colors would bleach out in the sun. I walked farther down to gain entrance onto the beach, got my feet wet, and then got some coffee to go from the sole surviving taco stand.

I asked if anyone had seen Zak.

—He made the coffee, they told me.

—Is he here? I asked.

—He's somewhere around.

Clouds drifted overhead. Memorial clouds. Passenger jets were taking off from JFK. Winch finished his tasks and we got back into the pickup truck and headed back across the channel, past the airport, over the bridge, and into the city. My dungarees were still damp from skirting the sea, and bits of sand shook out onto the floor that had been caught in the rolled-up folds. When I finished the coffee I couldn't part with the empty container. It occurred to me I could preserve the history of 'Ino, the lost boardwalk, and whatever came to mind in microscript upon the Styrofoam cup, like an engraver etching the Twenty-third Psalm on the head of a pin.

WHEN FRED DIED, we held his memorial in the Detroit Mariners' Church where we were married. Every November Father Ingalls, who wed us, held a service in memory of the twenty-nine crewmembers who went down in Lake Superior on the *Edmund Fitzgerald,* ending with ringing the heavy brotherhood bell twenty-nine times. Fred was deeply moved by this ritual, and as his memorial coincided with theirs, the father allowed the flowers and the model of the ship to be left on the stage. Father Ingalls presided over the service and wore an anchor around his neck in lieu of a cross.

The evening of the service, my brother, Todd, came upstairs for me, but I was still in bed.

—I can't do it, I told him.

——You have to, he said adamantly, and he shook me from my torpor, helped me to dress, and drove me to the church. I thought about what I would say, and the song "What a Wonderful World" came on the radio. Whenever we heard it Fred would say, Trisha, it's your song. Why does it have to be my song? I'd protest. I don't even like Louis Armstrong. But he would insist the song was mine. It felt like a sign from Fred, so I decided to sing "Wonderful World" a cappella at the service. As I sang I felt the simplistic beauty of the song, but I still didn't understand why he connected it with me, a question I had waited too long to ask. Now it's your song, I said, addressing a lingering void. The world seemed drained of wonder. I did not write poems in a fever. I did not see the spirit of Fred before me or feel the spinning trajectory of his journey.

My brother stayed with me through the days that followed. He promised the children he would be there for them always and would return after the holidays. But exactly a month later he had a massive stroke while wrapping Christmas presents for his daughter. The sudden death of Todd, so soon after Fred's passing, seemed unbearable. The shock left me numb. I spent hours sitting in Fred's favorite chair, dreading my own imagination. I rose and performed small tasks with the mute concentration of one imprisoned in ice.

Eventually I left Michigan and returned to New York with our children. One afternoon while crossing the street I noticed I was crying. But I could not identify the source of my tears. I felt a heat containing the colors of autumn. The dark stone in my heart pulsed quietly, igniting like a coal in a hearth. Who is in my heart? I wondered.

I soon recognized Todd's humorous spirit, and as I continued my walk I slowly reclaimed an aspect of him that was also myself—a natural optimism. And slowly the leaves of my life turned, and I saw myself pointing out simple things to Fred, *skies of blue, clouds of white,* hoping to penetrate the veil of a congenital sorrow. I saw his pale eyes looking intently into mine, trying to trap my walleye in his unfaltering gaze. That alone took up several pages that filled me with such painful longing that I fed them into the fire in my heart, like Gogol burning page by page the manuscript of *Dead Souls Two*. I burned them all, one by one; they did not form ash, did not go cold, but radiated the warmth of human compassion.

How Linden Kills the Thing
She Loves

✦

LINDEN IS RUNNING light-footed, swift. She stops, drawn to a perfectly formed tree in the center of a meadow. She is impermeable save for her Achilles' heel—Detective James Skinner, head of her unit, and a suppressed desire for his love. They once partnered in the field and clandestinely in bed, but that is seemingly behind them. Still, a pale shadow moves across her face when she is in his presence. As she approaches her front door she is surprised to find him waiting for her once more. Distances dissolve. Skinner comes to her human. Linden moves closer. In the hands of Skinner she is home.

A coin spins on its edge. How it falls is of little consequence. Heads you lose, tails you lose. Linden ignores the signs, believing she's in luck, striking a perfect balance of love and work, Skinner and her badge. The morning light illumines her rose-gold hair pulled back with a rubber band. Silhouettes of victims in an unfolding paper-doll stream momentarily dispel in the flame they have reignited.

The sun shifts. One more body burning, evidence uncovered, a ring tightening around her throat. Surrendering to love, Skinner and Linden are mutually exposed. In his eyes she suddenly sees other eyes, the horror of lurid depths. Forensic traces. Soiled slips. Hair ribbons soaked in shame.

The rain falls from the blue-eyed skies of Sarah Linden. She is washed with murderous clarity. Using all her God-given skills, she identifies Skinner, her mentor and her lover, as the serial killer.

Holder, her true confidant, pieces things together a beat behind her. With instinctive grace Holder traces her movements. Racing through the oppressive rain, he tracks them to Skinner's concealed lake house. The promise of a lovers' tryst now becomes the setting of an inexorable justice. Linden feels the vestiges of her joy floating among the dead. She will compassionately execute Skinner, ignoring Holder's pleas. He is cautious, protective; she is reckless. He watches in horror as Linden pulls the trigger, putting Skinner out of his misery, like a dying calf on the side of a road.

Stunned, I can only bow my head. I meld with the racing mind of Holder desperately trying to interpret her actions, foresee her future. My empty thermos remains by the bed wrapped in the ominous atmosphere of episode number 38. It is not long before I am confronted with the cruelest of all spoilers: there will be no episode 39.

The Killing season is over.

Linden has lost everything and now I am losing her. A television network has snuffed *The Killing*. There is the promise of a new show, yet another detective. But I am not ready to let her go and I do not want to move on. I want to watch as Linden plumbs the depths of the lake searching for feminine bones. What do we do with those that can be accessed and dismissed by a channel changer, that we love no less than a nineteenth-century poet or an admired stranger or a character from the pen of Emily Brontë? What do we do when one of them commingles with our own sense of self, only to be transferred into a finite space within an on-demand portal?

All is in limbo. An anguished moan rises from the black water. Swathed in pink industrial plastic, the dead await their champion—Linden of the Lake. But she has been relegated to no more than a statue in the rain with a gun. Having done the unpardonable, she will virtually lay her badge on the table.

A television series has its own moral reality. Pacing, I envision a spin-off: *Linden in the Valley of the Lost.* On the screen the black water surrounds the lake house. The lake takes on the shape of a diseased kidney.

Linden stares into the abyss where their sad remains lie.

It's the loneliest thing in the world, waiting to be found, she says.

Holder, numb with grief and insomnia, waits in that same car drinking the same cold coffee. Sitting vigil until she signals and he is again by her side as they tramp purgatory together.

Week by week a victim's story unfolds. Holder will connect the spatter of blood dots; she will root out the healing spring. The Linden tree will spread the scent of lime, purifying each girl shedding her plastic shroud and the linen strips of hell. But who will purify Linden? What dark maid will cleanse the chambers of her adulterated heart?

Linden is running. She abruptly stops and faces the camera. A Flemish Madonna with the eyes of a woman from the backwoods who has slept with the devil.

Divested of everything, it's of little consequence to her. She did it for love. There is only one directive: that the lost are found; that the thick leaves encasing the dead are parted and they are lifted into the arms of light.

Valley of the Lost

FRED HAD a cowboy, the only cowboy among his cavalry. He was molded from red plastic, slightly bowlegged, and poised to shoot. Fred called him Reddy. At night Reddy was not returned into a cardboard box with the rest of the components of Fred's small fortress but set on a low bookcase next to his bed where he could see him. One day as his mother was cleaning his room she dusted the bookcase and Reddy fell unnoticed and just disappeared. Fred searched for him for weeks but he was nowhere to be found. He silently called to Reddy as he lay in bed. When he set up his fort and arranged his men on the floor of his room, he felt Reddy near, calling to him. It was not his own voice but Reddy who called. Fred believed that, and Reddy became part of our common treasure, occupying a special place in the Valley of the Lost Things.

Several years later Fred's mother cleared out his old room. The floor was in such bad condition that several boards needed replacing. As the old boards were removed, all sorts of things emerged. And there, among the cobwebs and coins and bits of petrified gum, was Reddy, who had somehow fallen into a wide crack and slid out of sight, out of the reach of a boy's small hand. His mother returned Reddy, and Fred placed him on the bookcase in our bedroom where he could see him.

Some things are called back from the Valley. I believe Reddy called out to Fred. I believe Fred heard. I believe in their mutual jubilance. Some things are not lost but sacrificed. I saw my black coat in the Valley of the Lost on a random mound being picked over by desperate urchins. Someone good will get it, I told myself, the Billy Pilgrim of the lot.

Do our lost possessions mourn us? Do electric sheep dream of Roy Batty? Will my coat, riddled with holes, remember the rich hours of our companionship? Asleep on buses from Vienna to Prague, nights at the opera, walks by the sea, the grave of Swinburne in the Isle of Wight, the arcades of Paris, the caverns of Luray, the cafés of Buenos Aires. Human experience bound in its threads. How many poems bleeding from its ragged sleeves? I averted my eyes just for a moment, drawn by another coat that was warmer and softer, but that I did not love. Why is it that we lose the things we love, and things cavalier cling to us and will be the measure of our worth after we're gone?

Then it occurred to me. Perhaps I absorbed my coat. I suppose I should be grateful, considering its power, that my coat did not absorb me. Then I would seem to be among the missing though merely tossed over a chair, vibrating, holey.

Our lost things returning to the places from where they came, to their absolute origins: a crucifix to its living tree or rubies to their home in the Indian Ocean. The genesis of my coat, made from fine wool, spinning backwards through the looms, onto the body of a lamb, a black sheep a bit apart from the flock, grazing on the side of a hill. A lamb opening its eyes to the clouds that resemble for a moment the woolly backs of his own kind.

The moon was full and low like a wagon wheel, no doubt flanked by the two identical towers on Lafayette Street where the head of Picasso's girl with a ponytail dominates a small square. I washed and braided my hair and removed the coffee containers lining my bed, placed the scattered books and pages of notes in neat piles against the wall, removed my Irish linen from a wooden chest, and changed my bedding. I lifted the muslin veil that protects my Brancusi photographs from fading in the sun. A night shot of an endless column in the garden of Steichen and an immense marble teardrop. I wanted to look at them for a while before I turned out the light.

I dreamed I was somewhere that was also nowhere. It looked like a thoroughfare in Raleigh, with small highways crossing each other. No one was around, and then I saw Fred running, though he seldom ran. He didn't like to hurry. At the same moment something whizzed past him, a wheel on its side, racing as if alive across the highway. And then I saw the object's face—a clock with no hands.

I awoke and it was still dark. I lay there for a time reliving the dream, feeling other dreams stacked behind it. I slowly began to recall the entire body, telescoping backwards, letting my mind stitch the fleeting pieces together. I was high in the mountains. I trustingly followed my guide along a narrow, winding path. I noticed he was slightly bowlegged and he stopped abruptly.

—Look, he said.

We were on a high, straight drop. I froze, gripped by an irrational fear of the emptiness before me. He stood with confidence but I had trouble getting a true footing. I tried to reach for him but he turned and left.

—How can you leave me here? I cried. How shall I get back?

I called to him but he didn't answer. When I tried to move, loose earth and stone broke away. I could not see any way out except for falling or flying.

And then the physical terror lifted and I was on the ground, before a low, whitewashed structure with a blue door. A youth in a billowing white shirt approached me.

—How did I get here? I asked him.

—We called to Fred, he said.

I saw two men lingering by an old caravan with one wheel missing.

—Would you like some tea?

—Yes, I said. He motioned to the others. One of them went inside to prepare it. He heated the water on a brazier and stuffed a pot with mint and brought it to me.

—Would you like a saffron cake?

—Yes, I said, suddenly hungry.

—We saw you were in danger. We intervened and called to Fred. He swept you up and carried you here.

He is dead, I thought. How is it possible?

—There is a matter of a fee, said the youth. One hundred thousand dirhams.

—I'm not sure I have that much money, but I will get it.

I reached into my pocket and it was filled with money, exactly what he asked for, but the scene had shifted. I was alone on a stony path surrounded by chalky hills. I paused to reflect on what had happened. Fred had rescued me in a dream. And then suddenly I was back on the highway and I saw him in the distance trailing after the wheel with the face of a clock with no hands.

—Get it, Fred! I cried.

And the wheel collided with a massive cornucopia of lost things. It fell on its side, and Fred knelt and placed his hand on it. He flashed a huge smile, one of absolute joy, from a place with no beginning or end.

The Hour of Noon

✦

M Y FATHER WAS BORN in the shadows of the Bethlehem Steel Mill as the noon whistle blew. Thus he was born, in accordance with Nietzsche, at the appointed hour when certain individuals are granted the ability to grasp the mystery of the eternal recurrence of all things. My father's mind was beautiful. He seemed to see all philosophies with equal weight and wonder. If one could perceive an entire universe, the possibility of its existence seemed quite tangible. As real as the Riemann hypothesis, as belief itself, unfaltering and divine.

We seek to stay present, even as the ghosts attempt to draw us away. Our father manning the loom of eternal return. Our mother wandering toward paradise, releasing the thread. In my way of thinking, anything is possible. Life is at the bottom of things and belief at the top, while the creative impulse, dwelling in the center, informs all. We imagine a house, a rectangle of hope. A room with a single bed with a pale coverlet, a few precious books, a stamp album. Walls papered in faded

Hermann Hesse's typewriter, Montagnola, Switzerland

floral fall away and burst as a newborn meadow speckled with sun and a stream emptying into a greater stream where a small boat awaits with two glowing oars and one blue sail.

When my children were young I contrived such vessels. I set them to sail, though I didn't board them. I rarely left the perimeter of our home. I said my prayers in the night by the canal draped by ancient longhaired willows. The things I touched were living. My husband's fingers, a dandelion, a skinned knee. I didn't seek to frame these moments. They passed without souvenir. But now I cross the sea with the sole aim to possess within a single image the straw hat of Robert

Graves, typewriter of Hesse, spectacles of Beckett, sickbed of Keats. What I have lost and cannot find I remember. What I cannot see I attempt to call. Working on a string of impulses, bordering illumination.

I photographed the grave of Rimbaud when I was twenty-six. The pictures were not exceptional but contained the mission itself, which I had long forgotten. Rimbaud died in a Marseille hospital in 1891 at the age of thirty-seven. His last wish was to return to Abyssinia where he had been a coffee trader. He was dying and it was not possible for him to be carried aboard ship for the long journey. In his delirium he imagined himself on horseback in the high Abyssinian plains. I had a string of nineteenth-century blue glass trade beads from Harar and I got it in mind to take them to him. In 1973 I went to his gravesite in Charleville, near the bank of the Meuse River, and pressed the beads deep into the soil of a large urn that stood before his tombstone. Something of his beloved country near to him. I hadn't connected the beads with the stones I'd gathered for Genet, but I supposed they originated from the same romantic impulse. Presumptuous, perhaps, though not erring. I have since returned and the urn is no longer there, but I believe I am still the same person; no amount of change in the world can change that.

I believe in movement. I believe in that lighthearted balloon, the world. I believe in midnight and the hour of noon. But what else do I believe in? Sometimes everything. Sometimes nothing. It fluctuates like light flitting over a pond. I believe in life, which one day each of us shall lose. When we are young we think we won't, that we are different. As a child

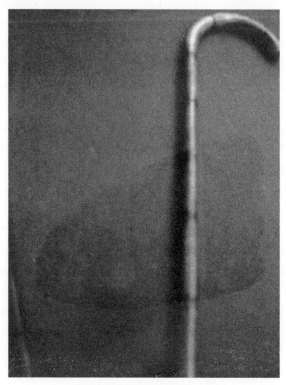

Virginia Woolf's walking stick

I thought I would never grow up, that I could will it so. And then I realized, quite recently, that I had crossed some line, unconsciously cloaked in the truth of my chronology. How did we get so damn old? I say to my joints, my iron-colored hair. Now I am older than my love, my departed friends. Perhaps I will live so long that the New York Public Library will be obliged to hand over the walking stick of Virginia Woolf. I would cherish it for her, and the stones in her pocket. But I would also keep on living, refusing to surrender my pen.

I removed my Saint Francis tau from around my neck, then braided my hair, still damp, and looked around. Home is a desk. The amalgamation of a dream. Home is the cats, my books, and my work never done. All the lost things that may one day call to me, the faces of my children who will one day call to me. Maybe we can't draw flesh from reverie nor retrieve a dusty spur, but we can gather the dream itself and bring it back uniquely whole.

I called to Cairo and she hopped onto the bed. I looked up and saw a singular star rise above my skylight. I tried to rise as well, but all at once gravity had the better of me and I was swept by the edges of a strange music. I saw the fist of a babe shaking a silver rattle. I saw the shadow of a man and the brim of his Stetson hat. He was toying with a kid's lariat, and then he knelt down, untied the knot, and laid it on the ground.

—Watch, he said.

The snake ate its tail, let go, and ate again. The lariat was a long string of slithering words. I leaned over to read what they said. My oracle. I checked my pocket but I had neither pen nor script.

—Some things, the cowpoke breathed, we save for ourselves.

It was the hour of showdown. The miraculous hour. I shielded my eyes from the punishing light, dusted off my jacket, and threw it over my shoulder. I knew exactly where I was. I fell out of the frame and saw what I was seeing. Same lone café, different dream. The dun-colored exterior had been repainted a bright canary yellow and the rusted gas pump was covered with what appeared to be a massive tea cozy. I just shrugged and sashayed in, but the place was unrecognizable. The tables and chairs and the jukebox were gone. The knotty pine panels had been stripped away and the faded walls were painted colonial blue with white wainscoting. There were crates of technical equipment, metal office furniture, and stacks of brochures. I leafed through a pile: Hawaii, Tahiti, and the Taj Mahal Casino in Atlantic City. A travel agency in the middle of nowhere.

I went into the back room but the coffeemaker, beans, wooden spoons, and earthenware mugs were all gone. Even the empty mescal bottles were gone. There were no ashtrays and no sign of my philosophic cowpoke. I sensed he had been heading this way and most likely, spotting the spanking-new paint job, just kept on going. I looked around. Nothing to hold me here, either, not even the dried carcass of a dead bee. I figured if I hustled I might spot the clouds of dust left behind where his old Ford flatbed passed. Maybe I could catch up with him and hitch myself a ride. We could travel the desert together, no agent required.

—I love you, I whispered to all, to none.

—Love not lightly, I heard him say.

And then I walked out, straight through the twilight, treading the beaten earth. There were no dust clouds, no signs of anyone, but I paid no mind. I was my own lucky hand of solitaire. The desert landscape unchanging: a long, unwinding scroll that I would one day amuse myself by filling. I'm going to remember everything and then I'm going to write it all down. An aria to a coat. A requiem for a café. That's what I was thinking, in my dream, looking down at my hands.

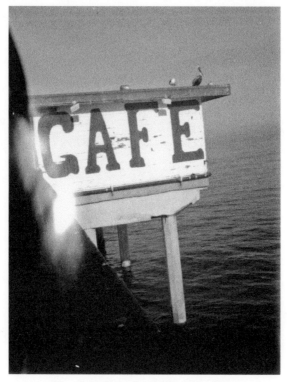

Wow Cafe, Ocean Beach Pier, Point Loma

ILLUSTRATIONS

PATTI SMITH is a writer, performer, and visual artist. She gained recognition in the 1970s for her revolutionary merging of poetry and rock. She has released twelve albums, including *Horses,* which has been hailed as one of the top one hundred debut albums of all time by *Rolling Stone.*

Smith had her first exhibit of drawings at the Gotham Book Mart in 1973 and has been represented by the Robert Miller Gallery since 1978. Her books include *Just Kids,* winner of the National Book Award in 2010, *Witt, Babel, Woolgathering, The Coral Sea,* and *Auguries of Innocence.*

In 2005, the French Ministry of Culture awarded Smith the title of Commandeur des Arts et des Lettres, the highest honor given to an artist by the French Republic. She was inducted into the Rock and Roll Hall of Fame in 2007.

In 1980, she married the musician Fred Sonic Smith in Detroit. They had a son, Jackson, and a daughter, Jesse. Smith resides in New York City.

A NOTE ON THE TYPE

This book was set in Granjon, a type named in compliment to Robert Granjon, a type cutter and printer active in Antwerp, Lyons, Rome, and Paris from 1523 to 1590. Granjon, the boldest and most original designer of his time, was one of the first to practice the trade of typefounder apart from that of printer.

Linotype Granjon was designed by George W. Jones, who based his drawings on a face used by Claude Garamond (ca. 1480–1561) in his beautiful French books. Granjon more closely resembles Garamond's own type than do any of the various modern faces that bear his name.

Composed by North Market Street Graphics,
Lancaster, Pennsylvania

Printed and bound by Berryville Graphics,
Berryville, Virginia

Designed by Cassandra J. Pappas

How to Ace the National Geographic Bee

Official Study Guide

Fifth Edition

by
Stephen F. Cunha

NATIONAL
GEOGRAPHIC

Washington, D.C.

In memory of John Joseph Ferguson and Ann Judge, *who perished aboard American Airlines Flight 77, which crashed into the Pentagon on September 11, 2001. They were traveling to California with six Washington, D.C., teachers and students as part of an educational field trip sponsored by the National Geographic Society. Joe and Ann were tireless, visionary supporters of the Society's education outreach programs. Their enduring work directly benefits countless teachers and students throughout North America.* —SFC

Cover design by Sanjida Rashid

Back cover: National Geographic Bee host Mo Rocca and National Geographic Society CEO Gary Knell with Geo Bee contestants in the National Geographic courtyard.

The text type is set in New Caledonia; headlines are set in Clarendon.

All questions and place-names were accurate and current at the date of their actual use in the National Geographic Bee.

Trade paperback ISBN: 978-1-4263-3080-3
Reinforced library binding ISBN: 978-1-4263-3081-0

Printed in the United States of America
17/WOR/1

Contents

Foreword

I wish I were in fourth grade again. Then I could compete in the National Geographic Bee.

You see, when I was growing up in Bethesda, Maryland, my favorite thing to do after school each day was to pull the encyclopedia volumes (ask your parents what those are) off the shelf, spread them on the family room floor, lie on my stomach on the red carpet, and page through each book, memorizing facts about different countries.

I learned their currencies. (Greece's drachma sounded so dramatic.) I studied their chief exports. (How else would I have known that Turkey is the world's largest source of sour cherries?) I marveled at their shapes. (Chile was so skinny I wondered if people there had to stand sideways to keep from stepping into Argentina.)

But I was especially proud that *I knew the capital of every country in the world.* "Name a country and I'll tell you the capital!" I'd beg my family, friends, and weary restaurant wait-staff. If they asked about Bolivia (two capitals), I'd get a special thrill. If they asked about South Africa (three capitals), my head would practically explode with excitement.

It was quite an accomplishment, if I do say so myself, and one that never really ended. In the early 1990s, when the Soviet Union fell apart, I nearly had a nervous breakdown. All those "Stans"! (My favorite remains Kyrgyzstan's capital, Bishkek. It sounds delicious.)

My world capital prowess didn't just help me stand out as a child. After graduating from college, I took a job at New York City's Macy's department store selling fragrances on commission; the more I'd sell, the more I was paid. Many of the customers were diplomats from the United Nations. I would politely say, "May I ask where you're from?"

"I am from the African nation of Burundi," replied one such diplomat reservedly.

"Oh, are you from … Bujumbura?" I inquired.

"Why, yes I am!" he said. "How do you know so much about my country?"

And invariably I'd make the sale … over and over and over again. Yes, world capitals helped me pay my rent.

In 2016, I was honored to host the National Geographic Bee in Washington, D.C. (If you're reading this book, I'm pretty sure you know it's the capital of the United States.) Meeting 54 competitors, all of whom know every world capital, felt like home.

More importantly, I discovered how deep the study of geography goes. (Deeper even than Siberia's Lake Baikal, which is the deepest lake in … well, you know.) It's about so much more than memorization. The 10 extraordinarily impressive finalists were able to call upon their knowledge of the planet's cartography, climate, culture, and more—and answer not just the "where" and "what" questions but also the "why" questions.

And I happen to know *why* you're reading this study guide. It's because you're curious about the world. You care about the world. And for that, all of the rest of us thank you.

Now if you'll excuse me, I've got some studying to do. I'm hosting again this year and really don't want to get shown up by a fourth grader.

Mo Rocca
Host, National Geographic Bee

CHAPTER 1

The Why of Where: Defining Geography

Imagine captaining a 17th-century merchant ship with a crew of 200 and a cargo hold stuffed with exotic goods from the Far East. You are London-bound to exchange your booty for gold coins and more shipping contracts from anxious merchants. Gazing across the Indian Ocean at sunrise, you take stock of the possible hazards that threaten success: pirates, sudden storms, rocky coastlines, and even mutiny. But the biggest danger of all is veering off course into an endless sea because you cannot plot your location accurately on the map.

Before John Harrison developed a special clock called the marine chronometer in the mid-1700s, sailors could not pinpoint their longitude—their location east or west of the prime meridian. Captains routinely lost hundreds of men and tons of cargo to starvation and storms while searching for a place to land. In Dava Sobel's wonderful book Longitude, *the author describes a dozen disasters,*

including that of Admiral Sir Clowdisley Shovell. The admiral lost four of his five warships and 2,000 troops in 1707 after misjudging his longitude in the Scilly Isles, off the southwestern tip of England. Adrift in dense fog, the ships "pricked themselves on rocks and went down like stones." Yikes!

Fortunately, Harrison's ingenious clock enabled navigators to determine longitude by comparing the time of day on board ship with noon in Greenwich, England, which was (and still is) located on the prime meridian (0° longitude). Because latitude—the distance north or south of the Equator—was easy to calculate by observing the stars, sailors could now see where their latitude and longitude intersected on the map and determine their exact geographic location in an open ocean where there are no landmarks. (You'll learn more about latitude and longitude in Chapter 3.)

Early continental explorers also suffered when they lacked geographical information. Poor Hannibal crossed the Alps in the wrong time of year and nearly froze to death. Lewis and Clark almost perished in the mountains of Idaho and Montana because they didn't know how vast the Rocky Mountains were. And what were those Vikings thinking when they attempted to grow barley in Iceland a thousand years ago?

Knowing where places are located is an important first step to learning geography and enjoying the Bee. Fortunately for us, using maps and finding latitude and longitude are much easier today than during poor Sir Clowdisley Shovell's lifetime.

However, geography is much more than places on a map. In the words of Alexander Graham Bell, one of the founders of the

National Geographic Society, geography is "the world and all that is in it." Place-names such as Brazil, Stockholm, Mount Everest, and Yangtze River are to geography what the alphabet is to reading. They open the gate for boundless and lifelong learning. Knowing where places are on a map is important, but the real heart of geography is understanding why people settle in a particular place, who their neighbors are, how they make a living, why they dress and speak the way they do, and what they do for fun. Developing this sense of place will raise a flat map to life.

Geographers investigate our global climate, landforms, economies, political systems, human cultures, and migration patterns. They are concerned not just with where something is located, but also with why it is there and how it relates to other things. A good geographer knows how to combine this information from many different sources and how to identify patterns that can help us understand our complex world. Geography explains why your grandmother moved to Tucson (warm and dry climate), how oil from Kuwait reaches Italy (by way of the Suez Canal), where tropical rain forests grow (near the Equator), who faces toward Mecca as they pray (Muslims), and which continent is the most populated (Asia). In a nutshell, geography is the "Why of Where" science that blends and enriches history, literature, mathematics, and science.

Although place-names of the world are now thoroughly mapped and available in atlases, maps, books, and even online, knowing where you are and the geographic characteristics of that place is just as important today as in earlier times.

Understanding people and environments influences the location of everything from Walmarts to hospitals to software manufacturing plants. City planners need population projections and environmental data before they can approve plans to build housing developments, office buildings, and shopping centers. Engineers must study water resources and the lay of the land before starting any project. (Even a small hill or creek can greatly increase construction costs.) Imagine trying to advertise a new product without knowing the composition (Hispanic, African American, Asian, European), age structure (teenagers or grandparents), and economic characteristics (farmers, factory workers, or professionals) of the people you want to buy it. Highway construction cannot proceed until facts about climate, soil, vegetation, and the number of people who will drive the proposed route are considered. Each day, kids everywhere awake in sheets of woven Egyptian cotton, pull on clothes stitched in Bangladesh, wolf down bananas grown in Central America, and grab schoolbooks printed in Singapore to board buses assembled in Michigan from parts made in Japan and Germany.

For more than a decade, the growth of our global society—the rising dependence of nations upon one another for trade and security—has made geographical studies more important than ever. Acronyms and abbreviations—such as NAFTA, GATT, EU, and WTO—are heard on the evening news. Schools from Alaska to Zambia stress second-language and culture studies to better prepare their students not just for a global economy but also for a more crowded planet where migration, tourism, and the

Internet connect our global family more each day. The global war on terrorism further underscores the great importance of more fully understanding the people of the world, how they live, what they believe, and the environment and resources we share.

Whether you are the secretary of state for the United States or the secretary of your class, knowing geography will help you understand the world.

CHAPTER 2

Bee Basics: Understanding the Contest

Through the Bee, I have become much more aware of the world around me, the problems that are facing it, and what can be done to solve these issues.
—SHRIYA YARLAGADDA, 2015 NATIONAL RUNNER-UP

This chapter marches through the annual Bee calendar from registration to the national finals. It explains who is eligible to participate and the format at the school, state, and national levels. (It is important to note that although the Bee provides an instruction booklet to each registered school, the booklet contains recommended procedures only. Schools sometimes have to make adjustments to fit their needs.) Understanding how the Bee works and following the advice at the end of the chapter will help you relax, have fun, and perform better.

REGISTRATION

Registering is easy. Schools must register each year by the deadline (usually mid-January). Registration fees are $100 until mid-December and $120 until registration closes. Check with school officials to see if your school is entered for the upcoming Bee or look

for your school on our website under the registration link. If you are a middle school student who rotates among classes, the social studies teacher is the best person to ask, followed by the principal. Schools must register *each* year by the deadline. More information on Bee registration appears on page 123 and on our website: natgeobee.org.

ELIGIBILITY

All U.S. schools with any of the grades four through eight may register for the Bee. Students enrolled in a conventional public or private school may not compete as part of a homeschool Bee. Homeschooling associations may register to have a county or area-wide Bee for homeschoolers in their area. A student may compete in a magnet school Bee only if enrolled full-time at the magnet school. Parents and teachers must pay close attention to these details to prevent a disqualification.

Students who are not over the age of 15 by September 1 of that school year may participate. The Bee is an open contest that does not separate students into age or grade-level categories. There must be a minimum of six student participants in a school to hold a school-level competition. Students may participate in no more than five years of the Bee.

SCHOOL-LEVEL BEES

In mid-October, Bee packets are available for download to registered schools. The packet contains the suggested procedures and the question booklet. A certificate and a medal for the school champion are mailed to registered schools. School officials then

select the days for their Bee, so long as the competition falls within the dates established by the Society—normally anytime between early October and early February.

School Bees are the responsibility of the schools. Their decisions are final. These Bees are usually broken into a Preliminary Competition, which normally takes place in individual classrooms, and the Final Competition, which is often held in the school assembly room (cafeteria, auditorium, gym, etc.).

Preliminary Competition

These rounds usually require an oral response. A teacher or other moderator reads the questions aloud. You will be asked one question per round and will have 15 seconds to answer each question. To keep the contest moving, you are allowed to ask to have a question repeated or a word spelled only two times during the Preliminary Competition. Such a request to the moderator must be made immediately.

Once the question has been repeated or the word spelled, you will have the remainder of your 15 seconds to answer the question. You must start to give your answer before the 15-second time limit is up. If you do not answer within the allotted time, the moderator will say, "Time," give the correct answer, and move on to the next student. One point is awarded for each correct response; a pass is counted as an incorrect response. There is no penalty for mispronunciations (or misspellings, in the event of a written response) so long as the moderator can determine you know the correct answer. The student with the most correct answers wins the chance to advance to the Final Round.

Tiebreakers

If there are ties in determining the finalists, officials will use a series of Preliminary Competition Tiebreaker Questions. Everyone involved begins with a clean slate—no hits and no misses. Students get the same question and write their answers on the paper provided. Again, there is no penalty for misspellings so long as the moderator can determine that the correct answer has been given. Questioning continues until the tie or ties have been broken.

Final Competition

The Final Competition consists of a Final Round and a Championship Round. If you are lucky enough to advance to this level, you may find yourself on a stage in the school auditorium. As with any contest or game, the pressure builds as you progress up the ladder. Expect some bright lights and audience noise, ranging from restrained gasps to thunderous applause.

In addition to the round-robin oral questions in the Preliminary Competition, the Final Round includes questions that require written responses (students are simultaneously asked the same question and respond by writing their answers on the paper provided). Other questions may involve graphs, maps, or photographs. If so, you will be given a copy of the visual to study up close before answering the question. But the biggest difference between the Preliminary Competition and the Final Round is that students are eliminated after giving their second incorrect answer. Once the third-place winner has been determined, the remaining two students advance to the Championship Round.

Championship Round

In the Championship Round, the two contestants start with a clean slate. Both are asked the same questions simultaneously and given 15 seconds to write their answers. The moderator then asks the students for their answers. The student with the most correct answers wins the school Bee. Tiebreaker questions may be necessary to determine the winner. The champion receives a medal and a certificate from the National Geographic Society, and every student who entered the school Bee receives a Certificate of Participation.

QUALIFYING TEST

To advance to the state Bee as a representative of his or her school, the school winner must take the online Qualifying Test. To access this test, the teacher administering the test must log into his or her registration account at natgeobee.org for the student to take the test online. This test should be given in a quiet location in the school building. It must be monitored by a teacher who is not a parent or guardian of the school Bee winner. The test has about 70 multiple-choice questions, covering the entire range of geographic inquiry, including a set that pertains to a map, table, or graph. There is a time limit of one hour. The test must be completed by the deadline, which is usually no later than the first week of February.

The National Geographic Society scores one Qualifying Test from each participating school. The top 100 students (more if there are ties) from each of the 50 states, the District of Columbia, the Department of Defense Dependents Schools, and the Atlantic and Pacific territories compete in their respective state

Bees. The National Geographic Society appoints state Bee coordinators to coordinate this portion of the contest. In early March, Society officials notify the teachers of the students who qualify for the state competition.

The state Bees can be held late March or early April. An adult must accompany each student to the state Bee. In most cases this is a teacher, parent, or legal guardian. Other adults may substitute with school approval. Expect the Bee to begin with an opening assembly jam-packed with all 100 state finalists, officials, teachers, and a zillion family members. The room is abuzz with excitement and nervous anticipation.

The contestants break into five groups of 20 students. The seating and room assignments are determined by random drawing before the Bee. Just as in the school-level competition, there are preliminary, final, and championship rounds (and tiebreakers if necessary). The Final and Championship Rounds are held in front of a large audience and are very exciting. Some rounds will include questions that require written responses on a sheet of paper. You should also expect questions that require interpreting information from a visual. This may be a photograph, illustration, map, satellite photo (e.g., from Google Earth), data table, or graph that is displayed on a large screen. You will be given a copy of the visual to study up close before answering the question. Once the Bee is under way, you will impress yourself with how many questions you can answer correctly! The same procedure that is recommended to schools for determining the

school-level winners is used to determine the state champions. The winner of each state Bee wins a trip to Washington, D.C., to compete in the national-level Bee.

THE NATIONAL-LEVEL BEE

State Bee winners meet at the headquarters of the National Geographic Society, in Washington, D.C., in May to compete for the title of national champion. The format for the national-level preliminary competition is similar to that of previous levels with rounds of questions, but there is an additional component called a GeoChallenge that is scored by a panel of judges. In general, the questions are harder, and there are more rounds involving visuals, such as photographs, maps, and graphs. The top ten winners of the Preliminary Competition compete in the Final Round. The format of the Final Round is different from earlier levels of the Bee. Instead of being eliminated after two incorrect answers, students earn points for correct answers and are eliminated at various checkpoints based on the lowest scores. The Final Round also includes GeoChallenge questions that are scored by a panel of judges. The Championship Round is similar to previous levels, with the top two students starting with a clean slate. Journalist and humorist Mo Rocca is the moderator for the Final and Championship Rounds. It's always fun to follow along and see how many questions you can answer; check the Bee website for broadcast information. The top three finishers take home college scholarships, and the champion also earns a prize trip. The total prize and scholarship monies awarded at the school, state, and national levels make the Bee one of the richest academic competitions on Earth.

The Canadian equivalent of the National Geographic Bee also features a series of competitions at the school, provincial or territorial, and national levels that are designed to test students' knowledge and skills in geography.

Currently there are two grade levels to the Challenge: Level 1 for grades four to six and Level 2 for grades seven to ten. Teachers register online for the Challenge; any number of students or classes within a school may compete. All registered schools receive an online instruction booklet, question and answer booklet, and prizes. The information is available in English and French.

The competition for Level 1 students ends at the school level. When the top student has been determined at the school level in Level 2 (this must be determined by the end of February), he or she will take the provincial/territorial online test to see if they will be invited to the national final. The top student in each province and territory will be recognized with a prize. The highest scoring students from this competition compete in the National Final in May. The top three scorers are declared the Canadian National Champions and receive scholarships.

BEE GREAT: ADVICE TO CONTESTANTS

The following list is the result of more than a decade of "Bee-ing" with students, teachers, and parents. Although my experience has been mostly at the state level, these tips will help at any level in almost any type of competition. They are included here to help make the Bee a truly memorable and fun event.

Relax! Cramming hurts your brain

The evening before and the morning of the Bee are prime times to relax, play with your dog, and go for a bike ride with a sibling or friend. Don't stay up the night before conversing with owls while attempting to cram in a few last-minute facts. This contest is fun, so rest up and dream of faraway lands.

Before then, set aside part of each day to prepare for the Bee. Remember that geography is an integrative subject that takes time to learn and appreciate. Avoid flipping flash cards on the way to the Bee. (Several times I have seen parents quizzing students just moments before the Bee!) This adds tension that can detract from the quality of your performance and your enjoyment of the competition.

Healthy body, healthy mind

Whether you live in Paris, Pyongyang, or Philadelphia, the best advice is to stay fit, eat a balanced diet, and avoid spending so much time hunting for facts online or looking things up in books that your physical fitness declines. A healthy body houses a sharper and more capable mind.

Many students at every level of the Bee find that eating before the contest is a difficult idea to stomach. Yet your brain is a big muscle, and to keep it working at full throttle requires high-octane fuel. That is to say, CHOW DOWN BEFORE THE BEE! Don't arrive hungry. An empty stomach will make any jitters you have feel much worse. This problem does not affect every student, but if you know that big events—even the fun ones—make it difficult to eat, then here is some food for thought.

First, eat a well-balanced dinner the night before the Bee. This way, unless your stomach is the size of a thimble, you'll have calories in your tank at least through noon the following day. Second, eat at least a small breakfast that includes some juice and something solid, such as fruit, carbohydrates (toast, muffins, cereal), or eggs. Try to avoid greasy and high-fat foods, as they are harder to digest and can make your tummy do backflips.

Dress for success

Although this is a special event, you don't need to rent a tux or a frilly evening gown. Even ties and dresses are rare. Most kids pull on something comfortable. Pants or a skirt with a clean shirt or blouse are a good choice. Of course, you'll want to look neat—advancing to the finals at any level could land you onstage.

Take a deep breath

It's easy to panic when you hear a question that freaks you out! "Oh no, I can't remember the largest city on Mars!" Forgetting to breathe or taking several gasps is a natural reaction. If this occurs, relax, take a deep breath, collect your thoughts, and then look for clues in the question that will help you figure out the correct answer. Remember, you have 15 seconds (except in the national finals) to answer. Believe it or not, that's a long time! Failing to take in oxygen will make it more difficult to think and will increase that feeling of alarm!

Listen to every question in each round

When competing in the oral rounds, listen to every question and every answer. You may pick up clues that will help you come up with the right answer when it's your turn.

Stand by your first answer

Unless you are certain of an error, stick with the first answer that comes to mind. Believe it or not, studies show that students who change their answers or get stuck trying to choose between two answers usually select a less accurate choice the second time.

Ignore your friends

While you're competing, don't look at people you know, especially just before and during your turn. Ask your friends, teacher, parents, and other family members to make themselves invisible by sitting as far away as possible. Also, tell them to photograph you *after* the Bee, not while you are trying to remember which country borders Zimbabwe on the east. (Mozambique, of course!)

Speak loudly and write with a big stick

Make your answers known in very decisive ways. Speak in a loud, clear voice. When a written answer is required, write clearly in LARGE, BOLD LETTERS. The teacher/moderator must be able to understand your answer and read your handwriting.

Remember: It is impossible to fail in the Bee. Just by taking part you are already a success!

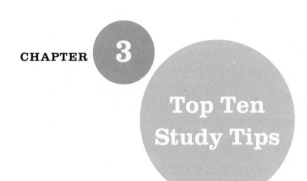

CHAPTER 3

Top Ten
Study Tips

*Since all aspects of
geography are inter-
connected, finding
something you love to
study will make it easier
and more interesting
to learn new things.*
—NEELAM SANDHU,
NATIONAL GEOGRAPHIC
WORLD GEOGRAPHY
CHAMPION (TEAM), 2013

*The ten trusty tips outlined in this chapter will help you
"Bee" ready. This powerful advice has been assembled
over many years from students just like you. A small
army of teachers added their two cents' worth, too.*

*Don't expect to learn everything about geography in
just one school year. Remember that you are eligible to
enter the Bee from the fourth through the eighth grade.
No one expects a fourth grader to know as much as an
eighth grader, but it's not impossible. Susannah Batko-
Yovino was only a sixth grader when she became the
national champion in 1990! By participating each year,
you will increase your knowledge of geography and self-
confidence. These ten study tips will teach you the basics
and how to build on them to recognize geographic
patterns. You'll be thinking like a geographer in no time!*

Getting started in geography is easy if you have the right tools. Spending a part of each day with these tools will expand your world in a hurry. A few pointers on using these are presented here. Advice about specific products and where to find them appears in Chapter 6.

A large **WORLD MAP** should be in every home. Concentrate first on learning the continents, oceans, and largest islands. Then focus on countries, capital cities, and major physical features (such as mountain ranges, lakes, and rivers), gradually adding other places and features to your vocabulary. Hang your world map next to your bed or on the closet door. Put smaller maps of each continent around your house. Position one in the bathroom so you can learn the countries of Africa while brushing your teeth. Laminated map place mats let you explore Italy while slurping spaghetti. You can also tape maps behind the front seat of your family car and visit South America on the way to school.

A good **ATLAS** is the next essential tool. These come in all sizes, with many excellent and reasonably priced volumes to match your skill level. Be sure to use one that is less than five years old so that it includes important name updates.

Look for three other features when choosing an atlas. First, it should have both physical maps (emphasizing natural features) and political maps (emphasizing country boundaries and cities). Second, make sure it includes an index (or gazetteer) that alphabetically lists place-names that appear on the maps. This will help you find unfamiliar locations. Finally, look for text that includes information about

each continent, country, and world region (such as Southeast Asia or Middle America), plus a section on geographic comparisons (longest rivers, largest cities, etc.).

BLANK OUTLINE MAPS are the third tool. These black-and-white line maps outline the continents and countries. Important physical features such as major rivers and mountain ranges may also appear. See Chapter 6 for tips on finding these maps online. Practice labeling countries, cities, rivers, mountains, and other geographic information as you learn it. Always start with the most obvious features and then add more detailed information as you progress. Blank maps are a great way to quiz yourself.

A **GEOGRAPHY REFERENCE BOOK** is another important tool. Although maps and atlases help you learn where Mongolia, Mauna Loa, and other places are located, a good geography reference book explains *why* they are located there, *who* lives there, *what* they do, and *how* the landscape came to be. These books usually arrange information in alphabetical order either by single topic (Agriculture, Alluvial Fan, Avalanche), or by category (Earth Science, Population, Wildlife). The most helpful ones enrich the text with numerous maps, photographs, charts and graphs, and a glossary of terms. A good reference book takes you to the next level of geographic learning by bringing maps to life. This marks the point where memorization evolves into real geographic exploration and discovery!

SATELLITE IMAGE SOURCES such as NASA's Visible Earth and the U.S. Geological Survey's EarthExplorer will round out your tool kit. Learning to maneuver about and interpret satellite images will help you visualize and build the mental maps described in Tip #4.

A good map is worth a thousand pictures. Expert map readers can absorb oceans of geographic information in a short time. But to understand all that a map can tell you, you must first learn the language of maps.

LATITUDE and **LONGITUDE** are the imaginary lines that divide Earth's surface into a grid. Under this system, both latitude and longitude are measured in terms of the 360 degrees of a circle. The latitude and longitude of a place are its **COORDINATES**. Coordinates mark the **ABSOLUTE LOCATION** of a place. Understanding coordinates, you can use a map to locate any point on Earth.

Latitude is the distance north or south of the **EQUATOR**, the line of 0° latitude that divides Earth into two equal halves called hemispheres. The top half is the **NORTHERN HEMISPHERE**, and the bottom half is the **SOUTHERN HEMISPHERE**. Lines of latitude are also called **PARALLELS** because they circle Earth without ever touching each other. From the Equator we measure latitude north and south to the poles. The **NORTH POLE** is located at 90° north latitude, and the **SOUTH POLE** is located at 90° south latitude.

There are other important parallels that you should learn. The parallel of latitude 23° 30' north of the Equator is called the **TROPIC OF CANCER**, and the parallel 23° 30' south of the Equator is the **TROPIC OF CAPRICORN**. The region between

these two parallels is called the **TROPICS.** The **SUBTROPICS** are the zones located between 23° 30' and about 40° north and south of the Equator.

The parallel of latitude 66° 30' north of the Equator is called the **ARCTIC CIRCLE,** and the parallel 66° 30' south of the Equator is the **ANTARCTIC CIRCLE.** The region between 66° 30' N and 90° N is called the Arctic; the region between 66° 30' S and 90° S is called the Antarctic. Both regions can simply be called polar.

Longitude is the distance east or west of the **PRIME MERIDIAN,** the point of 0° longitude. This is also the starting place for measuring distance both east and west around the globe. Lines of longitude are called **MERIDIANS.** They also circle Earth, but they converge at the poles.

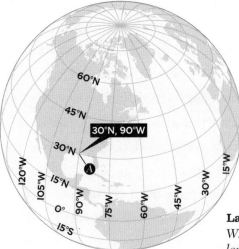

Latitude and Longitude
When used together, latitude and longitude form a grid that provides a system for determining the exact, or absolute, location of every place on Earth. For example, the absolute location of point A is 30° N, 90° W.

We also use the coordinate system to determine direction. When you face the North Pole (90° N), the sun rises to your right (east) and sets to your left (west). The south is behind you. These four points—north, south, east, and west—are **CARDINAL DIRECTIONS.** Any point *between* two cardinal directions is an **INTERMEDIATE DIRECTION.** For example, looking north and partly to the east is said to be looking northeast. But if you turn around and glance south and partly to the west, you are looking southwest.

A **GLOBE** is the only accurate representation of our spherical Earth. Think of a globe as a scale model of Earth with a paper or plastic map mounted on its spherical surface. Globes are great to study because, unlike most flat maps, they show continents and oceans in their true proportions. Size, shape, distance, and direction are all accurately represented. Projecting this round shape onto a flat sheet of paper to make a map distorts these elements. To solve the problem of distortion, mapmakers use a variety of **MAP PROJECTIONS** to portray our curved Earth on a flat sheet of paper. Each projection distorts Earth according to a mathematical calculation. Three commonly used projections are the Mercator, the Winkel Tripel, and the Goode's Interrupted Homolosine. The **MERCATOR** projection is helpful to navigators because it allows them to maintain a constant compass direction as they travel between two points, but it greatly exaggerates areas at higher latitudes. The **WINKEL TRIPEL** is a general-purpose projection popularly used for political, physical, and thematic maps because it minimizes distortion of both size and shape. The

GOODE'S INTERRUPTED HOMOLOSINE minimizes distortion of scale and shape by interrupting the globe. This type of equal-area projection is useful for mapping comparisons of various kinds of data, such as rain forests and population density.

MERCATOR

WINKEL TRIPEL

GOODE'S INTERRUPTED HOMOLOSINE

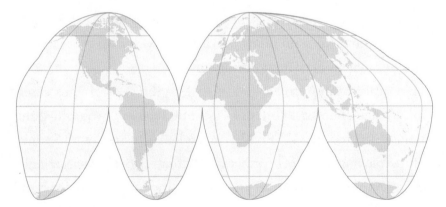

There are two main types of maps. **PHYSICAL MAPS** emphasize natural features such as mountains, rivers, lakes, deserts, and plains. Mapmakers often use shades of color to indicate different elevations. **POLITICAL MAPS** use lines to show boundaries between countries, points to show cities, and various other symbols to show roads, airports, canals, and other human-related features. Examples of these two kinds of maps are on the opposite page.

We use latitude and longitude to determine the absolute location of physical and political features and **RELATIVE LOCATION** to explain the underlying reasons for that precise location and to show the interconnection of geographic phenomena.

For example, the geographic grid pinpoints Chicago's absolute location at 41° N, 87° W. However, the Windy City's location on the shore of Lake Michigan is *relative* to the historic water commerce routes favored by early Native Americans and settlers. Without Lake Michigan, Chicago might not exist.

Similarly, Khartoum, the capital city of Sudan, is located at 15° N, 32° E, *relative* to the confluence of the Blue and the White Niles. Without the confluence of rivers, this city would not have become such an important economic center.

Physical features are located relative to the geologic processes that created them. For example, Mount Rainier, in Washington State, is located at 47° N, 122° W, relative to the two tectonic plates (moving slabs of Earth's crust) that created the Cascade Range. As a result, Mount Rainier shares the same geologic origin as the other volcanoes located north and south of it. Without the tectonic plate boundary, this part of the Pacific Northwest might

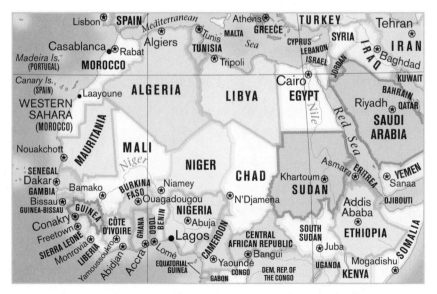

IMAGINARY LANDSCAPE

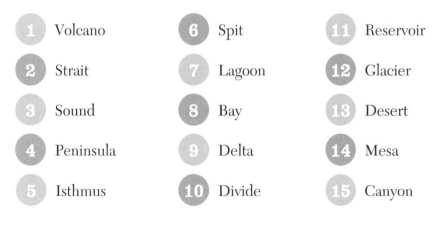

1	Volcano	6	Spit	11	Reservoir
2	Strait	7	Lagoon	12	Glacier
3	Sound	8	Bay	13	Desert
4	Peninsula	9	Delta	14	Mesa
5	Isthmus	10	Divide	15	Canyon

have a much different physical environment and human settlement pattern than we see today.

Use the world maps, atlases, and geographic reference books in your tool kit to learn more about these concepts and the language of maps. They are the building blocks for more learning and the source of many Bee questions.

The diagram of an imaginary landscape on the opposite page was used in a round of questions in a state-level Bee to quiz students on their ability to identify physical features. Students were asked to give the number that best represented a specific physical feature. Of course, they didn't have the benefit of being able to see the answers! They are provided for you so that you can use this as a study tool for learning some very basic physical terms. You will find definitions for each of these terms in your geographic reference book. Learn them and try to find examples of each on physical maps. You can be sure that geographic terms are a frequent topic for Bee questions.

Once you know how to read maps, the next step is to learn the most important place-names that go on them. This memorization develops your global sense of place. Learning place-names is like learning your ABCs. Without knowing the alphabet, you can't spell words. Without knowing place-names, you can't identify places and features on a map or understand the interrelationships between physical and human activities. Place-names are a necessary and important building block to greater geographic knowledge.

The number of place-names can be overwhelming. Organizing them into physical and political groups can be helpful. Start with the first categories in each group and work your way down. Don't just memorize a list of names and figures. Find each feature or place on the map and take time to learn about it and what it's near.

PHYSICAL FEATURES

THE CONTINENTS

| | AREA | | % of |
	(sq mi)	(sq km)	Earth's land
Asia	17,208,000	44,570,000	30.0
Africa	11,608,000	30,065,000	20.2
North America	9,449,000	24,474,000	16.5
South America	6,880,000	17,819,000	12.0
Antarctica	5,100,000	13,209,000	8.9
Europe	3,841,000	9,947,000	6.7
Australia	2,970,000	7,692,000	5.2

THE OCEANS

| | AREA | | % of Earth's |
	(sq mi)	(sq km)	water area
Pacific	65,436,200	169,479,000	46.8
Atlantic	35,338,500	91,526,400	25.3
Indian	29,839,800	74,694,800	20.6
Arctic	5,390,000	13,960,100	3.9

Note: The tables at the bottom of the previous page list the names of the continents and oceans in order by size. Although some geographers consider Europe and Asia as one continent called Eurasia, National Geographic counts them as two landmasses to make a total of seven continents. Likewise, some maps show a Southern Ocean around Antarctica. Others show this body of water as the continuation of the Atlantic, Pacific, and Indian Oceans.

HIGHEST POINT ON EACH CONTINENT

	feet	meters
Everest, Asia	29,035	8,850
Aconcagua, S. America	22,831	6,959
Denali (McKinley), N. America	20,310	6,190
Kilimanjaro, Africa	19,340	5,895
El'brus, Europe	18,510	5,642
Vinson Massif, Antarctica	16,066	4,897
Kosciuszko, Australia	7,310	2,228

LOWEST POINT ON EACH CONTINENT

	feet	meters
Bentley Subglacial Trench, Antarctica	-8,383	-2,555
Dead Sea, Asia	-1,385	-422
Lake Assal, Africa	-512	-156
Laguna del Carbón, S. America	-344	-105
Death Valley, N. America	-282	-86
Caspian Sea, Europe	-92	-28
Lake Eyre, Australia	-52	-16

TEN LARGEST SEAS

	AREA	
	(sq mi)	(sq km)
Coral	1,615,260	4,183,510
South China	1,388,570	3,596,390
Caribbean	1,094,330	2,834,290
Bering	972,810	2,519,580
Mediterranean	953,320	2,469,100
Sea of Okhotsk	627,490	1,625,190
Gulf of Mexico	591,430	1,531,810
Norwegian	550,300	1,425,280
Greenland	447,050	1,157,850
Sea of Japan (East Sea)	389,290	1,008,260

TEN LARGEST LAKES

	AREA	
	(sq mi)	(sq km)
Caspian Sea, Europe-Asia	143,200	371,000
Superior, N. America	31,700	82,100
Victoria, Africa	26,800	69,500
Huron, N. America	23,000	59,600
Michigan, N. America	22,300	57,800
Tanganyika, Africa	12,600	32,600
Baikal, Asia	12,200	31,500
Great Bear, N. America	12,100	31,300
Malawi, Africa	11,200	28,900
Great Slave, N. America	11,000	28,600

TEN LARGEST ISLANDS

	AREA (sq mi)	AREA (sq km)		AREA (sq mi)	AREA (sq km)
Greenland	836,000	2,166,000	Sumatra	165,000	427,300
New Guinea	306,000	792,500	Honshu	87,800	227,400
Borneo	280,100	725,500	Great Britain	84,200	218,100
Madagascar	226,600	587,000	Victoria	83,900	217,300
Baffin	196,000	507,500	Ellesmere	75,800	196,200

LONGEST RIVERS*

	miles	kilometers
Nile, Africa	4,160	6,695
Amazon, S. America	4,150	6,679
Chang Jiang (Yangtze), Asia	3,880	6,244
Mississippi-Missouri, N. America	3,710	5,970
Yenisey-Angara, Asia	3,610	5,810
Yellow (Huang), Asia	3,590	5,778

Antarctica has no flowing rivers.

* These lists name the longest river and the major mountain range on each continent. Rivers are listed longest to shortest. Mountain ranges are listed in alphabetical order.

MAJOR MOUNTAIN RANGES*

Alps, Europe

Andes, South America

Atlas Mountains, Africa

Great Dividing Range, Australia

Himalaya, Asia

Rocky Mountains, North America

Transantarctic Mountains, Antarctica

Ural Mountains form much of the boundary between Europe and Asia.

EARTH'S EXTREMES

Hottest Place: Dallol, Danakil Depression, Ethiopia; annual average temperature: 93°F (34°C)

Coldest Place: Ridge A, Antarctica; annual average temperature: -94°F (-70°C)

Wettest Place: Mawsynram, Assam, India; annual average rainfall: 467 in (1,187 cm)

Driest Place: Atacama Desert, Chile; rainfall barely measurable

Highest Waterfall: Angel Falls, Venezuela; 3,212 ft (979 m)

Largest Hot Desert: Sahara, Africa; 3,475,000 sq mi (9,000,000 sq km)

Largest Canyon: Grand Canyon, Colorado River, Arizona, U.S.A.; 277 mi (446 km) long along the river; 600 ft (180 m) to 18 mi (29 km) wide; about 1.1 mi (1.8 km) deep

Longest Reef: Great Barrier Reef, Australia; 1,429 mi (2,300 km)

Greatest Tidal Range: Bay of Fundy, Nova Scotia, Canada; 52 ft (16 m)

Most atlases list countries with statistical information, such as area and population, so that you can make your own chart of the largest and smallest by area and by population. Although area figures seldom change (unless there is a boundary change), population figures do. Use the country index starting on page 130 to look up this information, and go to the websites listed in Chapter 6 to keep up-to-date.

The countries of North America: North America is made up of 23 independent countries. It includes Canada, the United States, Mexico, the countries of Central America, and the islands of the West Indies. Greenland is geologically a large part of North America, but it is not a country. It is a dependency of Denmark.

The countries of South America: South America is made up of 12 independent countries and one French territory, French Guiana.

The countries of Europe: Russia is usually counted as one of Europe's 49 independent countries. Although most of its land is in Asia, most of its people and its capital city (Moscow) are west of the Ural Mountains in Europe.

The countries of Africa: Africa has 54 independent countries. Most people live along the Nile and south of the Sahara.

The countries of Asia: China is the largest country located entirely in Asia and also the most populous of Asia's 48 countries.

Australia, New Zealand, and Oceania: Australia is a continent and a country. Geographers often include it and New Zealand with the islands of the south and central Pacific and call this region Oceania. Australia is the largest and most populous of the 14 independent countries in this region.

Antarctica: This is the only continent that has no independent countries and no permanent population.

Studying geographic shapes and place-names will eventually fix mental maps in your brain. You'll be able to picture not only where a place is but also what's near it, who lives there, and lots more. The ability to produce mental images of the world characterizes all Bee champions. This requires atlas and reference book use and a good understanding of map scale.

MAP SCALE makes it possible to figure out what distance on Earth's surface is represented by a given length on a map. Large-scale maps show a limited geographic area such as a neighborhood or city in great detail. The scale on such a map may be expressed as a ratio such as 1:1,500, meaning that every inch on the map represents 1,500 inches on the ground. (That's 125 feet or less than half a football field.) This allows the cartographer to include street names, parks, and creeks. A large-scale map of the United States wouldn't fit in your backpack. In fact, you'd need a dump truck!

Small-scale maps have much less detail but cover a greater geographical area, such as a state, mountain range, or continent. The scale here may read 1:5,000,000 (one inch represents five million inches on the ground—a very long crawl). This level of detail is the only way to cover a large area such as a continent or the world so that you can study it as a whole.

The next step is adding more physical and cultural depth to these mental maps. The following categories will get you started.

Vegetation Zones, or Biomes: There are four main categories of vegetation zones: forest, grassland, desert, and tundra. Start with these and then expand your knowledge by learning about the different types of vegetation within these categories. Vegetation is closely linked to climate.

Climate Zones: Climate is the long-term average weather conditions of a place. Most climate maps show at least five different zones: tropical, dry, temperate, continental, and polar. As you build your knowledge, you will become familiar with subcategories, such as tropical wet and dry, arid and semiarid, marine west coast, and Mediterranean.

Population Density: Population density is the average number of people living in each square mile or kilometer of a place. The population density of a country is calculated by dividing its population by its area. Asia is the most densely populated continent; Australia is the least densely populated continent (excluding Antarctica). Check out your maps and see if you can figure out why!

Religion: All of the world's major religions—Christianity, Hinduism, Judaism, Buddhism, and Islam—as well as Shinto, Taoism, and Confucianism originated in Asia. They spread around the world as people migrated to new areas.

Languages: There are thousands of languages in the world, but there are only 12 major language families. Languages in the Indo-European family, which includes English, Russian, and German,

are spoken over the widest geographic area. Mandarin Chinese is spoken by the most people. Can you figure out why?

ECONOMIC FEATURES

World Economy: Familiarize yourself with terms such as primary, secondary, tertiary, and quaternary, as well as developed and developing, industrialized and nonindustrialized.

Commerce: Learn the major crops, minerals, and products that countries on each continent produce and export. Then take note of major trade alliances, such as NAFTA (North American Free Trade Agreement), the EU (European Union), WTO (World Trade Organization), and OPEC (Organization of the Petroleum Exporting Countries).

Transportation: Study maps, charts, and graphs to learn about major trade routes by land, sea, and air.

Filling in your mental maps will take some time, so be patient. Find a study method that works for you and then hop to it!

Conquering place-names prepares you to tackle the biggest and most rewarding challenge of preparing for the Bee: learning about the world's primary physical and cultural patterns. Understanding how the world functions as an interconnected and dynamic system is what geography is all about. Studying these patterns prepares you to combine and layer more complex geographic information onto your basic mental maps. This takes time, but the rewards are great. The following suggestions are designed to help you reach this level.

COMBINE INFORMATION

Good geographers combine information from different sources to arrive at logical conclusions. They understand the basic patterns of climate, geology, vegetation, human settlement, migration, and commerce. Combining these patterns with a knowledge of regions and place-names will empower you to answer very specific questions that otherwise might have been a choice between two guesses. At the very least it will enable you to make an educated guess when you don't know the answer. The question analyses that follow explain how this works.

1. Which city recently suffered a severe earthquake, Tokyo or Omaha?

You may not recall any recent earthquakes, but you know that Tokyo is in Japan, an island country off the east coast of Asia,

*along the tectonic Ring of Fire. Omaha is a city in Nebraska, a state located in the middle of the North American plate. Since more earthquakes occur around the rim of the Pacific Ocean than anywhere else, you correctly answer **Tokyo.***

2. Which is Germany's most important export crop, wheat or palm oil?

*Using your mental maps, you know that Germany is a midlatitude country in western Europe. You also know that palm trees grow in warm tropical climates and that wheat grows in more temperate regions, like the American Midwest. Given Germany's location, you reason that it is more likely to have a temperate rather than tropical climate, and you correctly answer **wheat.***

LEARN PATTERNS ON THE LAND

Interpreting a landscape is very different from memorizing names on a map. Geographers use **THEMATIC MAPS** to show patterns on the land. They start with a physical or a political base map and add layers of information to show whatever geographic theme they wish to emphasize—everything from world population and energy consumption (see map opposite, top) to shark attacks and local weather predictions.

CARTOGRAMS are special kinds of thematic maps. On them, the size of a country is based on a statistic other than land area. In the cartogram shown opposite, population determines the size of each country. This is why Nigeria, Africa's most populous country, is shown much larger than Algeria, Africa's largest country in area.

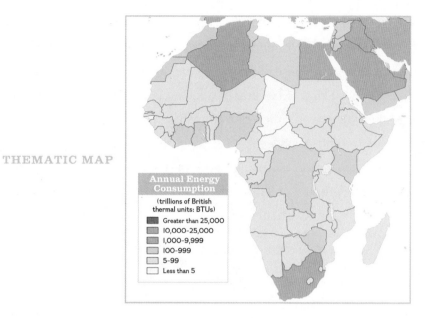

THEMATIC MAP

Annual Energy Consumption
(trillions of British thermal units: BTUs)

- Greater than 25,000
- 10,000–25,000
- 1,000–9,999
- 100–999
- 5–99
- Less than 5

CARTOGRAM

Algeria

Nigeria

World Population, 2014
1 block = 1 million people

Population Growth Rate
(as a percentage of total population)

- More than 2.9%
- 2.0 to 2.9%
- 1.0 to 1.9%
- 0 to 0.9%
- Population decline

Graphs are another important tool that geographers use to convey information, and you can expect to encounter various kinds in the Bee. A special kind of bar graph called a population pyramid (below, top) shows the distribution of a country's population by sex and age. A more traditional style of bar graph shows the most commonly spoken languages. A climate graph (opposite page) is a combination bar and line graph that shows monthly averages of precipitation and temperature for a particular place.

POPULATION
PYRAMID

MOST
COMMONLY
SPOKEN
LANGUAGES

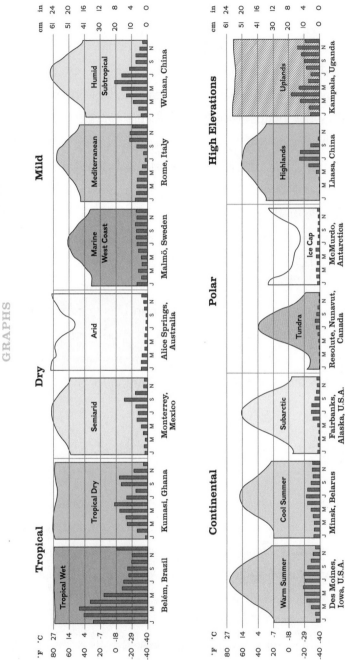

CLIMATE GRAPHS

Geography is all around you! The first place to look is in school. History uniformly incorporates geography in discussing wars (the Russian winter froze the German Army in World War II), slavery (wind belts made the triangular trade possible), and ecological disasters (poor farming techniques and drought triggered the Dust Bowl during the 1930s). You will also find geography concepts in literature (Mark Twain, Robert Service, Laura Ingalls Wilder), science classes (especially Earth science and biology), mathematics (latitude and longitude, population studies, sun angles, etc.), and fine arts (dance, music, and paintings are all reflections of culture). You can even find geography in your school cafeteria (tacos, spaghetti, and rice). With good mental maps and the ability to combine information from different sources, you can spend your entire school day in excellent preparation for the Bee!

TIP # **Use Your Geographic Eyes**

When you can think like a geographer and understand the major patterns that influence our physical environment, culture, and economy, it's time for some field observation. The following suggestions will get your nose out of the books and into the real world.

BECOME AN OBSERVANT MALL RAT
Stores are filled with goods from every corner of the world. The

origin of these products and their movement around the globe tells us much about where raw materials such as wood, minerals, and cotton come from; who makes them into finished products such as furniture, baseball bats, and shirts; and who buys them. They also furnish clues about labor use, population growth rates, and the huge difference in wealth between rich and poor countries.

Combining information from product labels and packaging with your mental maps represents advanced geographic thinking. You can practice this in stores, at school, and at home by reading the labels and packaging on products to find out where the raw materials used to make them came from and who made them.

For example, many computers are manufactured in China from European and Japanese components. They carry a U.S.A. label and are packaged in boxes made in Mexico. Most toys are manufactured in China. Much of our clothing is stitched in Mexico, Central America, or Asia. Many books are printed in Singapore. After much practice, you will find it easier to predict which country names will appear on boxes and labels. This is great evidence that your mental maps are becoming more detailed!

Check out stores that sell furniture (look for exotic woods), electronics (identify manufactured goods with components from multiple regions), and indigenous art (something that comes from everywhere). A century ago, Americans prized goods made overseas for their exotic qualities. Today, it would be extraordinarily difficult to outfit a home with products made only in North America. Global connections are the heart of the world's economy.

STOMACH MORE GEOGRAPHY

Grocery stores offer products from everywhere. Look for New Zealand kiwis, Colombian coffee, Central Asian spices, Swiss chocolate, and Mexican avocados among the zillion other products from around the world that arrive in your local food store.

Be aware that geographic place-names incorporated into product labels can sometimes lead you astray. For instance, check out fine china from Ireland, India ink bottled in South America, chile peppers grown in Mexico, English muffins baked from Nebraska wheat, and Canadian bacon from hogs raised in Iowa!

ATTEND COMMUNITY AND LOCAL EVENTS

Local communities are a great resource for learning more about your world. Keep an eye out for free concerts and lectures. Visit your museums and library display cases. If you have a college or university nearby, watch for public lectures and exhibits.

TIP # **8** Stay Current With Current Events

Current events questions query knowledge about natural disasters (floods, wildfires, tsunamis, earthquakes, volcanic eruptions, etc.), cultural and political upheaval (Libya, South Sudan, Syria, Turkey, Ukraine), international agreements (the Paris Agreement, Kyoto Protocol, Law of the Sea Treaty, Intellectual Piracy), and discoveries (archaeological finds, new plant species, energy, etc.). Almost any topic in the news, especially if it involves more than one of the categories just

mentioned, is fair game for the Bee. Stories that have been the subject of recent Bee questions include the spread of AIDS, the Beijing Olympics, Iran's nuclear ambitions, and the Arab Spring.

For our purposes, we can divide current events into ongoing topics—such as climate change, immigration, and oil exploration—and breaking news stories, such as Nobel Prize announcements, international border closures, and national elections.

Your local and regional media (newspapers, TV, radio) are great ways to keep tabs on our rapidly changing world. Online news sites are also good sources, and they report events from many different perspectives. Bookmark online domestic and international newspapers so you can easily access and quickly scan them. Many of them appear in several languages, including English. They also offer great maps, photos, archived back issues, and links to related sites.

TIP #9 Read, Read, Read

Bee champions share a passion for reading. They read books, magazines, newspapers, cereal boxes, websites—anything they can lay their eyes on. They read at school, at Grandma's, and on buses, trains, and airplanes. They read on weekends and throughout the summer. Reading helps to build your mental maps of people and places around the world. At the same time, reading becomes more geographic once you have good mental maps that enliven and enrich almost any story or news item. You can add to

your mental maps as you read by keeping a map handy. Use it to find new places and features and to understand relationships between the land and the people.

Play Games

Chapter 6 evaluates several games that use a quiz format like the Bee's to test your knowledge of geography. The Bee website offers geography questions to give you an idea of what the questions in the contest are like.

Playing these games offers several advantages. First, they simulate the Bee by asking questions from diverse topics that require an answer in a fixed amount of time. Second, they can help you identify your weak areas so that you can concentrate on improving those skills. A final advantage is that many of these games require multiple players, which doubles the opportunity to learn, promotes discussion, and lets you benefit from the knowledge of others.

There are other kinds of fun and productive study aids. Some, such as flash cards, are helpful for testing basic facts. Others are great for gathering interesting geo-tidbits. These should be treated as supplements to your learning.

CHAPTER **4**

Conquering the Questions

Building a mental map of a region I was being asked a question about helped me focus in on the region and develop a visual answer.
—AKHIL REKULAPELLI, 2014 NATIONAL CHAMPION

This chapter presents questions that have been used at the school, state, and national levels of the Bee. Most are from the preliminary competitions, as questions there are organized by geographic categories. Samples of map, graph, and photo questions are also included.

The objective here is not to provide questions and answers for you to memorize. Rather, it is to make you familiar with the kinds of questions asked in the Bee and show you how to look for clues within the questions that can help you come up with the right answers. Learning how to recognize the clues will reinforce the need to master the ten study tips outlined in Chapter 3. It is important to remember that the purpose of the Bee is to test your knowledge of geography. This means you don't have to worry about "trick" questions. Just take your time and think things through. Even if you answer incorrectly, you will learn something new for next time.

Before plunging into the questions, here are a few pointers to remember about the contest. First, remember the Bee is mostly an oral competition (there are a few exceptions), so you usually won't have the benefit of seeing the questions in writing. It is important to listen carefully. The moderator will read each question only once, and you want to be sure to hear all the clues that might help you answer correctly.

Second, be sure to listen to the entire question before answering. Don't assume that you know what is going to be asked. You have only one chance to respond. Once you say your answer out loud, it cannot be taken back.

Third, don't let difficult-sounding words intimidate or sidetrack you. If the moderator trips over the pronunciation, he or she should automatically repeat the entire question. If you think having a word spelled will help you, then ask the moderator to spell it out. Just be aware that you can interrupt the competition only two times to ask to have either a question repeated or a word spelled. This rule applies to the Preliminary Competition and to the Final Round at each level of the Bee.

Finally, always speak very clearly with your best pronunciation. Don't worry if microphones are present, because they make you sound very cool and extra important!

Some Bee rounds involve questions from a single topic, such as cultural geography; others are a mix of many topics. At the school and state levels, a few rounds of questions usually offer a choice of two answers so that you have a fifty-fifty chance of answering correctly. This is to help you relax. Gradually, the questions

become more difficult as you progress from round to round and from one level to the next. After all, the Bee is a contest, and ultimately only one student can be the champion. But if you stay cool, use your study tips, and look for clues, you'll be surprised at how many questions you will be able to answer correctly.

The questions that follow are organized first by the level of the Bee in which they were used and then by the round in which they appeared. Since the titles of rounds can change from year to year, and since the sample questions are taken from several different years, the titles listed here are only representative of what you might encounter. You may also notice that some questions could fit in more than one category. This overlap is just the nature of the competition. The titles of the rounds will give you a general idea of the focus of the questions included in them. The first question in each round is followed by a discussion in italics that points out clues and reminds you of the study tips that will lead you to the correct answer (in bold type). For the remaining questions in the round you are on your own. You will find the answers starting on page 125.

As you go through the questions, jot down new terms, facts, and place-names. Keep your study tools handy so you can put questions in their geographic context. Try timing yourself to get practice in answering within the 15-second time limit (12 seconds for the national Final Round questions). Since much of the Bee is an oral competition, consider having someone read the questions to you. That will teach you to listen carefully for clues. Most of all, have fun!

Round 1: State Savvy

1. Which state borders Lake Michigan—Virginia or Illinois? *You know that Lake Michigan is one of the Great Lakes, and also that Virginia borders the Atlantic Ocean, far from the Great Lakes. So you correctly answer* **Illinois.**

2. Which state has a longer border with Canada—North Dakota or Vermont?

3. Which state has a smaller population—New York or Wyoming?

4. Key West is a resort city located on an island chain that is part of which state—Rhode Island or Florida?

5. The San Andreas [sahn an-DRAY-us] Fault is located in which state—California or Washington?

6. The city of Baton Rouge [bat-un ROOHZH] is located on the Mississippi River in which state—Ohio or Louisiana?

7. The Aleutian [a-LOOH-shun] Islands are part of which state—Hawaii or Alaska?

8. Which state is the leading producer of oil and natural gas— Texas or Missouri?

9. Lexington and Bowling Green are cities located in which state—Kentucky or Delaware?

10. Which state is located in the Great Plains—Kansas or Oregon?

Round 2: U.S. Road Trip

1. To which state would you travel to visit Gettysburg and also watch the Pirates play baseball in Pittsburgh—Iowa or Pennsylvania? *Even if you are not sure about Gettysburg or you are not a fan of baseball, the main clue here is the major city of Pittsburgh, which you know is in **Pennsylvania.***

2. To visit a desert museum in Tucson [TOOH-sahn] or hike the red rocks of Sedona, you would travel to which state—Arizona or Utah?

3. Which state would you visit to ride the Ferris wheel on Navy Pier and see President Abraham Lincoln's home in Springfield—Illinois or Nebraska?

4. To stroll the San Antonio River Walk or watch the Cowboys play football near Dallas, you would travel to which state—Montana or Texas?

5. Which state would you visit to swim in the Lake of the Ozarks and climb the Gateway Arch in St. Louis—Oklahoma or Missouri?

6. To which state would you travel to visit historic Mount Vernon and explore caverns in the Shenandoah Valley—Rhode Island or Virginia?

7. To visit Jackson Hole and climb Devils Tower, you would travel to which state—North Dakota or Wyoming?

8. To visit Seneca Caverns in the Allegheny Mountains and tour a restored coal mine in Beckley, you would travel to which state—West Virginia or Iowa?

9. If you wanted to visit Mount St. Helens National Volcanic Monument and go sailing on Puget [PYOO-jet] Sound, you would travel to which state—Washington or South Dakota?

10. The city of Nashville, located on the Cumberland River, is home to the Grand Ole Opry in which state—Tennessee or Kentucky?

Round 3: Discover National Parks

1. Visitors to Channel Islands National Park in California can take a boat tour to see which animal—penguin or gray whale? *Using your knowledge of animals, you know that penguins live in a cold environment, but coastal California has a mild climate. Therefore, you correctly answer the **gray whale.***

2. Visitors to Voyageurs National Park in Minnesota can hike through what kind of vegetation—spruce trees or cacti?

3. Which animal roams the high mountain meadows of Olympic National Park in Washington—elk or jaguar?

4. At dusk in summer, visitors to Carlsbad Caverns National Park in New Mexico can watch thousands of which animal fly from the cave—cardinals or bats?

5. Which climate type is found in Denali National Park and Preserve in Alaska—subarctic or tropical wet?

6. Visitors to Biscayne National Park in Florida can go fishing and lobstering along the shore of which kind of habitat—mangrove or desert?

7. Which animal roams the slopes of Lassen Volcanic National Park in California—black bear or polar bear?

8. The tide pools at Acadia National Park in Maine are home to which animal—sea star or giant squid?

9. Yellowstone National Park in the western United States is home to the world's largest collection of which geothermal feature—geyser or glacier?

10. Visitors to Congaree [KAHN-guh-ree] National Park in South Carolina can paddle a canoe past which kind of vegetation— arctic moss or bald cypress?

Round 4: Weird But True!

1. In France, ketchup is banned in elementary schools. It's weird but true! France is located on which continent that borders the Bay of Biscay? *Not sure about the Bay of Biscay? Close your eyes and draw on your mental map of the world. Where is France? Yes, you remember it is a country in western* **Europe.**

2. In Singapore, chewing gum is only available with a prescription. It's weird but true! Singapore is part of which continent that is crossed by the Mekong River?

3. A koala sleeps for up to 22 hours a day. It's weird but true! Koalas live in the states of Queensland and New South Wales on which continent?

4. In Morocco, goats climb trees to get their favorite fruit. It's weird but true! Morocco is located on which continent that includes the Atlas Mountains?

5. Of all new cars sold in Brazil, 90 percent use fuel made from sugarcane. It's weird but true! Brazil is located on which continent that borders the Caribbean Sea?

6. The numbers we write with today were invented in India 2,000 years ago. It's weird but true! India is located on which continent that borders the Arabian Sea?

7. More earthquakes occur in Alaska than in any other U.S. state. It's weird but true! Alaska is located on which continent that borders Hudson Bay?

8. Elephants can swim for up to six hours without resting. It's weird but true! Elephants can be found in Tanzania and Zambia on which continent?

9. You can ride a Ferris wheel underground in Romania. It's weird but true! Romania is located on which continent that is crossed by the Danube River?

10. Surgeons sometimes use sea coral to replace human bone. It's weird but true! The world's largest coral reef system, the Great Barrier Reef, is located off the coast of which continent?

Round 5: Geo Extremes

1. Some of the world's tallest mountains are located in which Asian country—Israel or Nepal? *It's time for your mental map again. Visualize the location of Israel—a relatively flat, dry country on the eastern shore of the Mediterranean Sea—so you correctly answer* **Nepal.**

2. Which country is Africa's largest by area—Algeria or Malawi [ma-LAH-wee]?

3. The world's largest salt flat is located in the Altiplano region in which country—Guatemala or Bolivia?

4. Which country is one of the leading producers of oil in the world—the United States or Oman?

5. The world's longest road tunnel is located northeast of Bergen in which Scandinavian country—Italy or Norway?

6. The world's hottest inhabited place, with a record high annual average temperature of 93 degrees, is located near Eritrea [er-ih-TREE-ah] in which country—Ethiopia or Croatia?

7. Which is Africa's most populous country—Nigeria or Sudan?

8. Which landlocked country is located farther from an ocean— Paraguay or Kazakhstan?

9. Tugela [too-gay-luh] Falls, the highest waterfall in Africa, is located near the border between Lesotho [leh-soo-too] and which other country—Eritrea or South Africa?

10. What is the largest island by area in the Caribbean Sea—Cuba or Jamaica?

Round 6: Odd One Out

1. Which country is not crossed by the Tropic of Capricorn— Brazil, Egypt, or Australia? *You need to take this question apart to arrive at the answer. You know that the Tropic of Capricorn is south of the Equator. Your mental map tells you that Australia and much of Brazil lie south of the Equator, so they must be the ones crossed by the Tropic of Capricorn, and* **Egypt** *is the odd one out.*

2. Which country does not border the Indian Ocean—Tanzania, Indonesia, or Uzbekistan?

3. Which country is not mostly Christian—Italy, Pakistan, or Brazil?

4. Which country is not made up of a group of islands—Japan, Thailand, or the Philippines?

5. Which country does not border Lake Victoria—Tanzania, Uganda, or Nigeria?

6. Which country does not have a border along the Red Sea—Egypt, Syria, or Eritrea?

7. Which country does not share a border with Panama—Costa Rica, Nicaragua, or Colombia?

8. Which country does not border the Adriatic Sea—Germany, Italy, or Croatia?

9. Which country is not located near the Tsushima [TSOO-SHEE-MAH] Current—Japan, South Korea, or Indonesia?

10. Which country does not include an area of humid subtropical climate—China, Uruguay, or Chad?

Round 7: Awesome Adventures

1. You can whiz along one of the world's longest series of zip lines in the Snowdonia Mountains in Wales in which European country? *You don't know where the Snowdonia Mountains are? Not a problem! You know that Wales is a part of the **United***

Kingdom of Great Britain and Northern Ireland, so you know the correct answer.

2. Runners travel more than 150 miles in an annual desert race called the Gobi March. This race takes place south of Mongolia in which Asian country?

3. Bicyclists enjoy paths around Lake Constance, a body of water that lies on the border between Switzerland, Germany, and which other country?

4. You can strap on a hang glider's harness and soar over the city of Rio de Janeiro in which South American country?

5. Climbers can explore the ice on the Athabasca [a-thuh-BAS-kuh] Glacier. This massive river of ice is located in the Rocky Mountains in Alberta in which country?

6. Adventurers experience eight seconds of free fall while bungee jumping into Nevis Gorge on South Island. This island is part of which country located in the South Pacific?

7. Extreme kayakers maneuver through jagged rocks and rapids on the Bashkaus River, located in Siberia in which country?

8. Climb one of the tallest sand dunes in the world in a desert that borders the Atlantic Ocean in which country south of Angola?

9. Climb one of Europe's highest peaks, Mont Blanc. This mountain is located on the border between France, Switzerland, and which other country?

10. Volunteers can feed, walk, and wash elephants at wildlife sanctuaries near Kathmandu in which small Asian country?

Tiebreaker Questions

1. Name the desert that covers much of the area between Los Angeles and Death Valley in southern California. *This question requires you to recall the location of major deserts in the United States. You remember that the Mojave and Sonoran Deserts are in Southern California, but much of the Sonoran Desert extends into Mexico, so you correctly answer* **Mojave Desert.**

2. What is another term used for lines of longitude?

3. What is the name of the channel between the Atlantic and Pacific Oceans that separates South America's mainland from Tierra del Fuego?

4. The Edwards Plateau, Brazos River, and Padre Island are all physical features found in which U.S. state?

5. In 1697, Spain ceded control of what is now Haiti to which country?

6. What is the official language of Libya, Yemen, and Mauritania?

7. The Danube River flows for about 1,800 miles before emptying into what body of water?

8. The Ganges [GAN-jeez] Plain extends across much of the northern portion of which country?

The questions in the final round are similar to those in the Preliminary Competition, except they are more difficult. The questions are not grouped into geographic categories. Instead, it is a good bet that each question will test your knowledge about a different geographic subject. The exception to this is the series of questions that pertains to a map, graph, or other visual aid.

1. Which state is bordered by Lake Erie and Kentucky?

2. The Great Salt Lake is located in which state that borders Idaho?

3. Corpus Christi and Houston are cities in which state that borders Oklahoma?

4. Which state that borders Connecticut is the smallest state in the United States?

5. Which state is bordered by Lake Superior and North Dakota?

6. The Yukon River flows through which state that borders Canada?

7. Syracuse and Buffalo are cities in which state that borders Pennsylvania?

8. Which state includes the Pacific islands of Oahu and Maui?

9. Stonehenge, an ancient group of standing stones, is located near Salisbury in what country?

10. The Sydney Opera House, with its distinctive roof resembling the sails of a ship, is a landmark in which country?

11. Zürich is a major banking center in which European country?

12. The St. Lawrence River flows out of the easternmost of the Great Lakes. Name this lake.

13. What berries are harvested from flooded bogs in some parts of the northern United States and Canada?

14. Saris [SAR-ees], garments made of lengths of cloth that are wrapped and draped around the body, are the traditional clothing of women in which country that borders Pakistan?

15. Gondolas floating on canals are associated with which city in northern Italy?

16. Name the largest island in the Greater Antilles.

The response for the next question is written. During the competition a piece of paper is provided for you. You will have 15 seconds to write your answer.

17. The classic film *The Wizard of Oz* features a young girl named Dorothy who experiences a powerful tornado in her home state where Topeka is the capital. In this story, Dorothy lives in which state located north of Oklahoma?

Map Questions

To answer the questions below, you will have to use the map showing the U.S. National Water Trails system on the following spread. This round tests your ability to identify U.S. states by locating the trails that exist along rivers, lakes, and other waterways around the country. During the Bee you will be given 15 seconds to study the map before answering your question.

1. Canoers paddling down the Hudson River Greenway Water Trail can see historic sites and wildlife marshes. This water trail is located in which state that borders Vermont?

2. The Black Canyon Water Trail is located along a rugged section of the Colorado River on the border between Arizona and which other state?

3. Kayakers can see crawfish and alligators along the Bayou Teche [BYE-oo TESH] Paddle Trail. This trail is located in which state that borders the Gulf of Mexico?

4. You can explore a stretch of the mighty Mississippi River near the Twin Cities by visiting the Mississippi National River and Recreation Area Water Trail. This trail is located in which state that borders North Dakota?

5. Paddlers can see marine mammals on the Kitsap Peninsula Water Trail. This trail travels through parts of Puget [PYOO-jet] Sound, located in which Pacific state?

6. The Red Rock Water Trail, located along Lake Red Rock, features rocky cliffs and bluffs. This trail is located in which state that borders Nebraska?

U.S. National Water Trails System

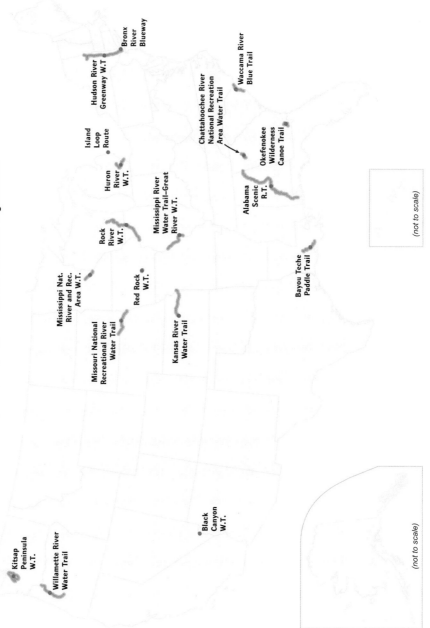

Kitsap Peninsula W.T.

Willamette River Water Trail

Black Canyon W.T.

Mississippi Nat. River and Rec. Area W.T.

Missouri National Recreational River Water Trail

Red Rock W.T.

Kansas River Water Trail

Rock River W.T.

Huron River W.T.

Island Loop Route

Mississippi River Water Trail–Great River W.T.

Hudson River Greenway W.T.

Bronx River Blueway

Waccama River Blue Trail

Chattahoochee River National Recreation Area Water Trail

Alabama Scenic R.T.

Okefenokee Wilderness Canoe Trail

Bayou Teche Paddle Trail

(not to scale)

(not to scale)

Championship Round

1. Gray wolves were once wiped out from Yellowstone National Park, but they have made a comeback in recent years because of conservation efforts. Yellowstone National Park is located in Wyoming, Montana, and which other state?

2. In the popular Harry Potter book series by J. K. Rowling, Harry catches the train to Hogwarts at the Kings Cross station in what major European city?

Championship Tiebreaker Questions

1. Earth's coldest place, with an annual average temperature of -94°F, is located at Ridge A on which continent?

2. Name the most populous city in Siberia.

QUALIFYING TEST

The online Qualifying Test determines which students qualify for the state Bee. The 70 questions, including a set pertaining to a map, graph, or other visual aid, cover a wide variety of geographic topics. Each question offers a choice of four answers, and you must choose the answer you think is correct. Remember, the only time that you will take this test is if you are the winner of your School Bee.

1. How long does it take Earth to make one orbit around the sun?
   - O 1 month
   - O 1 day
   - O 1 week
   - O 1 year

2. Properties such as Boardwalk, Baltic Avenue, and Marvin Gardens in the classic board game Monopoly are named for places in what city known for its hotels and casinos?

   O Atlantic City

   O Las Vegas

   O New Orleans

   O Salt Lake City

3. Which device invented in 1837 by blacksmith John Deere allowed farmers to raise crops on large areas of the Midwest?

   O barbed wire

   O cotton gin

   O steel plow

   O telegraph

4. Since the industrial revolution, which environmental problem has caused chemical weathering that has damaged marble stonework on many buildings?

   O acid rain

   O desertification

   O greenhouse effect

   O ozone depletion

5. In which country is 26 percent of its population, more than in any other country, age 65 and older?

   O Afghanistan

   O India

   O Japan

   O Malaysia

6. A thick liquid gel obtained from what succulent plant is some-times used to treat burns and other skin conditions?

O aloe

O eucalyptus

O indigo

O poppies

7. What material was used to make traditional clogs worn by people in the Netherlands to keep their feet dry when walking through soggy areas?

O felt

O leather

O rubber

O wood

8. Some automobile companies are producing small numbers of fuel cell vehicles that are powered by what gas?

O carbon dioxide

O hydrogen

O nitrogen

O oxygen

9. Fruit trees in which state have been affected by citrus green-ing, a disease spread by small insects?

O Alaska

O Florida

O Maine

O Utah

10. Which route would you most likely take to travel from the Lincoln Memorial to the Jefferson Memorial?

  ○ Potomac Parkway to Constitution Avenue

  ○ 23rd Street to Ohio Drive

  ○ Independence Avenue to 17th Street

  ○ Constitution Avenue to Virginia Avenue

Analogies

The Qualifying Test almost always has a series of analogies in which you are asked to compare two things that have something in common. For example, in the analogy "The peso is to Mexico

as the WHAT is to Japan?" the answer is yen because yen is the currency of Japan, just as the peso is the currency in Mexico. See if you can figure out the following analogies.

1. Lemurs are to Madagascar as giant tortoises are to WHAT?
   O Aleutian Islands
   O Easter Island
   O Galápagos Islands
   O Hawaiian Islands

2. Goulash is to Hungary as curry is to WHAT?
   O India
   O Japan
   O France
   O Mexico

3. Species are to animals as dialects are to WHAT?
   O languages
   O religions
   O climates
   O soils

STATE-LEVEL PRELIMINARY ROUNDS

At the state level, before the official questioning begins, there is a warm-up round to help you relax. Your answers to these questions do not count. As with the school level, the first few rounds at the state level offer a choice of answers.

Round 1: State Savvy

1. Which state has two panhandles—Iowa or West Virginia? *Close your eyes and visualize the map of the United States. You picture each state and realize that Iowa is almost box-shaped, so you correctly answer **West Virginia.***

2. Which state is divided into parishes instead of counties— Maryland or Louisiana?

3. Which state receives more annual precipitation on average— Vermont or Utah?

4. Which state includes part of a generally flat grassland region called the High Plains—Colorado or Virginia?

5. Which state has experienced population increases from retir- ees seeking a warm climate—Arizona or Pennsylvania?

6. Which state borders two Canadian provinces—Maine or Idaho?

7. Which state is made up of land ceded to the United States by Mexico—Utah or Wisconsin?

8. Which state has a longer frost-free period during an average year—South Dakota or Texas?

9. The Boise River has its source in the Sawtooth Range of which state—Idaho or Ohio?

10. Trade winds contribute to the mild, tropical climate in which state—Tennessee or Hawaii?

Round 2: Our National Monuments

1. Booker T. Washington National Monument preserves the farm where this educator was born into slavery. It is located southeast of Roanoke in which state? *The question tells you Washington was born into slavery, so you know this must be a southern state. The important clue is the city of Roanoke. So use your mental map of southeastern states and correctly identify that Roanoke is in **Virginia.***

2. Grand Portage National Monument, once an important fur-trading center, is located near both the Ontario border and Lake Superior in which present-day U.S. state?

3. Timpanogos [tim-puh-NO-guhs] Cave National Monument, containing many colorful mineral formations, is a cave system located in the Wasatch [WAH-sach] Range of which state?

4. A well-preserved fossil bed from roughly 40 million years ago can be found at John Day Fossil Beds National Monument, located near the city of Bend in which state?

5. Prehistoric mounds constructed in the shapes of mammals and birds can be found in Effigy Mounds National Monument, located northeast of Cedar Falls in which state?

6. George Washington Carver's boyhood home is preserved in the national monument bearing his name, located near Joplin in the southwestern part of which state?

7. Castle Clinton National Monument, a historic fort and now the ticketing office for ferries to Ellis Island, is located in Battery Park in which state?

8. Markers honoring both Native American warriors and members of the U.S. Army can be found at Little Bighorn Battlefield National Monument, located near Billings in which state?

9. Ancient tribes mined flint to make tools at what is now Alibates [ah-leh-BAH-tays] Flint Quarries National Monument, located north of Amarillo in which state?

10. Russell Cave National Monument protects a cave system that has evidence of human habitation beginning nearly 10,000 years ago. This monument is located northeast of Birmingham and near the Tennessee River in which southern state?

Round 3: Weird But True!

1. The heaviest cauliflower on record weighed more than a bulldog. It's weird but true! This cauliflower was grown in a greenhouse near the Pennines [PEN-nines] range in which European island country? *The question asks for an island country in Europe, so pull out your mental list of island countries to arrive at the answer. The list is short and you realize, correctly, the answer is the* **United Kingdom.**

2. The pudu [POO-doo]—a small kind of deer—runs in a zigzag pattern to escape predators. It's weird but true! This vulnerable species can be found in the Patagonia region, including the Chubut [choo-BOOT] province of which South American country?

3. One kind of mushroom resembles a human brain. It's weird but true! Brain mushrooms are poisonous but still considered a delicacy in which northern European country that includes Lake Saimaa [SAHY-mah]?

4. The coati [koh-AH-tee], a member of the raccoon family, can rotate its ankles 180 degrees. It's weird but true! The coati can be found in Chirripó National Park in the northern part of the Cordillera de Talamanca [kor-dee-YAIR-uh DAY tah-lah-MAHN-kah] in which Central American country?

5. Some old jets are placed in airplane graveyards. It's weird but true! One such airplane graveyard is located in Alice Springs, near the MacDonnell Ranges in which country?

6. The Pac-Man frog can lift three times its own body weight with its tongue. It's weird but true! This frog lives in the rain forest near Manaus [mah-NAUS] in which South American country?

7. Sputnik 1, the first satellite in space, was about the size of a beach ball. It's weird but true! This satellite was launched in 1957 from a site in what present-day country that includes Lake Balkhash [bal-KASH]?

8. The southern cassowary bird has claws nearly the length of an iPhone. It's weird but true! This bird lives on the island of Ceram [SAY-rahm] in the Maluku [mah-LOO-koo] province of which Asian country?

9. The cherimoya [cher-uh-MOY-uh] fruit, native to South America, tastes like bubble gum. It's weird but true! This fruit grows near the city of Loja [LOH-ha] in which country that borders Peru?

10. Polar bears sometimes communicate by touching noses. It's weird but true! This vulnerable species lives on the Queen Elizabeth Islands in which North American country?

Round 4: Odd Item Out

1. Which country is not landlocked—Mongolia, Nepal, or North Korea? *You know that "landlocked" means no direct access to water. Pull up that mental map again! Visualize each country and you will correctly identify* **North Korea,** *which borders water on two sides.*

2. Which country does not border Bhutan—Afghanistan, China, or India?

3. Which country does not experience a tropical wet climate—Brazil, Indonesia, or Kenya?

4. Which country does not border the Adriatic Sea—Italy, Sweden, or Albania?

5. Which country does not share a border with Bangladesh—India, Myanmar, or Vietnam?

6. Which country does not contain part of the Kalahari Desert—Tanzania, Namibia, or Botswana?

7. Which island country is not part of the Greater Antilles—Cuba, Barbados, or Jamaica?

8. In which country is ranching not a major economic activity—Italy, Australia, or the United States?

9. Which country does not have a Muslim majority—Egypt, Iran, or Russia?

10. Which country does not border the Black Sea—Georgia, Turkey, or Turkmenistan?

Round 5: Protecting Wildlife

1. The island of Java, located south of Borneo, is home to a critically endangered population of which animal—lions or rhinoceros? *You know that lions and rhinoceros once lived in Africa and Asia, but you remember that lions now live only south of the Sahara. So by elimination, one type of **rhinoceros** must be found in Java.*

2. Scientists are working to determine the economic impact of dam construction on the Mekong River system in Southeast Asia, which threatens the habitat of which animal—fin whale or river dolphin?

3. Punta Izopo is a protected area on the Caribbean coast of Honduras. This area is known for its vast mangrove forests that are home to which animal—snowy egret or chimpanzee?

4. Namibia, the first country to include environmental protection in its constitution, is home to which animal that has one of the world's longest migrations—zebra or hippo?

5. Public access is restricted in Canada's Suffield National Wildlife Area, a vast prairie grassland in Alberta that is home to which endangered animal—river otter or kangaroo rat?

6. Usually calm and nonaggressive, which animal has about half of its known population living in the Virunga [vee-RUN-gah] region of East Africa—condor or mountain gorilla?

7. Many groups are working to designate the Gulf of Corcovado, located off the southwestern coast of Chile, as a marine protected area. This area is an important feeding ground for which animal that is the largest on the planet—elephant or blue whale?

8. Wildlife groups are working to establish safe zones in New Zealand waters for which seabird that breeds only in these areas—Chatham [CHAH-tum] albatross or blue heron?

9. Cumbernauld Glen is a popular conservation area for viewing which protected animal, one of the largest remaining carnivores in Great Britain—arctic fox or badger?

10. The Sonoran Desert, which stretches across northern Mexico and the southern United States, is home to which endangered big cat—tiger or jaguar?

Round 6: Forces of Nature

1. Scientists warn that rising sea levels and decreasing freshwater resources may lead to a natural disaster in an African country where the Aswan High Dam is located. Name this country. *You know that the Aswan High Dam was built to regulate the flow of the Nile River as it passes through Egypt. Therefore, you correctly answer* **Egypt.**

2. In the summer of 2010, severe flooding left millions of people homeless, including many between the cities of Multan [mul-TAHN] and Karachi [kuh-RAH-chee] in which Asian country?

3. In 2006, Typhoon Durian caused mudslides around Mayon [mah-YAWN], a volcano on the island of Luzon. This island is part of which Asian country?

4. In 2015, a magnitude 8.3 earthquake and accompanying tsunami affected the city of Coquimbo [koh-KEEM-boh] and surrounding areas in which country that borders Argentina?

5. In 2007, flooding affected thousands of people in the central provinces of Durazno and Treinta y Tres [train-tah e trase] in South America's second smallest country by area. Name this country.

6. In 1931, an island country experienced the deadliest earthquake in its history, centered near the city of Napier on Hawke Bay. Name this country.

7. Following Hurricane Mitch in 1998, a country improved its disaster preparations and was able to reduce the damage from landslides and flooding that occurred a decade later. Name this country that borders Guatemala and Nicaragua.

8. In 2009, a plague of caterpillars destroyed crops and contaminated water supplies in a country on Africa's Atlantic coast. Name this country that borders Sierra Leone and Guinea.

9. In 2004, a tsunami destroyed many fishing operations in an island country separated from India by the Gulf of Mannar. Name this country.

10. In 1999, landslides killed tens of thousands of people north of Caracas [kah-RAH-kas] on the Caribbean coast of which South American country?

Round 7: Watery Planet

1. Which body of water is part of the Panama Canal—Lake Managua or Lake Gatún [gah-TOON]? *You remember that Managua is the capital of Nicaragua, so Lake Managua must also be in Nicaragua, and you correctly answer* **Lake Gatún.**

2. Which body of water lies north of Arnhem [ARN-hem] Land, one of the rainiest regions of Australia—Tasman Sea or Arafura [ah-rah-FOO-rah] Sea?

3. Which body of water borders Equatorial Guinea's island of Bioko [bee-OH-koh]—Gulf of Sidra or Bight of Bonny?

4. Which body of water forms an arm of the Yellow Sea—Bo Hai [HI] or Gulf of Tonkin?

5. Which body of water is known for its considerable oil and natural gas deposits—Scotia Sea or North Sea?

6. Over which body of water do many tropical storms pass on their way from the West Indies to the North American mainland—Yucatán Channel or Gulf of Guayaquil [gwi-yuh-KEEL]?

7. Which body of water is crossed by the Arctic Circle—Norwegian Sea or Baltic Sea?

8. Which body of water is located along a disputed border in West Asia—Lake Nasser or Sea of Galilee?

9. Which body of water lies southwest of the South Shetland Islands—Timor Sea or Bellingshausen [BELL-ingz-how-zen] Sea?

10. Which body of water lies west of Naples, Italy—Tyrrhenian [teh-REE-nee-en] Sea or Ionian Sea?

Round 8: World Music

1. Rap music called Rap-e [RAH-pee] Farsi sometimes critiques the government in which country south of the Caspian Sea? *Using your mental map, you know that Iran lies south of the Caspian Sea, and you recall that Farsi is a major language there. So you correctly answer* **Iran.**

2. Gamelan [GA-muh-lan] orchestras composed of gongs struck by mallets provide the music for many temple ceremonies on the island of Bali in which country?

3. Maracas, or rattles made from gourds, are important to many songs and dances in the country that includes Lake Maracaibo [mah-rah-KI-boh]. Name this country.

4. The duduk [doo-DOOK], a type of oboe traditionally made from apricot wood, is especially important in the area around the city of Yerevan [yer-eh-VAHN] in which country?

5. Bhangra [BAHN-gruh] is a syncopated kind of music played by farmers in the state of Punjab in which country that borders Nepal?

6. Vimbuza [vim-BOO-zah], which combines dances and drum music, is an important healing ritual for the Tumbuka [TOOM-boo-kah] people living in which African country formerly known as Nyasaland [NYAH-sah-land]?

7. Bomba, a form of music and dance that combines Andean guitar and rhythms from Africa, is traditional in a country that borders Peru and Colombia. Name this country.

8. Bachata [ba-SHA-ta], a style of slow romantic music, developed among the poor communities in what Caribbean country that borders Haiti?

9. Calypso music, which often has lyrics that comment on social conditions, originated in which Caribbean country southeast of Grenada [gruh-NAY-duh]?

10. Timbila [tim-BEE-luh], or wooden xylophones, are traditionally played in the Chopi [SHAH-pee] communities in which country that borders South Africa and Tanzania?

Tiebreaker Questions

1. Lake Assal [ah-SAHL], west of the Gulf of Aden, lies about 500 feet below sea level and is the lowest point on which continent? *The Gulf of Aden lies south of the Arabian Peninsula, which is part of Asia. But Lake Assal is west of the gulf and according to your mental map that means it is in Djibouti, which is in **Africa.***

2. A ryokan [ree-oh-kun], a type of traditional inn, has been operating for nearly 1,300 years in Komatsu [koh-maht-soo]. Komatsu is on the island of Honshu in what country?

3. The European Food Safety Authority is located in the city of Parma in what country?

4. Flightless, nocturnal parrots called kakapos [ka-ka-pohs] live in island sanctuaries in the Fiordland and Stewart Island areas of what country?

5. The Falkland Islands, an overseas territory of the United Kingdom, are also claimed by Argentina. These islands are located in which major ocean?

6. The 2010 World Cup final was held at Soccer City Stadium in the most populous city in South Africa. Name this city.

7. James Bay, which borders Ontario and Quebec, is a southern extension of what body of water?

8. The Persian New Year is a national holiday in a country that includes the site of Persepolis [per-SEP-uh-lis], which was once the capital of ancient Persia. Name this present-day country.

STATE-LEVEL FINAL ROUND

The only rounds of questions organized by topics in the State Finals are those that deal with a theme or visual materials, such as maps, graphs, or photographs. The following randomly selected examples are designed to give you an idea of what you can expect for these kinds of rounds.

1. The city of Tuskegee is southeast of Lake Martin in what state that borders Georgia?

2. Manassas and Fredericksburg are Civil War battle sites in what state?

3. A state known for its Cajun culture includes the towns of Lake Charles and Lafayette. Name this state.

4. Kilauea [kee-lau-WAY-ah], an active volcano, is near the coast in the southeastern part of what state?

5. Padre Island National Seashore lies on a barrier island south of Corpus Christi in what state?

6. Santa Monica Pier, the official western end of Route 66, is in what state?

7. Buzzards Bay and Nantucket Sound border what state?

8. Sioux City and the city of Council Bluffs are close to Nebraska in what neighboring state?

9. You can eat oyaki dumplings while riding a train to the mountain city of Nagano [nah-GAH-noh] in which country?

10. Nantes [NANTS], located on the Loire [LWAHR] River, was the home of writer Jules Verne and is located in which country?

11. Arequipa [ar-uh-KEE-pah], a center for Andean textiles, is located in which country that borders Brazil?

12. Jaipur [JI-poor], known as the "pink city" due to the color of the stone used for its buildings, is located in which Asian country?

13. Lake Lucerne is located in the Alps in which European country?

14. The tropical island of Negros [NAY-grohs] borders the Sulu Sea and is part of which Asian island country?

15. Milford Sound, a fjord carved by glacial erosion, borders South Island in which Southern Hemisphere country?

16. Eucalyptus forests can be found in the state of Victoria in which country?

The response for the next question is written. During the competition a piece of paper will be provided for you. You will have 15 seconds to write your answer.

17. Recent world weather patterns have been influenced by El Niño, which is characterized by unusually warm water temperatures in which ocean?

Map Questions

To answer the questions below, you will have to use the map showing locations of National Parks. During the Bee you will be given 15 seconds to study the map and give your answer.

1. You can hike steep switchbacks on Old Rag Mountain and see dramatic views of the Blue Ridge Mountains in Shenandoah National Park. Give the number of this park and name the state.

2. In Zion National Park, located in the Colorado Plateau region, you can rappel down 100-foot cliffs and go canyoneering in the slot canyons. Give the number of this park and name the state.

3. You can kayak and fish for trout on Jackson Lake, a glacial lake located in Grand Teton National Park near Jackson Hole. Give the number of this park and name the state.

4. Visitors to Biscayne National Park can see colorful fish while snorkeling through its shallow reefs in the Atlantic Ocean. Give the number of this park and name the state.

5. Sandboarding is a popular activity in Great Sand Dunes National Park and Preserve, located in the northern part of the Sangre de Cristo Mountains. Give the number of this park and name the state.

6. You can soar in a biplane above the rocky shores of Acadia National Park, which includes Mount Desert Island. Give the number of this park and name the state.

7. Visitors can bathe in the spring waters in Hot Springs National Park, located in the Ouachita [WAH-sheh-tah] Mountains. Give the number of this park and name the state.

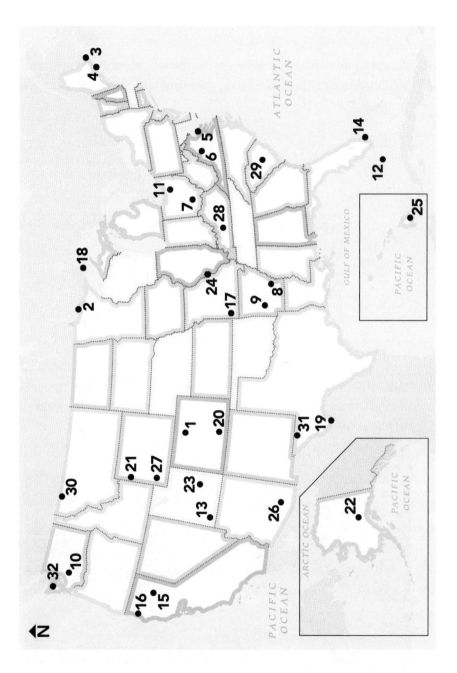

Photo Questions

1. Photographer John Stanmeyer captured Mount Bromo and Mount Semeru [seh-MER-oo] erupting simultaneously on the island of Java in which country?

2. This African penguin got up close and personal with photographer Thomas Peschak on Mercury Island. This island is located off the coast of which country that includes Walvis Bay?

3. Photographer Paul Nicklen discovered these baby arctic foxes sitting outside their den in Svalbard [SVAHL-bar], an archipelago that belongs to which Scandinavian country?

4. This tiger shark was spotted by photographer Brian Skerry off the coast of which Caribbean country in the West Indies with Nassau as its capital?

Championship Round

1. In the newest *Star Wars* movie, *The Force Awakens,* desert scenes of the fictional planet of Jakku were filmed in a country that borders both Oman and Saudi Arabia. Name this country on the Persian Gulf.

2. In 2015, scientists sent a camera into Kavachi [kuh-VAH-chee], an underwater volcano in the Pacific Ocean, and were surprised to discover two shark species inside despite the threat of eruptions. This volcano is located near the New Georgia Islands in which country?

Championship Tiebreaker Questions

1. Santa Maria Island, where Portuguese settlers planted grapes as far back as 1430, is part of what island chain?

2. What country is the only predominantly Muslim country to have a currency called the rupee?

NATIONAL-LEVEL PRELIMINARY ROUNDS

The following questions are representative of the questions and geographic categories in the National Preliminary Competition.

Round 1: Globetrotter

1. The Benue [BAYN-way] and Kaduna [KAH-doo-NAH] Rivers are major tributaries of which West African river?

2. Mount Damavand [dahm-ah-VAHND], at more than 18,000 feet, is the highest point in which West Asian country?

Round 2: Dare to Explore

1. Although he did not succeed in finding the Northwest Passage, which British explorer sailed near a large Arctic island that now bears his name—Francis Drake or William Baffin?

2. Which female British explorer traveled throughout West Africa during the late 19th century, writing two books about her experiences—Meave Leakey or Mary Kingsley?

Round 3: Rankings

1. Place these countries in order according to their literacy rates from highest to lowest: Egypt, Indonesia, Philippines.

2. Place these lakes in order according to their longitude from west to east: Lake Balaton [BAH-lah-ton], Lake Constance, Lake Ladoga [la-DOH-ga].

Round 4: Weird But True!

1. A prison in Brazil's most populous city uses geese as an alarm system—they honk at anyone roaming the grounds! Name this major city.

2. Canadians like to eat dulse [duhls], a dried red seaweed. Dulse is served in some restaurants in which major city located along the Burrard [buh-RARD] Inlet?

Round 5: Your World

1. In January 2016, a European country announced that it had produced 42 percent of its electricity from wind power in 2015, the highest proportion ever achieved by a country. Many of these wind farms are located in the Jutland [JUT-lund] region in which country?

2. In January 2016, a country that borders the Aegean Sea held its annual Camel Wrestling Championship, an ancient tradition where camels fight each other. This competition is held in Selçuk [SEL-juk] in which country?

Round 6: Destinations of a Lifetime
1. Visit the tallest pyramid in the Yucatán Peninsula in the ancient Maya city of Cobá [ko-BAH]. Cobá is located southwest of Cancún in which Mexican state?

2. An island that is part of an overseas territory of the United Kingdom is a stopping point for birds and seals crossing the South Atlantic. It is also where the explorer Ernest Shackleton is buried. Name this large island.

Round 7: Geography Rocks!
1. Which mineral is a good conductor of electricity and is named after the island of Cyprus—copper or cobalt?

2. Some rare specimens of a gem from the Dominican Republic look blue when viewed under direct sunlight but golden brown when viewed under incandescent light. Is this gem amber or kunzite [KOON-zite]?

Round 8: World National Parks (Map Questions)

Look at the map on the previous page to give the number of the park and name the country where it is located.

1. Khao Yai [kow-yai] National Park, covering an area of more than 800 square miles and home to tropical wildlife, such as elephants and tigers, lies at the southern end of the Phetchabun [pet-chah-BOON] Range. Give the number of this park and name the country where it is located.

2. Canaima [kah-NEI-mah] National Park, covering over 11,500 square miles, is mainly located in a region called La Gran Sabana and includes the world's tallest waterfall. Give the number of this park and name the state where it is located.

Round 9: City Situation

1. Which clue correctly describes the location of Calgary, Canada?

   on the shores of Lake Ontario

   on the banks of the Bow River

   on the banks of the Red River

2. Which clue correctly describes the location of Baghdad, Iraq?

   west of Kuwait City

   west of Mosul

   on the banks of the Tigris River

Round 10: Analogies

1. Abuja [ah-BOO-jah] is to Lagos [LAH-gos] as Astana [ah-STAH-nah] is to WHAT?

2. Vesuvius is to Italy as Tajumulco [tah-hoo-MUHL-koh] is to WHAT?

GeoChallenges

At the national level, students will encounter GeoChallenges, or special questions that require critical thinking. Students will be asked to synthesize their geographic knowledge and apply it accurately, compellingly, and creatively. GeoChallenges often require an extended response in either oral or written form. The response is scored by a panel of judges based on criteria such as accuracy, reasoning, and presentation. Over time, more of these types of questions will be introduced in the Bee at all levels.

EXAMPLE:

The question below poses a real-world scenario that requires an extended oral response. After hearing the question, the student has 15 seconds to reflect, and then has 45 seconds to answer. A panel of judges will score the response based on accuracy, reasoning, and presentation.

QUESTION:

You're the owner of a riverboat cruise company that operates worldwide, and business is booming. You're looking for a popular new cruise destination. You know your customers care about a warm climate, scenery, and accessibility to the port of departure. You've narrowed the selection to three rivers: Lena River, Vistula River, and Zambezi River. Which river is the best choice for your new cruise, and why?

EXAMPLE RESPONSE:

I would choose the Zambezi River as the destination for my new riverboat cruise. It's located in the tropics, so it has a warm climate most of the year. The Lena River and Vistula River are not as warm. The Zambezi also has great scenery, with interesting wildlife along the route. And I know it's accessible because there are several major airports in the area. As a bonus, the cruise could include an excursion to Victoria Falls, one of the world's most popular tourist destinations. Overall, I think the Zambezi River is the best choice for the new cruise.

CHAPTER **5**

Tips From Bee Finalists

Use every resource you have to help your geographical journey.
—LUCY CHAE, 2015 NATIONAL TOP TEN; 2016 MASSACHUSETTS STATE RUNNER-UP

This chapter provides advice from Bee champions about the best ways to get involved in learning about geography, what to study, how to relax, and more!

Have fun! Despite what some may think, learning can be fun, especially when it involves trivia. My favorite way to study was by taking online quizzes because they helped reinforce what I knew, and made me realize what I didn't know or forgot. And the feeling of accomplishment after getting all the questions to a particularly hard quiz correct makes all the studying worth it. But more important than taking quizzes, reading books, or even looking at maps, is having the drive to learn as much as you can about the world.

Asha Jain, 2013 State Bee Champion, Wisconsin (7th Grade); 2013 Top Ten National Finalist; 2013 Team USA Member, World Championships, 1st Place; 2014 State Bee Champion, Wisconsin (8th Grade); 2014 Top Ten National Finalist

Whenever you participate in any competition, you are bound to fail at least a few times before you achieve success. This is definitely something that happened to me. When I was in fifth grade, I unfortunately missed a question during the preliminary rounds at the state level and was eliminated, even though the previous year, I had made it all the way to fourth place in my state. When you experience disappointments like this, you begin to question if studying for the Bee is even worth the time. However, if you are truly passionate about geography, you need to be able to set defeats behind you and allow them to inspire you to be better. I was able to realize that I had a passion for learning about the world and a goal to be the best. I used this failure as motivation, won my state bee the next year, and became the 2015 National Geographic Bee Runner-Up.

Shriya Yarlagadda, 2013, 2014, and 2015 State Bee Champion, Michigan (4th–6th Grade); 2015 National Runner-Up (6th Grade)

· ·

My first tip is to definitely trust your gut … Something that I initially struggled with during my Bee saga was impulsively changing my answers, which often deviated quite greatly from the correct answer which had been my instinct. Therefore, I adopted a policy where I always stuck to my first answer, and only ever changed it if I felt as though I had a lapse of judgment or, whilst confirming my answer, determined a flaw.

Another tip is to build a mental map. Building a mental map of a region I was being asked a question about helped me focus in on the region and develop a visual answer. For example, whenever there was a question about borders, or any question on the location of a city, state, river in relation to another landform, [a mental map] enabled me to determine the answer quite easily, as after years of compiling information, constructing a rough map of the world becomes routine.

My third and final tip is to do what works for you. While studying for the Bee, strategies will be thrown at you from all sides, and sometimes it can be overwhelming. Many times, after compiling these strategies, I would try them while being quizzed by my parents, sister, or friends, and quickly discovered what worked for me. There really is no one cookie-cutter method for winning the Bee, but the one way to find the method that you feel works best is not to just read it out of a book but to apply it in practice.

Akhil Rekulapelli, 2013–2014 State Bee Champion, Virginia (7th– 8th Grade); 2014 National Champion (8th Grade)

. . . .

It's important to study as much as you can. This also helps you feel less nervous on the competition day, because you'll feel more prepared. Taking breaks and getting some physical exercise while studying is also important and will actually help you retain the geographic information for a longer period of time.

One of the things that I struggled with was controlling my nerves during the competition. A technique I found effective was taking slow, deep breaths and focusing on my questions alone. Visualizing myself performing well also helped me to calm down. Also, don't be afraid to reach out to your parents, teachers, friends, other contestants, or even past Bee participants for advice about the competition. Think of the Bee as a team effort—everyone wants you to succeed! Lastly, forget about the competition. Geography is a fascinating and extremely relevant topic. No matter how you place in the Bee, you will have an improved knowledge of the world for the rest of your life.

Grace Rembert, 2013, 2015, and 2016 State Bee Champion; 2016 Top Ten National Finalist (8th Grade)

In my three-year history of participating in the National Geographic Bee, I have several tidbits of advice I can give to upcoming Bee participants. Although the title depicts the competition as a "Geography Bee," it is much more than just geography. The Nat Geo Bee is all about relating people, cultures, and the environment and applying them to geographical elements of certain regions around the world. When I study and prepare for the Bee, I'll scan maps with my mind, but I won't completely memorize the exact layout of a certain map. Even though I think [composing] a visualization of a map in your head is necessary for success in the Geography Bee, I think it is better to evaluate and [make] connections to the real world while analyzing maps. I also think a great study method is reading country and state indexes. These small sections of information are excellent for Bee preparation as they don't exclusively highlight geographical details. They include cultural, environmental, climate, and geopolitical information. Over the last year, the CIA *World Factbook* has become a favorite for studying.

A final tip for Geo Bee preparation is having a strong grasp of geographical reasoning. Personally, I think geographical reasoning is much more useful than memorizing geographical facts, because it challenges your mind to apply what you've learned. These are only a few of the study tips I use, but I hope they are useful in your geography preparation.

Thomas Wright, 2016 State Champion and Top Ten National Finalist (7th Grade), Wisconsin

. . . .

View the Bee as an adventure, and you, the adventurer. When adventurers discover a new place, they don't just take a quick glance and move on. Instead, they look for something interesting, and spend time to learn more about it. Similarly, when learning about a new place, don't be shy to stray away from the major facts. If you find a certain fact intriguing, read more about it, until you are satisfied with what you have

learned. I found that often it was the information that I learned in these digressions that made me successful at competition.

Vansh Jain, 2009, 2010, and 2012 State Bee Champion, Wisconsin; 2009 Top Ten National Finalist (5th Grade); 2010 Top Ten National Finalist (6th Grade); 2012 Second Place National Bee (8th Grade); Three-time Top Ten National Finalist

· ·

Two items were crucial in my Bee preparation: a small atlas and my phone. I always glanced at my atlas after finishing my work at school; constant reinforcement of your mental map is beneficial. Also, I always had oodles of geography-related Wikipedia articles open on my phone's Internet browser. I could read about exports of Zambia anytime on the bus ride home! These small things throughout my day really added up.

Most importantly, look up the things you don't know. If you hear something and don't know where it is located, take the opportunity to learn. I don't think we appreciate the Internet enough—basically everything is available. But don't turn your back on good old paper maps! Use every resource you have to help your geographical journey.

Lucy Chae, 2015 State Bee Champion, Massachusetts (7th Grade); 2015 Top Ten National Finalist; 2016 Massachusetts State Runner-Up (8th Grade)

· ·

I prepared for the Bee by having my family go through questions in the *National Geographic Bee Official Study Guide, Afghanistan to Zimbabwe,* and *The Geography Bee Complete Preparation Handbook,* looking at atlases, and watching TV programs, especially the History and Travel

Channels. Before the competition, I contacted the previous state winner for New Jersey to see what tips he had.

Evan Meltzer, 2006 State Bee Champion, New Jersey (8th Grade)

. . . .

When preparing for the Bee, remember that the competition is not just about memorization: It requires an in-depth understanding of the United States and the world. While memorizing capitals will help with some questions, one of the best ways to prepare is by looking through maps and atlases and gaining a general idea of what places look like spatially. Preparing this way allows you to think spatially in the competition, which is something that helped me succeed. Additionally, keep in mind that while there is a time limit for answering questions, you can significantly benefit from taking your time on each one. Once you hear a question, think of an answer, confirm it mentally, and then say it aloud. Fifteen seconds is plenty of time to think about the question, so don't answer in the first one or two seconds. Also, if you can't understand a question clearly, don't hesitate to ask for a spelling or repetition. If you think it could make the difference between a right and wrong answer, it is in your best interest to use this option. Taking advantage of the time and options you have when answering a question can help you minimize mistakes and give you a competitive advantage.

Pranit Nanda, 2011 State Bee Runner-Up (5th Grade), 2012 State Bee Champion (6th Grade), Colorado; 2013 Top Ten National Finalist (7th Grade); 2014 Top Ten National Finalist (8th Grade)

. . . .

My first and most important tip is to be passionate! When preparing for the Bee, it's so important to find the aspects of geography that you're most curious about. Personally, my favorite part about geography was

discovering all the unique and beautiful cultures across the globe. By learning about cultures, I was able to integrate other aspects of geography into my study routine by exploring where these cultural and ethnic groups lived, how they lived, who they interacted with, etc. Since all aspects of geography are interconnected, finding something you love to study will make it easier and more interesting to learn new things.

My second piece of advice is to just have fun with it. While that sounds clichéd, finding new and exciting ways to study is really what helped me become immersed in geography, which ultimately made me compete better. During my spring vacation between Nationals and States, my whole family would have a "multicultural week," when we would go out to a new ethnic restaurant each night and watch foreign films as I learned about various regions of the world. By doing this, I got to truly understand the places I was learning about, and even discovered my favorite international cuisine (Thai) and movie (*North Face*, a German film that I highly recommend). Also, be sure to keep up with current events by watching the news. It's the best way not only to be an informed global citizen, but also to understand where and why global issues are occurring.

Neelam Sandhu, 2012–2013 State Bee Champion, New Hampshire (7th–8th Grade); 2012–2013 Top Ten National Finalist (7th–8th Grade); 2013 National Geographic World Geography Champion (Team), St. Petersburg, Russia (8th Grade)

. . . .

There are a few tips I would like to share with all future aspirants. One is that it's never too late to start the journey of geography. If you put [in] a lot of effort and hard work, then success could come. Second, is to never get intimidated by the older folks, always believe in yourself and have confidence, but at the same time don't be overconfident. Third, if you are [made]

nervous by the audience, then I recommend you look down or concentrate on a spot in the room and listen to the question, or close your eyes.

Another tip is to never blurt out the answer to a question; always process it in your mind and then give your firm answer. If you don't know the question, there will always be clues, which you can connect or relate to a certain country or place. Lastly, if you are a beginner in the Nat Geo Bee, I would prefer starting with basic facts, like U.S. states and features and at least the currency, capital, and major geographic features. A start is to have a large world wall map. Best wishes to you all geo explorers!

Ameya Mujumdar, Florida, 2014 National Runner-Up (5th Grade)

Studying geography for me meant studying maps, first identifying all the major physical features and then, one by one, studying each of those features more closely to understand the details surrounding them … start studying first with simple maps like [the] *National Geographic Kids Atlas*, and as you get more comfortable you can graduate to [a] more comprehensive atlas. Studying should be done starting with the simplest things and then adding layers upon that foundation. Keep a Word document for the facts so you can revise old information while also adding new facts. Whenever [you are] studying, find some fun facts about different countries, which helps to make studying interesting. Use blank maps and make sure you get a mental map of various features and locations. Sometimes the amount of material that needs to be covered seems difficult and also frustrating, so keep a mark of your progress which will help in those situations. Just remember all the studying improves your knowledge and makes you better aware of the world around [you]. That in itself is the reward you get from geography. In addition, you will know what it feels like to succeed through hard work and preparation.

Saketh Jonnalagadda, 2016 National Runner-Up (6th Grade)

Many centuries ago the great Mongol ruler Genghis Khan united his nomad tribes into a formidable army. His Golden Horde swept across the Central Asian steppe on horseback, terrorizing and plundering settlements from the Caspian Sea to the Pacific Ocean. They devastated cities, redirected rivers, and left deserts crowded with fleeing refugees. The Chinese built the Great Wall to keep the "barbarians" out, the Persians hid from them, and the Europeans fell like matchsticks. At the time of Genghis Khan's death in 1227, he controlled one of the greatest land empires the world has ever known.

Mr. Khan succeeded because, unlike the Europeans, his army did not wear heavy armor or burden itself with supply wagons that could break down. The Mongols traveled exceptionally light and fast. Their excellent use of geographic information made this possible. Mongol scouts went out months ahead of the main army, secretly gathering

crucial information about terrain, vegetation, and settlements. This later assured the best routes, food for the men and ponies, and great hideaways. In a nutshell (or saddlebag), the Mongol scouts were simply the best.

Although great for the 13th century, Genghis's information was meager compared with what our current atlases, globes, and reference books can provide. Throw in television, the Internet, e-mail, and cell phones that allow instant information to flow around the globe, and you have an advantage that might have turned back even the Golden Horde.

The Mongols aside, just imagine how historic news headlines might have read if our current geographic information and communications technology had been available long ago. We might have seen: "GPS Navigation Guides Columbus to New World (film and details at 11:00)!" "Paul Revere E-Mails Alert From North Church!" "Custer's Lieutenant Faxes Map of Indian Camps." "Cell Phone Saves Captain Scott at South Pole."

The good news today is that for modest barter or a quick crusade to your local library, even ordinary peasants can obtain geographic learning materials the great Khan would have loved (and probably even killed for). An exhaustive list would make a book in itself, so this one simply highlights proven resources that will help you learn to think like a geographer.

ATLASES

Even if you're not scheming to plunder European villages, a good world atlas belongs in every ger, or yurt. This is the standard reference

for Bee preparation, and it should include a full set of political, physical, and thematic maps (population, economic, climate, etc.). Also, look for country profiles, information about the oceans, plate tectonics, time zones, geographic comparisons, and more.

Our rapidly changing world alters the political landscape very quickly, so beware if your atlas is more than five years old, as some country names and boundaries may be outdated. The same is true for population figures and similar statistics. The rule of thumb is always to look for the most recent edition. Also, check to see if a less expensive paperback edition is available.

Large World Atlases
National Geographic Atlas of the World, 10th Edition. National Geographic Books, Washington, D.C., 2014.
A superb collection of political, physical, urban, regional, and ocean-floor maps; thematic maps covering topics such as climate patterns, plate tectonics, population, economic trends, and world cultures; country profiles; satellite imagery; information on temperature and rainfall; geographic comparisons; and a comprehensive index.

Midsize World Atlases
National Geographic Family Reference Atlas of the World, 4th Edition. National Geographic Books, Washington, D.C., 2015.
A comprehensive, family-friendly atlas with sections about the world, continents, oceans, and space. It includes an expansive thematic section with maps, graphs, charts, photographs, and an extensive list of geographic comparisons.

Rand McNally Goode's World Atlas, 23rd Edition. Rand McNally & Co., Skokie, IL, 2016.

A comprehensive world atlas that includes a wide variety of thematic maps, world and regional maps, geographic comparison tables, and explanations of map scale, map projections, and Earth-sun relationships.

National Geographic Collegiate Atlas of the World, 2nd Edition. National Geographic Books, Washington, D.C., 2011.

This detailed atlas features excellent world and regional maps. The many thematic maps (e.g., Health and Literacy, Defense and Conflict, Protected Lands) are a real strength.

Children's and Student World Atlases

National Geographic Student World Atlas, 4th Edition. National Geographic Kids Books, Washington, D.C., 2014. (Grades 6–10)

Packed with informative thematic maps that explore the world's physical and human systems, focusing on geology, climate, vegetation, population, economies, food, energy, and mineral resources. For each continent there are three sets of maps (physical and political, climate and precipitation, population and predominant economies) plus a photo essay. Websites are included for finding additional information and updating statistics.

National Geographic Kids World Atlas, 4th Edition (updated). National Geographic Kids Books, Washington, D.C., 2013. (Grades 3–7)

Winner of the Parents' Choice Gold Award, this atlas contains world

thematic maps, photo essays, satellite images, physical and political maps of each continent, country profiles, geographic comparisons, a glossary, and a comprehensive index.

Specialty Atlases

National Geographic Concise Atlas of the World, 4th Edition. National Geographic Books, Washington, D.C., 2016.

National Geographic Global Atlas: A Comprehensive Picture of the World Today With More Than 300 New Maps, Infographics, and Illustrations. National Geographic Books, Washington, D.C., 2013.

National Geographic Kids United States Atlas, 5th Edition. National Geographic Kids Books, Washington, D.C., 2017.
Superb U.S., state, and regional maps explain the primary geographical relationships in the United States. This fifth edition features concise state profiles, photographic essays on each region and state, and thematic spreads on topics such as natural disasters, immigration, and climate change.

Atlas of Global Development: A Visual Guide to the World's Greatest Challenges, 4th Edition. World Bank Publications, Washington, D.C., 2013.
Easy-to-read world maps, tables, and graphs highlight key social, economic, and environmental data for the world's economies. Topics include infant mortality, gross domestic product, female labor, drinking water, forest cover, and CO_2 emissions.

Student Atlas of World Politics, 10th Edition. McGraw/Dushkin, New York, NY, 2012.

Emphasizes current affairs that reflect recent developments in political geography and international relations. This collection of maps and data is particularly useful for exploring the relationships between geography and world politics.

GEOGRAPHIC REFERENCE BOOKS

Merriam-Webster's Geographical Dictionary, Revised 3rd Edition. Merriam-Webster, Inc., Springfield, MA, 2007.

Provides an alphabetical listing of more than 54,000 places and features, with concise information about each plus hundreds of maps and tables.

The National Geographic Bee Ultimate Fact Book: Countries A to Z. Andrew Wojtanik. National Geographic Kids Books, Washington, D.C., 2012.

This updated book is full of facts about 195 countries that the author compiled to help him study for and win the 2004 National Geographic Bee.

National Geographic United States Encyclopedia. National Geographic Kids Books, Washington, D.C., 2015.

Organized by geographic regions, this book is packed with specially designed maps and concise essays that explore the history, climate, natural resources, and physical features of each region, each state, the District of Columbia, and the territories.

ALMANACS

The World Almanac and Book of Facts 2017. Sarah Janssen. World Almanac Books, New York, NY, 2016.

Abundant information on essential topics, such as animals, computers, inventions, movies and television, religion, and sports. This fact book includes many photographs, illustrations, and maps, along with puzzles, brainteasers, and other activities.

The World Almanac and Book of Facts 2017. Sarah Janssen. World Almanac Books, New York, NY, 2017.

A classic annual with a price that drops during the year. Crammed with global facts from farm imports to volcanic activity to baseball batting averages.

National Geographic Almanac of World History, 3rd Edition. Patricia Daniels and Stephen G. Hyslop. National Geographic Books, Washington, D.C., 2014.

Through essays, detailed maps, charts, and time lines, this book traces world history from the dawn of humanity to the 21st century.

National Geographic Kids Almanac 2017. National Geographic Kids Books, Washington, D.C., 2016.

This colorful page-turner is packed with fun-to-browse features, useful reference material, homework help developed by educators, and quirky facts. Every chapter is updated annually with new content: animal photography; cool inventions; adventure; nature; maps of the continents; hundreds of facts and figures; and fascinating stories about incredible creatures, space, vacations, and more.

GEOGRAPHY TEXTBOOKS

Fourth- through eighth-grade social studies textbooks are a great source for learning about geography. As your skills improve, check out the textbooks for more advanced levels. Don't be afraid of college textbooks. They may be more difficult to read, but if you understand geography fundamentals they offer a comprehensive and advanced tutorial on most topics. You can find these texts in bookstores, especially college and secondhand bookstores. Or surf the Internet for the best bargains (search under "used college textbooks"). College and university libraries shelve textbooks. Many state and community colleges will allow you to obtain a library card so you can borrow books. If a book was published in the last five years, check for a companion website with chapter summaries and a dizzying array of self tests.

LITERATURE

Reading nonfiction books on just about any topic—exploration, sports, survival, wars, biography, or even regional cookbooks!—can help expand your geographic knowledge. Even fiction has to have a setting, and most authors carefully research the background for their plots. This means that just about anything you read can add to your geographic knowledge.

ONLINE RESOURCES

There are many great stops on our rapidly emerging information superhighway. Beware that URL addresses change frequently. If you have trouble finding any, consult one of the popular Internet search engines, such as Google (google.com), Yahoo! (yahoo.com), and

Bing (bing.com), and simply request the site name. In any search engine, entering key words such as geography games, geography facts, or geography maps, will produce an array of sites to explore and learn about our world.

Check out the main National Geographic website—nationalgeographic.com—or one of the following:

National Geographic Bee: nationalgeographic.com/bee: a site that offers five new National Geographic Bee questions each day

UN Atlas of the Oceans: oceansatlas.org
An excellent source of readily accessible and up-to-the-minute information about oceans. Designed for government policy experts and students alike, this site provides information relevant to the sustainable development of the oceans, from basic explanations to intricate data sets.

Quintessential Instructional Archive: quia.com/shared/geography
A good flash card quiz site, with plenty of other interactive games. Navigate the pull-down menu for dozens of worthwhile activities.

World Resources Institute: wri.org
Click on Climate and Energy.

Geography: thoughtco.com/geography-4133035
This site offers free downloads and links to other geography sites, outline maps, and current events.

Population Reference Bureau: prb.org
The best source for world population, with interactive population pyramids, a quiz, recent news, country data, and links to other sites.

The CIA *World Factbook*:
cia.gov/library/publications/the-world-factbook
Downloadable maps, current information, and background data on every country.

NASA Space Place for Kids: spaceplace.nasa.gov
This site features information on Earth's surface, weather, oceans, and more. It includes games and activities.

United Nations: un.org
Full of country facts, statistics, current events, maps, and more.

Newspapers online: onlinenewspapers.com
This site features thousands of links to all of the world's online newspapers and other sources of information. A great source for current events from a global perspective. Many are published in languages native to the region, but nearly every highly populated country and many regional papers offer an English edition.

Kids and Climate Change Canada: canada.ca/en/services/environment/weather/climatechange/climate-action/kids-climate-change
Check out the useful resources on this page and try taking the "Kids Challenge" and taking part in the "Creative Social Media Mission."

Canadian Geographic Education: cangeoeducation.ca
Canada's top site to learn about its people and places. Offers quizzes.

National Atlas of Canada: atlas.gc.ca
Great technical information, maps, and educational materials.

California Geographical Survey World Atlas of Panoramic
Aerial Images:
californiageographicalsurvey.com/world_atlas
Test your knowledge of mountains, rivers, peninsulas, and all the
rest—from space! Accurate and downloadable, these images offer a
perspective very different from maps.

Google Earth: google.com/earth
Curious about what La Paz, the Nile River, or the Fedchenko
Glacier actually looks like from above? Google Earth takes you there.
First, download the free software, and then use the images to build
your mental map of the world.

GREAT GEO GAMES

Carmen Sandiego. The Learning Company.
This clever quiz game tests your geographic knowledge, from the
United States and beyond.

Brain Quest—Know the States! Game. Educational Insights,
Rancho Dominguez, CA.
An entertaining board game that teaches locations, capital cities,
American culture, and scenic features for all 50 states.

Name That Country. Educational Insights,
Rancho Dominguez, CA.

A board game that uses names, salutations, or special features on postcards to help you identify countries and capitals. The game can be played at varying levels of difficulty and tests knowledge of rivers, major cities, languages, and currencies.

Go Travel: Africa, South America. Travel by Games, Clinton, IA.

These fun card games test your knowledge of the history, geography, people, plants, animals, and problems on these continents.

GeoSafari Talking Globe. Educational Insights,
Rancho Dominguez, CA.

A talking geography quiz game and globe all in one. The 5,000-interactive-question database challenges players about their world knowledge. An advanced version offers 10,000 questions.

OTHER STUDY AIDS

Globes

Globes are available from a variety of manufacturers. Be sure to check the product date before ordering. Those produced by National Geographic can be found on the Society's website (nationalgeographic.com) or by calling 1-800-647-5463.

Magazines

National Geographic magazine, *National Geographic Kids, National Geographic Explorer, Canadian Geographic, Time for Kids* (TFK),

and newsweeklies, such as *Time, Newsweek,* and *U.S. News & World Report,* include great articles, maps, graphs, and pictures.

Television

Programming on the National Geographic Channel, PBS (*Nature, Bill Nye the Science Guy, Kratts' Creatures,* etc.), CNN, C-SPAN, the Discovery Channel, the History Channel, and nightly news broadcasts will greatly expand your world.

Mo Rocca's *Innovation Nation* on CBS will widen your worldview by introducing you to people from all over the world who are creating innovative solutions to real problems.

CD-ROMs

The National Geographic Society, Rand McNally, GeoSafari, Hammond, and George F. Cram offer many digital versions of their world atlases, picture libraries, and other specific topics (history, world regions, exploration, etc.). Be sure to check the operating system requirements before purchasing any software.

Blank Outline Maps

Free downloads are available online from the following:
National Geographic Education:
nationalgeographic.org/education/mapping/outline-map/
Arizona Geographic Alliance: geoalliance.asu.edu/maps
Search online to locate additional blank outline maps.

Note to Teachers

The National Geographic Society developed the National Geographic Bee in response to concern about the lack of geographic knowledge among young people in the United States. In a ten-country Gallup survey conducted for the Society in 1988 and 1989, Americans 18 to 24 (the youngest group surveyed) scored lower than their counterparts in the other nine countries. Shocked by such poor results, the National Geographic Society spearheaded a campaign to return geography to American classrooms. Since 1989, the Bee has been one of several projects designed to encourage the teaching and study of geography. With more than two million fourth through eighth graders entering each year, the Bee is one of the nation's most popular academic contests.

Some parents and even a few teachers think the Bee might resemble an orderly Trivial Pursuit contest. Indeed, kids who correctly answer questions on topics such as glacial erosion, Hinduism, location, and changing political blocks humble a new flock of adults every year. The annual assembly of teachers,

parents, and media is impressed not just with what the contestants know right off the bat but also with how they methodically answer questions that at first appear to stump them. This ability to think like a geographer—to integrate physical, cultural, and economic knowledge—shines through at every level of the Bee.

Teaching young people to think like geographers provides them with a vital understanding of the connections that exist among ourselves, our global neighbors, and the physical environment that supports us all. The U.S. Congress has recognized this important role by designating geography as one of ten core academic subjects included in federal education acts that have been passed into law since 1994. Unfortunately, in the No Child Left Behind Act that was passed in 2001, geography lacks the designated funding mandates that accompany other core academic subjects. Ongoing efforts by the National Geographic Society and others seek to improve this situation so that teachers can receive the support they need to provide crucial geographic education.

The National Geographic Society also offers many forms of support to teachers who seek to enhance the geographic education they provide to students. The national K–12 geography standards, published as *Geography for Life: National Geography Standards,* 2nd Edition (2012), are a comprehensive presentation of what students should know and be able to do as the result of their educational experiences. Accompanying these voluntary national standards are *Path Toward World Literacy: A Standards-Based Guide to K–12 Geography* and the Road Map Project, which present a scope and sequence for teaching geography along with

explanations and activities that assist teachers, curriculum writers, parents, and the general public to effectively integrate the geography standards into the school curriculum. The National Geography Standards have been incorporated into the curriculum frameworks of almost all of the 50 U.S. states.

In addition to the national K–12 geography standards, a Network of Alliances for Geographic Education—partnerships between university faculty and K–12 educators (nationalgeographic.org/education/programs/geography-alliances)—has chapters in most U.S. states and provides training and support for educators. Whether teaching a stand-alone geography class or wishing to incorporate geography into other subjects such as history, science, or vocational education, teachers can tap into a wealth of resources through the Geographic Alliance Network. It offers opportunities for professional development training, ready-to-use lesson plans and other teaching resources, and interaction with a community of professionals at the local school, state, and university levels who provide the mentoring, contacts, assistance, and camaraderie that help to energize the daily task of teaching.

National Geographic also offers an education site and EdNet (nationalgeographic.com/foundation/geographic_literacy.html), an online community that provides education news, resources, discussion, and much more. The education site provides links to maps, activities, and other programs for educators at National Geographic.

Contact information for schools to register for the Bee, obtain the geography standards, locate a state alliance, or obtain online geography education information appears below. These are the

perfect places to receive answers to your questions and to explore the world of possibilities in geography education.

Whether you are an experienced geo-educator or a newcomer, the Bee is a sure bet to stir student interest in the "Why of Where." Running the contest is simple. The Society provides registered schools with an instruction booklet, the questions and answers, certificates, and prizes. Think of the Bee as an open door to a world of fun and productive learning.

GEOGRAPHIC SUPPORT COORDINATES

To register for the National Geographic Bee

U.S. schools with students in grades 4–8 may visit natgeobee.org starting in August to register their school for the Bee. Only a school employee can register a school. The early-bird registration fee is $100 (cost in 2016) for schools that register before mid-December, and schools can pay by check or credit card. From mid-December to mid-January, the registration fee increases to $120 (cost in 2016), and schools may pay by credit card only. For the most current information, visit natgeobee.org or e-mail ngbee@ngs.org.

For information about the Canadian Geographic Challenge go to

challenge.canadiangeographic.ca/en

To find your state geographic alliance office and for other education resources, go to

nationalgeographic.org/education

To order *Geography for Life: National Geography Standards*, go to

ncge.org/geography-for-life

To order *Path Toward World Literacy: A Standards-Based Guide to K–12 Geography*, go to

amazon.com/TOWARD-WORLD-LITERACY-STANDARDS-BASED-GEOGRAPHY/dp/0792284410

To order more copies of the fifth edition of *How to Win the National Geographic Bee: Official Study Guide* or *The National Geographic Bee Ultimate Fact Book: Countries A to Z* (by 2004 Bee winner Andrew Wojtanik) go to shop.nationalgeographic.com/category/books **or any place that books are sold.**

Answers

Round 1: State Savvy
1. Illinois
2. North Dakota
3. Wyoming
4. Florida
5. California
6. Louisiana
7. Alaska
8. Texas
9. Kentucky
10. Kansas

Round 2: U.S. Road Trip
1. Pennsylvania
2. Arizona
3. Illinois
4. Texas
5. Missouri
6. Virginia
7. Wyoming
8. West Virginia
9. Washington
10. Tennessee

Round 3: Discover National Parks
1. gray whale
2. spruce trees
3. elk
4. bats
5. subarctic
6. mangrove
7. black bear
8. sea star
9. geyser
10. bald cypress

Round 4: Weird But True!
1. Europe
2. Asia
3. Australia
4. Africa
5. South America
6. Asia
7. North America
8. Africa
9. Europe
10. Australia

Round 5: Geo Extremes
1. Nepal
2. Algeria
3. Bolivia
4. United States
5. Norway
6. Ethiopia
7. Nigeria
8. Kazakhstan
9. South Africa
10. Cuba

Round 6: Odd One Out
1. Egypt
2. Uzbekistan
3. Pakistan
4. Thailand
5. Nigeria
6. Syria
7. Nicaragua
8. Germany
9. Indonesia
10. Chad

Round 7: Awesome Adventures
1. United Kingdom
2. China
3. Austria
4. Brazil
5. Canada
6. New Zealand
7. Russia
8. Namibia
9. Italy
10. Nepal

Tiebreaker Questions
1. Mojave [mo-HAH-vee] Desert
2. meridians
3. Strait of Magellan
4. Texas
5. France
6. Arabic
7. Black Sea
8. India

SCHOOL-LEVEL FINAL
1. Ohio
2. Utah
3. Texas
4. Rhode Island
5. Minnesota
6. Alaska
7. New York
8. Hawaii
9. United Kingdom
10. Australia
11. Switzerland
12. Lake Ontario
13. cranberries
14. India
15. Venice
16. Cuba
17. Kansas

Map Questions
1. New York
2. Nevada
3. Louisiana
4. Minnesota
5. Washington
6. Iowa

Championship Round
1. Idaho
2. London

Championship Tiebreaker
1. Antarctica
2. Novosibirsk
[noh-vuh-suh-BEERSK]

QUALIFYING TEST
1. 1 year
2. Atlantic City
3. steel plow
4. acid rain
5. Japan
6. aloe
7. wood
8. hydrogen
9. Florida
10. 23rd Street to Ohio Drive

Analogies
1. Galápagos Islands
2. India
3. languages

STATE-LEVEL PRELIMINARY

Round 1: State Savvy
1. West Virginia
2. Louisiana
3. Vermont
4. Colorado
5. Arizona
6. Maine
7. Utah
8. Texas
9. Idaho
10. Hawaii

Round 2: Our National Monuments
1. Virginia
2. Minnesota
3. Utah
4. Oregon
5. Iowa
6. Missouri
7. New York
8. Montana
9. Texas
10. Alabama

Round 3: Weird But True!
1. United Kingdom
2. Argentina
3. Finland
4. Costa Rica
5. Australia
6. Brazil
7. Kazakhstan
8. Indonesia
9. Ecuador
10. Canada

Round 4: Odd Item Out
1. North Korea
2. Afghanistan
3. Kenya
4. Sweden
5. Vietnam
6. Tanzania
7. Barbados
8. Italy
9. Russia
10. Turkmenistan

Round 5: Protecting Wildlife

1. rhinoceros
2. river dolphin
3. snowy egret
4. zebra
5. kangaroo rat
6. mountain gorilla
7. blue whale
8. Chatham albatross
9. badger
10. jaguar

Round 6: Forces of Nature

1. Egypt
2. Pakistan
3. Philippines
4. Chile
5. Uruguay
6. New Zealand
7. Honduras
8. Liberia
9. Sri Lanka
10. Venezuela

Round 7: Watery Planet

1. Lake Gatún
2. Arafura Sea
3. Bight of Bonny
4. Bo Hai
5. North Sea
6. Yucatán Channel
7. Norwegian Sea
8. Sea of Galilee
9. Bellingshausen Sea
10. Tyrrhenian Sea

Round 8: World Music

1. Iran
2. Indonesia
3. Venezuela
4. Armenia
5. India
6. Malawi
7. Ecuador
8. Dominican Republic
9. Trinidad and Tobago
10. Mozambique

Tiebreaker Questions

1. Africa
2. Japan
3. Italy
4. New Zealand
5. Atlantic Ocean
6. Johannesburg
7. Hudson Bay
8. Iran

STATE-LEVEL FINAL

1. Alabama
2. Virginia
3. Louisiana
4. Hawaii
5. Texas
6. California
7. Massachusetts
8. Iowa
9. Japan
10. France
11. Peru
12. India
13. Switzerland
14. Philippines
15. New Zealand
16. Australia
17. Pacific Ocean

Map Questions
1. 6, Virginia
2. 13, Utah
3. 21, Wyoming
4. 14, Florida
5. 20, Colorado
6. 4, Maine
7. 9, Arkansas

Photo Questions
1. Indonesia
2. Namibia
3. Norway
4. Bahamas

Championship Round
1. United Arab Emirates
2. Solomon Islands

Championship Tiebreaker
1. Azores
2. Pakistan

NATIONAL-LEVEL PRELIMINARY

Round 1: Globetrotter
1. Niger River
2. Iran

Round 2: Dare to Explore
1. William Baffin
2. Mary Kingsley

Round 3: Rankings
1. Philippines, Indonesia, Egypt
2. Lake Constance, Lake Balaton, Lake Ladoga

Round 4: Weird But True!
1. São Paulo
2. Vancouver

Round 5: Your World
1. Denmark
2. Turkey

Round 6: Destinations of a Lifetime
1. Quintana Roo
2. South Georgia

Round 7: Geography Rocks!
1. copper
2. amber

Round 8: World National Parks (Maps Questions)
1. 30, Thailand
2. 29, Venezuela

Round 9: City Situation
1. on the banks of the Bow River
2. on the banks of the Tigris River

Round 10: Analogies
1. Almaty
2. Guatemala

**Countries
of the World
Index**

Earth's surface is approximately 70.9% water and 29.1% land. The National Geographic Society recognizes four oceans (in order of size): Pacific, Atlantic, Indian, and Arctic; and seven continents (in order of size): Asia, Africa, North America, South America, Antarctica, Europe, and Australia (including the islands of Oceania).

The U.S. Department of State recognizes 195 independent states, as well as 72 dependent areas and territories spread across six continents. Antarctica has no permanent population. It is used for peaceful purposes only and is governed under the terms of the Antarctic Treaty System. Africa has 54 countries; Europe has 49* countries; Asia has 48* countries; North America has 23 countries; Australia/Oceania has 14 countries; and South America has 12 countries.

The world population, which is estimated to be 7,323,187,457 (July 2016),† is growing at an annual rate of 1.06%. The five most populous countries are China, India, the United States, Indonesia, and Brazil. The five least populous countries are the Holy See (Vatican City), Nauru, Tuvalu, Palau, and Monaco. More than half of

the world's people live in urban areas. An estimated 7,100 languages are spoken in the world. The most widely spoken as first languages are Chinese, Spanish, English, Arabic, and Hindi. The most widely observed religions are Christianity, Islam, and Hinduism.

In the country index to follow, you will find a number next to each country name. This number corresponds with each country's location on the continent map at the beginning of each section.

*Five countries are shared by Europe and Asia: Azerbaijan, Georgia, Kazakhstan, Russia, and Turkey.

†CIA *World Factbook* (July 2016)

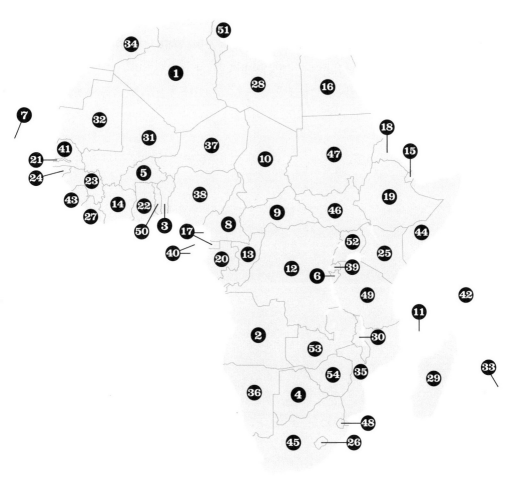

❶ ALGERIA

Area: 919,595 mi²
   (2,381,740 km²)
Capital: Algiers
Population: 40,263,711
Population growth rate: 1.8%
Urban population: 70.7%
Official language: Arabic
Religion: Muslim

❷ ANGOLA

Area: 481,354 mi²
   (1,246,700 km²)
Capital: Luanda
Population: 20,172,332
Population growth rate: 2.7%
Urban population: 44%
Official language: Portuguese
Religion: Christian

❸ BENIN

Area: 43,484 mi² (112,622 km²)
Capital: Porto-Novo
Population: 10,741,458
Population growth rate: 2.8%
Urban population: 44%
Official language: French
Religions: Christian, Muslim

❹ BOTSWANA

Area: 224,607 mi²
   (581,730 km²)
Capital: Gaborone
Population: 2,209,208
Population growth rate: 1.2%
Urban population: 57.4%
Official language: Setswana
Religion: Christian

❺ BURKINA FASO

Area: 105,869 mi²
   (274,200 km²)
Capital: Ouagadougou
Population: 19,512,533
Population growth rate: 3.0%
Urban population: 29.9%
Official language: French
Religion: Muslim

❻ BURUNDI

Area: 10,745 mi² (27,830 km²)
Capital: Bujumbura
Population: 11,099,298
Population growth rate: 3.3%
Urban population: 12.1%
Official languages: Kirundi,
   French
Religion: Christian

❼ CABO VERDE

Area: 1,557 mi² (4,033 km²)
Capital: Praia
Population: 533,432
Population growth rate: 1.4%
Urban population: 65.5%
Official language: Portuguese
Religion: Christian

❽ CAMEROON

Area: 183,568 mi²
(475,440 km²)
Capital: Yaoundé
Population: 24,360,803
Population growth rate: 2.6%
Urban population: 54.4%
Official languages: English,
French
Religion: Christian

❾ CENTRAL AFRICAN REPUBLIC

Area: 240,535 mi²
(622,984 km²)
Capital: Bangui
Population: 5,507,257
Population growth rate: 2.1%
Urban population: 40.0%
Official language: French
Religion: Indigenous beliefs

❿ CHAD

Area: 495,755 mi² (1,284,000 km²)
Capital: N'Djamena
Population: 11,852,462
Population growth rate: 1.9%
Urban population: 22.5%
Official languages: French,
Arabic
Religion: Muslim

⓫ COMOROS

Area: 863 mi² (2,235 km²)
Capital: Moroni
Population: 794,678
Population growth rate: 1.7%
Urban population: 28.3%
Official languages: Arabic,
French, Shikomoro
Religion: Muslim

⓬ CONGO, DEMOCRATIC REPUBLIC OF THE

Area: 905,355 mi² (2,344,858 km²)
Capital: Kinshasa
Population: 81,331,050
Population growth rate: 2.4%
Urban population: 42.5%
Official language: French
Religion: Christian

13 CONGO, REPUBLIC OF THE

Area: 132,047 mi²
(342,000 km²)
Capital: Brazzaville
Population: 4,852,412
Population growth rate: 2.1%
Urban population: 65.4%
Official language: French
Religion: Christian

14 CÔTE D'IVOIRE

Area: 124,504 mi²
(322,463 km²)
Capital: Yamoussoukro
Population: 23,740,424
Population growth rate: 1.9%
Urban population: 54.2%
Official language: French
Religion: Muslim

15 DJIBOUTI

Area: 8,958 mi² (23,200 km²)
Capital: Djibouti
Population: 846,687
Population growth rate: 2.2%
Urban population: 77.3%
Official languages: French,
Arabic
Religion: Muslim

16 EGYPT

Area: 386,662 mi²
(1,001,450 km²)
Capital: Cairo
Population: 94,666,993
Population growth rate: 2.5%
Urban population: 43.1%
Official language: Arabic
Religion: Muslim

17 EQUATORIAL GUINEA

Area: 10,831 mi² (28,051 km²)
Capital: Malabo
Population: 759,451
Population growth rate: 2.5%
Urban population: 39.9%
Official languages: Spanish,
French
Religion: Christian

18 ERITREA

Area: 45,406 mi² (117,600 km²)
Capital: Asmara
Population: 5,869,869
Population growth rate: 0.8%
Urban population: 22.6%
Official languages: Tigrinya,
Arabic, English
Religion: Muslim

⑲ ETHIOPIA

Area: 426,373 mi²
(1,104,300 km²)
Capital: Addis Ababa
Population: 102,374,044
Population growth rate: 2.9%
Urban population: 19.5%
Official language: Amharic
Religion: Christian

⑳ GABON

Area: 103,347 mi²
(267,667 km²)
Capital: Libreville
Population: 1,738,541
Population growth rate: 1.9%
Urban population: 87.2%
Official language: French
Religion: Christian

㉑ THE GAMBIA

Area: 4,363 mi² (11,300 km²)
Capital: Banjul
Population: 2,009,648
Population growth rate: 2.1%
Urban population: 59.6%
Official language: English
Religion: Muslim

㉒ GHANA

Area: 92,098 mi² (238,533 km²)
Capital: Accra
Population: 26,908,262
Population growth rate: 2.2%
Urban population: 54.0%
Official language: English
Religion: Christian

㉓ GUINEA

Area: 94,926 mi² (245,857 km²)
Capital: Conakry
Population: 12,093,349
Population growth rate: 2.6%
Urban population: 37.2%
Official language: French
Religion: Muslim

㉔ GUINEA-BISSAU

Area: 13,948 mi² (36,125 km²)
Capital: Bissau
Population: 1,759,159
Population growth rate: 1.9%
Urban population: 49.3%
Official language: Portuguese
Religion: Muslim

25 KENYA

Area: 224,081 mi² (580,367 km²)
Capital: Nairobi
Population: 46,790,758
Population growth rate: 1.8%
Urban population: 25.6%
Official languages: English, Kiswahili
Religion: Christian

26 LESOTHO

Area: 11,720 mi² (30,355 km²)
Capital: Maseru
Population: 1,953,070
Population growth rate: 0.3%
Urban population: 27.3%
Official languages: Sesotho, English
Religion: Christian

27 LIBERIA

Area: 43,000 mi² (111,369 km²)
Capital: Monrovia
Population: 4,299,944
Population growth rate: 2.4%
Urban population: 49.7%
Official language: English
Religion: Christian

28 LIBYA

Area: 679,362 mi² (1,759,540 km²)
Capital: Tripoli
Population: 6,541,948
Population growth rate: 1.8%
Urban population: 78.6%
Official language: Arabic
Religion: Muslim

29 MADAGASCAR

Area: 226,658 mi² (587,041 km²)
Capital: Antananarivo
Population: 24,430,325
Population growth rate: 2.5%
Urban population: 35.1%
Official languages: French, Malagasy
Religion: Christian

30 MALAWI

Area: 45,747 mi² (118,484 km²)
Capital: Lilongwe
Population: 18,570,321
Population growth rate: 3.3%
Urban population: 16.3%
Official languages: English, Chichewa
Religion: Christian

31 MALI

Area: 478,841 mi²
(1,240,192 km²)
Capital: Bamako
Population: 17,467,108
Population growth rate: 3.0%
Urban population: 39.9%
Official language: French
Religion: Muslim

32 MAURITANIA

Area: 397,955 mi²
(1,030,700 km²)
Capital: Nouakchott
Population: 3,677,293
Population growth rate: 2.2%
Urban population: 59.9%
Official language: Arabic
Religion: Muslim

33 MAURITIUS

Area: 788 mi² (2,040 km²)
Capital: Port Louis
Population: 1,348,242
Population growth rate: 0.6%
Urban population: 39.7%
Official languages: English,
Creole
Religion: Hindu

34 MOROCCO

Area: 172,414 mi²
(446,550 km²)
Capital: Rabat
Population: 33,655,786
Population growth rate: 1.0%
Urban population: 60.2%
Official language: Arabic
Religion: Muslim

35 MOZAMBIQUE

Area: 308,642 mi² (799,380 km²)
Capital: Maputo
Population: 25,930,150
Population growth rate: 2.5%
Urban population: 32.2%
Official language: Portuguese
Religion: Christian

36 NAMIBIA

Area: 318,261 mi² (824,292 km²)
Capital: Windhoek
Population: 2,436,469
Population growth rate: 2.0%
Urban population: 46.7%
Official languages: English,
indigenous African languages
Religion: Christian

㊲ NIGER

Area: 489,191 mi²
  (1,267,000 km²)
Capital: Niamey
Population: 18,638,600
Population growth rate: 3.2%
Urban population: 18.7%
Official language: French
Religion: Muslim

㊳ NIGERIA

Area: 356,669 mi²
  (923,768 km²)
Capital: Abuja
Population: 186,053,386
Population growth rate: 2.4%
Urban population: 47.8%
Official language: English
Religion: Muslim

㊴ RWANDA

Area: 10,169 mi² (26,338 km²)
Capital: Kigali
Population: 12,988,423
Population growth rate: 2.5%
Urban population: 28.8%
Official languages:
  Kinyarwanda, French, English
Religion: Christian

㊵ SÃO TOMÉ AND PRÍNCIPE

Area: 372 mi² (964 km²)
Capital: São Tomé
Population: 197,541
Population growth rate: 1.8%
Urban population: 65.1%
Official language: Portuguese
Religion: Christian

㊶ SENEGAL

Area: 75,955 mi² (196,722 km²)
Capital: Dakar
Population: 14,320,055
Population growth rate: 2.4%
Urban population: 43.7%
Official language: French
Religion: Muslim

㊷ SEYCHELLES

Area: 176 mi² (455 km²)
Capital: Victoria
Population: 93,186
Population growth rate: 0.8%
Urban population: 53.9%
Official languages: Seychellois
  Creole, English, French
Religion: Christian

43 SIERRA LEONE

Area: 27,699 mi² (71,740 km²)
Capital: Freetown
Population: 6,018,888
Population growth rate: 2.4%
Urban population: 39.9%
Official language: English
Religion: Muslim

44 SOMALIA

Area: 246,201 mi² (637,657 km²)
Capital: Mogadishu
Population: 10,817,354
Population growth rate: 1.9%
Urban population: 39.6%
Official languages: Somali,
    Arabic
Religion: Muslim

45 SOUTH AFRICA

Area: 470,693 mi² (1,219,090 km²)
Capitals: Pretoria, Cape Town,
    Bloemfontein
Population: 53,300,704
Population growth rate: 1.0%
Urban population: 64.8%
Official languages: Afrikaans,
    English, indigenous African
    languages
Religion: Christian

46 SOUTH SUDAN

Area: 248,777 mi² (644,329 km²)
Capital: Juba
Population: 12,530,717
Population growth rate: 3.9%
Urban population: 18.8%
Official languages: English,
    Arabic
Religions: Christian, animist

47 SUDAN

Area: 718,723 mi²
    (1,861,484 km²)
Capital: Khartoum
Population: 36,729,501
Population growth rate: 1.7%
Urban population: 33.8%
Official languages: Arabic,
    English
Religion: Muslim

48 SWAZILAND

Area: 6,704 mi² (17,364 km²)
Capitals: Mbabane, Lobamba
Population: 1,451,428
Population growth rate: 1.1%
Urban population: 21.3%
Official languages: English,
    siSwati
Religion: Christian

49 TANZANIA

Area: 365,755 mi² (947,300 km²)
Capitals: Dodoma, Dar es Salaam
Population: 52,482,726
Population growth rate: 2.8%
Urban population: 31.6%
Official languages: Kiswahili, English
Religion: Christian

50 TOGO

Area: 21,925 mi² (56,785 km²)
Capital: Lomé
Population: 7,756,937
Population growth rate: 2.7%
Urban population: 40.0%
Official language: French
Religions: Christian, Muslim

51 TUNISIA

Area: 63,170 mi² (163,610 km²)
Capital: Tunis
Population: 11,134,588
Population growth rate: 0.9%
Urban population: 66.8%
Official language: Arabic
Religion: Muslim

52 UGANDA

Area: 93,065 mi² (241,038 km²)
Capital: Kampala
Population: 38,319,241
Population growth rate: 3.2%
Urban population: 16.1%
Official language: English
Religion: Christian

53 ZAMBIA

Area: 290,587 mi² (752,618 km²)
Capital: Lusaka
Population: 15,510,711
Population growth rate: 2.9%
Urban population: 40.9%
Official languages: English, indigenous African languages
Religion: Christian

54 ZIMBABWE

Area: 150,872 mi² (390,757 km²)
Capital: Harare
Population: 14,546,961
Population growth rate: 2.2%
Urban population: 32.4%
Official languages: Shona, Ndebele, English indigenous African languages
Religion: Christian

ASIA

❶ AFGHANISTAN

Area: 251,827 mi²
(652,230 km²)
Capital: Kabul
Population: 33,332,025
Population growth rate: 2.3%
Urban population: 26.7%
Official languages: Dari,
Pashto
Religion: Muslim

❷ ARMENIA

Area: 11,484 mi² (29,743 km²)
Capital: Yerevan
Population: 3,051,250
Population growth rate:
−0.18%
Urban population: 62.7%
Official language: Armenian
Religion: Christian

❸ AZERBAIJAN

Area: 33,436 mi² (86,600 km²)
Capital: Baku
Population: 9,872,765
Population growth rate: 0.9%
Urban population: 54.6%
Official language: Azerbaijani
Religion: Muslim

❹ BAHRAIN

Area: 293 mi² (760 km²)
Capital: Manama
Population: 1,378,904
Population growth rate: 2.3%
Urban population: 88.8%
Official language: Arabic
Religion: Muslim

❺ BANGLADESH

Area: 57,321 mi² (148,460 km²)
Capital: Dhaka
Population: 156,186,882
Population growth rate: 1.1%
Urban population: 34.3%
Official language: Bangla
Religion: Muslim

❻ BHUTAN

Area: 14,824 mi²
(38,394 km²)
Capital: Thimphu
Population: 750,125
Population growth rate: 1.1%
Urban population: 38.6%
Official language: Dzongkha
Religion: Lamaistic Buddhist

⑦ BRUNEI

Area: 2,226 mi² (5,765 km²)
Capital: Bandar Seri Begawan
Population: 436,620
Population growth rate: 1.6%
Urban population: 77.2%
Official language: Malay
Religion: Muslim

⑧ CAMBODIA

Area: 69,898 mi² (181,035 km²)
Capital: Phnom Penh
Population: 15,957,223
Population growth rate: 1.6%
Urban population: 20.7%
Official language: Khmer
Religion: Buddhist

⑨ CHINA

Area: 3,705,407 mi²
    (9,596,960 km²)
Capital: Beijing
Population: 1,373,541,278
Population growth rate:
    0.4%
Urban population: 55.6%
Official language: Mandarin
Religions: Buddhist,
    unaffiliated

⑩ CYPRUS

Area: 3,572 mi² (9,251 km²)
Capital: Nicosia
Population: 1,205,575
Population growth rate: 1.4%
Urban population: 66.9%
Official languages: Greek,
    Turkish
Religion: Christian

⑪ GEORGIA

Area: 26,911 mi² (69,700 km²)
Capital: Tbilisi
Population: 4,928,052
Population growth rate:
    −0.05%
Urban population: 53.6%
Official language: Georgian
Religion: Christian

⑫ INDIA

Area: 1,269,219 mi²
    (3,287,263 km²)
Capital: New Delhi
Population: 1,266,883,598
Population growth rate: 1.2%
Urban population: 32.7%
Official language: Hindi
Religion: Hindu

13 INDONESIA

Area: 735,358 mi²
(1,904,569 km²)
Capital: Jakarta
Population: 258,316,051
Population growth rate: 0.9%
Urban population: 53.7%
Official language: Bahasa
Indonesia
Religion: Muslim

14 IRAN

Area: 636,372 mi²
(1,648,195 km²)
Capital: Tehran
Population: 82,801,633
Population growth rate: 1.2%
Urban population: 73.4%
Official language: Persian
Religion: Muslim

15 IRAQ

Area: 169,235 mi² (438,317 km²)
Capital: Baghdad
Population: 38,146,025
Population growth rate: 2.9%
Urban population: 69.5%
Official languages: Arabic,
Kurdish
Religion: Muslim

16 ISRAEL

Area: 8,019 mi² (20,770 km²)
Capitals: Jerusalem, Tel
Aviv-Yafo
Population: 8,174,527
Population growth rate: 1.5%
Urban population: 92.1%
Official language: Hebrew
Religion: Jewish

17 JAPAN

Area: 145,914 mi²
(377,915 km²)
Capital: Tokyo
Population: 126,702,133
Population growth rate: –0.19%
Urban population: 93.5%
Official language: Japanese
Religions: Shinto, Buddhist

18 JORDAN

Area: 34,495 mi² (89,342 km²)
Capital: Amman
Population: 8,185,384
Population growth rate: 0.8%
Urban population: 83.7%
Official language: Arabic
Religion: Muslim

⑲ KAZAKHSTAN

Area: 1,052,090 mi²
(2,724,900 km²)
Capital: Astana
Population: 18,360,353
Population growth rate: 1.1%
Urban population: 53.2%
Official languages: Kazakh,
Russian
Religion: Muslim

**⑳ KOREA, NORTH
(DEMOCRATIC PEOPLE'S
REPUBLIC OF)**

Area: 46,540 mi² (120,538 km²)
Capital: Pyongyang
Population: 25,115,311
Population growth rate: 0.5%
Urban population: 60.9%
Official language: Korean
Religion: None

**㉑ KOREA, SOUTH
(REPUBLIC OF)**

Area: 38,502 mi² (99,720 km²)
Capital: Seoul
Population: 50,924,172
Population growth rate: 0.5%
Urban population: 82.5%

Official language: Korean
Religions: Christian, Buddhist

㉒ KUWAIT

Area: 6,880 mi² (17,818 km²)
Capital: Kuwait City
Population: 2,832,776
Population growth rate: 1.5%
Urban population: 98.3%
Official language: Arabic
Religion: Muslim

㉓ KYRGYZSTAN

Area: 77,202 mi² (199,951 km²)
Capital: Bishkek
Population: 5,727,553
Population growth rate: 1.1%
Urban population: 35.7%
Official language: Kyrgyz
Religion: Muslim

㉔ LAOS

Area: 91,429 mi² (236,800 km²)
Capital: Vientiane
Population: 7,019,073
Population growth rate: 1.5%
Urban population: 38.6%
Official language: Lao
Religion: Buddhist

25 LEBANON

Area: 4,015 mi² (10,400 km²)

Capital: Beirut

Population: 6,237,738

Population growth rate: 0.9%

Urban population: 87.8%

Official language: Arabic

Religions: Muslim, Christian

26 MALAYSIA

Area: 127,355 mi²
(329,847 km²)

Capital: Kuala Lumpur

Population: 30,949,962

Population growth rate: 1.4%

Urban population: 74.7%

Official language: Bahasa
Malaysia

Religion: Muslim

27 MALDIVES

Area: 115 mi² (298 km²)

Capital: Male

Population: 392,960

Population growth rate: –0.17%

Urban population: 45.5%

Official language: Dhivehi

Religion: Muslim

28 MONGOLIA

Area: 603,909 mi²
(1,564,116 km²)

Capital: Ulaanbaatar

Population: 3,031,330

Population growth rate: 1.3%

Urban population: 72.0%

Official language: Khalkha
Mongol

Religion: Buddhist

29 MYANMAR (BURMA)

Area: 261,228 mi² (676,578 km²)

Capital: Yangon (Rangoon)

Population: 56,890,418

Population growth rate: 1.0%

Urban population: 34.1%

Official language: Burmese

Religion: Buddhist

30 NEPAL

Area: 56,827 mi² (147,181 km²)

Capital: Kathmandu

Population: 29,033,914

Population growth rate: 1.2%

Urban population: 18.6%

Official language: Nepali

Religion: Hindu

31 OMAN

Area: 119,499 mi² (309,500 km²)
Capital: Muscat
Population: 3,355,262
Population growth rate: 2.1%
Urban population: 77.6%
Official language: Arabic
Religion: Muslim

32 PAKISTAN

Area: 307,374 mi² (796,095 km²)
Capital: Islamabad
Population: 201,995,540
Population growth rate: 1.5%
Urban population: 38.8%
Official languages: Urdu, English
Religion: Muslim

33 PHILIPPINES

Area: 115,831 mi² (300,000 km²)
Capital: Manila
Population: 102,624,209
Population growth rate: 1.6%
Urban population: 44.4%
Official languages: Filipino, English
Religion: Christian

34 QATAR

Area: 4,473 mi² (11,586 km²)
Capital: Doha
Population: 2,258,283
Population growth rate: 2.6%
Urban population: 99.2%
Official language: Arabic
Religion: Muslim

35 SAUDI ARABIA

Area: 830,000 mi² (2,149,690 km²)
Capital: Riyadh
Population: 28,160,273
Population growth rate: 1.5%
Urban population: 83.1%
Official language: Arabic
Religion: Muslim

36 SINGAPORE

Area: 269 mi² (697 km²)
Capital: Singapore
Population: 5,781,728
Population growth rate: 1.9%
Urban population: 100.0%
Official languages: Mandarin, English, Malay, Tamil
Religion: Buddhist

37 SRI LANKA

Area: 25,332 mi² (65,610 km²)
Capital: Colombo
Population: 22,235,000
Population growth rate: 0.8%
Urban population: 18.4%
Official languages: Sinhala,
Tamil
Religion: Buddhist

38 SYRIA

Area: 71,498 mi² (185,180 km²)
Capital: Damascus
Population: 17,185,170
Population growth rate:
1.6%
Urban population: 57.7%
Official language: Arabic
Religion: Muslim

39 TAJIKISTAN

Area: 55,637 mi² (144,100 km²)
Capital: Dushanbe
Population: 8,330,946
Population growth rate: 1.7%
Urban population: 26.8%
Official language: Tajik
Religion: Muslim

40 THAILAND

Area: 198,117 mi²
(513,120 km²)
Capital: Bangkok
Population: 68,200,824
Population growth rate: 0.3%
Urban population: 50.4%
Official language: Thai
Religion: Buddhist

41 TIMOR-LESTE

Area: 5,743 mi² (14,874 km²)
Capital: Dili
Population: 1,261,072
Population growth rate: 2.4%
Urban population: 32.8%
Official languages: Tetum,
Portuguese
Religion: Christian

42 TURKEY

Area: 302,535 mi²
(783,562 km²)
Capital: Ankara
Population: 80,274,604
Population growth rate: 0.9%
Urban population: 73.4%
Official language: Turkish
Religion: Muslim

43 TURKMENISTAN

Area: 188,456 mi²
(488,100 km²)
Capital: Ashgabat
Population: 5,291,317
Population growth rate: 1.1%
Urban population: 50.0%
Official language: Turkmen
Religion: Muslim

44 UNITED ARAB EMIRATES

Area: 32,278 mi² (83,600 km²)
Capital: Abu Dhabi
Population: 5,927,482
Population growth rate: 2.5%
Urban population: 85.5%
Official language: Arabic
Religion: Muslim

45 UZBEKISTAN

Area: 172,742 mi²
(447,400 km²)
Capital: Tashkent
Population: 64,430,428
Population growth rate: 0.9%
Urban population: 36.4%
Official language: Uzbek
Religion: Muslim

46 VIETNAM

Area: 127,881 mi²
(331,210 km²)
Capital: Hanoi
Population: 95,261,021
Population growth rate:
0.95%
Urban population: 33.6%
Official language: Vietnamese
Religion: Buddhist/None

47 YEMEN

Area: 203,850 mi²
(527,968 km²)
Capital: Sana'a
Population: 27,392,779
Population growth rate: 2.4%
Urban population: 34.6%
Official language: Arabic
Religion: Muslim

AUSTRALIA/ OCEANIA

❶ AUSTRALIA

Area: 2,988,902 mi²
(7,741,220 km²)
Capital: Canberra
Population: 22,992,654
Population growth rate: 1.1%
Urban population: 89.4%
Official language: English
Religion: Christian

❷ FIJI

Area: 7,056 mi² (18,274 km²)
Capital: Suva
Population: 915,303
Population growth rate: 0.6%
Urban population: 53.7%
Official languages: English,
Fijian
Religion: Christian

❸ KIRIBATI

Area: 313 mi² (811 km²)
Capital: Tarawa
Population: 106,925
Population growth rate: 1.1%
Urban population: 44.3%
Official language: English
Religion: Christian

❹ MARSHALL ISLANDS

Area: 70 mi² (181 km²)
Capital: Majuro
Population: 73,376
Population growth rate: 1.6%
Urban population: 72.7%
Official languages:
Marshallese, English
Religion: Christian

❺ MICRONESIA, FEDERATED STATES OF

Area: 271 mi² (702 km²)
Capital: Palikir
Population: 104,719
Population growth rate: –0.5%
Urban population: 22.4%
Official language: English
Religion: Christian

❻ NAURU

Area: 8 mi² (21 km²)
Capital: Yaren District (no
official capital)
Population: 9,591
Population growth rate: 0.5%
Urban population: 100.0%
Official language: Nauruan
Religion: Christian

7 NEW ZEALAND

Area: 103,799 mi² (268,838 km²)
Capital: Wellington
Population: 4,474,549
Population growth rate: 0.8%
Urban population: 86.3%
Official languages: English,
Maori, New Zealand Sign
Language
Religion: Christian, no religion

8 PALAU

Area: 177 mi² (459 km²)
Capital: Ngerulmud
Population: 21,347
Population growth rate: 0.4%
Urban population: 87.1%
Official languages: Palauan,
English
Religion: Christian

9 PAPUA NEW GUINEA

Area: 178,704 mi² (462,840 km²)
Capital: Port Moresby
Population: 6,791,317
Population growth rate: 1.8%
Urban population: 13.0%
Official languages: Tok Pisin,
English, Hiri Motu
Religion: Christian

10 SAMOA

Area: 1,093 mi² (2,831 km²)
Capital: Apia
Population: 198,926
Population growth rate: 0.6%
Urban population: 19.1%
Official language: Samoan
Religion: Christian

11 SOLOMON ISLANDS

Area: 11,157 mi² (28,896 km²)
Capital: Honiara
Population: 111,219
Population growth rate: 2.0%
Urban population: 22.3%
Official languages:
Melanesian pidgin, English
Religion: Christian

12 TONGA

Area: 288 mi² (747 km²)
Capital: Nuku'alofa
Population: 106,513
Population growth rate: –0.01%
Urban population: 23.7%
Official languages: Tongan,
English
Religion: Christian

⑬ TUVALU

Area: 10 mi² (26 km²)
Capital: Funafuti
Population: 10,959
Population growth rate: 0.9%
Urban population: 59.7%
Official languages: Tuvaluan, English
Religion: Christian

⑭ VANUATU

Area: 4,706 mi² (12,189 km²)
Capital: Port-Vila
Population: 277,554
Population growth rate: 1.9%
Urban population: 26.1%
Official languages: Bislama, English, French
Religion: Christian

EUROPE

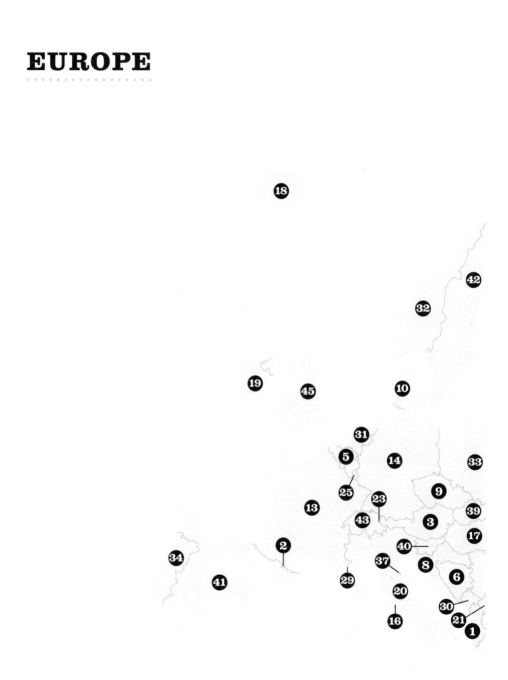

❶ ALBANIA

Area: 11,100 mi² (28,748 km²)
Capital: Tirana
Population: 3,038,594
Population growth rate: 0.3%
Urban population: 57.4%
Official language: Albanian
Religion: Muslim

❷ ANDORRA

Area: 181 mi² (468 km²)
Capital: Andorra la Vella
Population: 85,660
Population growth rate: 0.1%
Urban population: 85.1%
Official language: Catalan
Religion: Christian

❸ AUSTRIA

Area: 32,383 mi² (83,871 km²)
Capital: Vienna
Population: 8,711,770
Population growth rate: 0.5%
Urban population: 66.0%
Official language: German
Religion: Christian

❹ BELARUS

Area: 80,155 mi² (207,600 km²)
Capital: Minsk
Population: 9,570,376
Population growth rate: –0.21%
Urban population: 76.7%
Official languages: Russian,
Belarusian
Religion: Christian

❺ BELGIUM

Area: 11,787 mi² (30,528 km²)
Capital: Brussels
Population: 11,409,077
Population growth rate: 0.7%
Urban population: 97.9%
Official languages: Dutch,
French, German
Religion: Christian

❻ BOSNIA AND HERZEGOVINA

Area: 19,767 mi² (51,197 km²)
Capital: Sarajevo
Population: 3,861,912
Population growth rate: –0.14%
Urban population: 39.8%
Official languages: Bosnian,
Serbian, Croatian
Religions: Muslim, Christian

❼ BULGARIA

Area: 42,811 mi² (110,879 km²)
Capital: Sofia
Population: 7,144,653
Population growth rate: –0.60%
Urban population: 73.9%
Official language: Bulgarian
Religion: Christian

❽ CROATIA

Area: 21,851 mi² (56,594 km²)
Capital: Zagreb
Population: 4,313,707
Population growth rate: –0.50%
Urban population: 59.0%
Official language: Croatian
Religion: Christian

❾ CZECH REPUBLIC (CZECHIA)

Area: 30,451 mi² (78,867 km²)
Capital: Prague
Population: 10,644,842
Population growth rate: 0.14%
Urban population: 73.0%
Official language: Czech
Religion: Unspecified/None

❿ DENMARK

Area: 16,639 mi² (43,094 km²)
Capital: Copenhagen
Population: 5,593,785
Population growth rate: 0.2%
Urban population: 87.7%
Official language: Danish
Religion: Christian

⓫ ESTONIA

Area: 17,463 mi² (45,228 km²)
Capital: Tallinn
Population: 1,258,545
Population growth rate: –0.54%
Urban population: 67.5%
Official language: Estonian
Religion: None

⓬ FINLAND

Area: 130,559 mi²
  (338,145 km²)
Capital: Helsinki
Population: 5,498,211
Population growth rate: 0.4%
Urban population: 84.2%
Official languages: Finnish,
  Swedish
Religion: Christian

⑬ FRANCE

Area: 212,935 mi² (551,500 km²)

Capital: Paris

Population: 66,836,154

Population growth rate: 0.4%

Urban population: 79.5%

Official language: French

Religion: Christian

⑭ GERMANY

Area: 137,847 mi²
(357,022 km²)

Capital: Berlin

Population: 23,740,424

Population growth rate: –0.16%

Urban population: 75.3%

Official language: German

Religion: Christian

⑮ GREECE

Area: 50,949 mi² (131,957 km²)

Capital: Athens

Population: 10,773,253

Population growth rate: –0.03%

Urban population: 78.0%

Official language: Greek

Religion: Christian

⑯ HOLY SEE (VATICAN CITY)

Area: 0.17 mi² (0.44 km²)

Capital: Vatican City

Population: 1,000

Population growth rate: 0.0%

Urban population: 100.0%

Official languages: Italian,
Latin, French

Religion: Christian

⑰ HUNGARY

Area: 35,918 mi²(93,028 km²)

Capital: Budapest

Population: 9,874,784

Population growth rate: –0.24%

Urban population: 71.2%

Official language: Hungarian

Religion: Christian

⑱ ICELAND

Area: 39,769 mi² (103,000 km²)

Capital: Reykjavík

Population: 335,878

Population growth rate: 1.2%

Urban population: 94.1%

Official languages: Icelandic,
English

Religion: Christian

⑲ IRELAND

Area: 27,133 mi² (70,273 km²)
Capital: Dublin
Population: 4,952,473
Population growth rate: 1.2%
Urban population: 63.2%
Official languages: English, Gaelic
Religion: Christian

⑳ ITALY

Area: 116,348 mi² (301,340 km²)
Capital: Rome
Population: 62,007,540
Population growth rate: 0.2%
Urban population: 69.0%
Official language: Italian
Religion: Christian

㉑ KOSOVO

Area: 4,203 mi² (10,887 km²)
Capital: Pristina
Population: 1,883,018
Population growth rate: N/A
Urban population: N/A
Official languages: Albanian, Serbian
Religion: Muslim

㉒ LATVIA

Area: 24,938 mi² (64,589 km²)
Capital: Riga
Population: 1,965,686
Population growth rate: −1.07%
Urban population: 67.4%
Official language: Latvian
Religion: Christian

㉓ LIECHTENSTEIN

Area: 62 mi² (160 km²)
Capital: Vaduz
Population: 37,937
Population growth rate: 0.8%
Urban population: 14.3%
Official language: German
Religion: Christian

㉔ LITHUANIA

Area: 25,212 mi² (65,300 km²)
Capital: Vilnius
Population: 2,854,235
Population growth rate: −1.06%
Urban population: 66.5%
Official language: Lithuanian
Religion: Christian

25 LUXEMBOURG

Area: 998 mi² (2,586 km²)
Capital: Luxembourg
Population: 582,291
Population growth rate: 2.1%
Urban population: 90.2%
Official languages:
    Luxembourgish, French,
    German
Religion: Christian

26 MACEDONIA

Area: 9,928 mi² (25,713 km²)
Capital: Skopje
Population: 2,100,025
Population growth rate: 0.2%
Urban population: 57.1%
Official languages:
    Macedonian, Albanian
Religion: Christian

27 MALTA

Area: 122 mi² (316 km²)
Capital: Valletta
Population: 415,196
Population growth rate: 0.3%
Urban population: 95.4%
Official languages: Maltese,
    English
Religion: Christian

28 MOLDOVA

Area: 13,070 mi² (33,851 km²)
Capital: Chisinau
Population: 3,510,485
Population growth rate: –1.04%
Urban population: 45.0%
Official language: Moldovan
Religion: Christian

29 MONACO

Area: 0.8 mi² (2 km²)
Capital: Monaco
Population: 30,581
Population growth rate: 0.2%
Urban population: 100.0%
Official language: French
Religion: Christian

30 MONTENEGRO

Area: 5,333 mi² (13,812 km²)
Capital: Podgorica
Population: 644,578
Population growth rate: –0.35%
Urban population: 64.0%
Official language:
    Montenegrin
Religion: Christian

31 NETHERLANDS

Area: 16,040 mi² (41,543 km²)
Capitals: Amsterdam, The Hague
Population: 17,016,967
Population growth rate: 0.4%
Urban population: 90.5%
Official language: Dutch
Religion: Christian

32 NORWAY

Area: 125,021 mi² (323,802 km²)
Capital: Oslo
Population: 5,265,158
Population growth rate: 1.1%
Urban population: 80.5%
Official language: Norwegian
Religion: Christian

33 POLAND

Area: 120,728 mi² (312,685 km²)
Capital: Warsaw
Population: 38,523,261
Population growth rate: –0.11%
Urban population: 60.5%
Official language: Polish
Religion: Christian

34 PORTUGAL

Area: 35,556 mi² (92,090 km²)
Capital: Lisbon
Population: 10,833,816
Population growth rate: 0.1%
Urban population: 63.5%
Official languages: Portuguese, Mirandese
Religion: Christian

35 ROMANIA

Area: 92,043 mi² (238,391 km²)
Capital: Bucharest
Population: 21,599,736
Population growth rate: –0.32%
Urban population: 54.6%
Official language: Romanian
Religion: Christian

36 RUSSIA

Area: 6,601,668 mi² (17,098,242 km²)
Capital: Moscow
Population: 142,355,415
Population growth rate: –0.06%
Urban population: 74.0%
Official language: Russian
Religions: Christian, Muslim

37 SAN MARINO

Area: 24 mi² (61 km²)
Capital: San Marino
Population: 33,285
Population growth rate: 0.8%
Urban population: 94.2%
Official language: Italian
Religion: Christian

38 SERBIA

Area: 29,913 mi² (77,474 km²)
Capital: Belgrade
Population: 7,143,921
Population growth rate: –0.46%
Urban population: 55.6%
Official language: Serbian
Religion: Christian

39 SLOVAKIA

Area: 18,933 mi² (49,035 km²)
Capital: Bratislava
Population: 5,445,802
Population growth rate: 0.01%
Urban population: 53.6%
Official language: Slovak
Religion: Christian

40 SLOVENIA

Area: 7,827 mi² (20,273 km²)
Capital: Ljubljana
Population: 1,978,029
Population growth rate: –0.29%
Urban population: 49.6%
Official language: Slovenian
Religion: Christian

41 SPAIN

Area: 195,124 mi² (505,370 km²)
Capital: Madrid
Population: 48,563,476
Population growth rate: 0.8%
Urban population: 79.6%
Official language: Castilian
  Spanish
Religion: Christian

42 SWEDEN

Area: 173,860 mi² (450,295 km²)
Capital: Stockholm
Population: 9,880,604
Population growth rate: 0.8%
Urban population: 85.8%
Official language: Swedish
Religion: Christian

43 SWITZERLAND

Area: 15,937 mi² (41,277 km²)
Capital: Bern
Population: 8,179,294
Population growth rate: 0.7%
Urban population: 73.9%
Official languages: German,
French, Italian, Romansch
Religion: Christian

44 UKRAINE

Area: 233,032 mi² (603,550 km²)
Capital: Kyiv
Population: 44,209,733
Population growth rate: –0.39%
Urban population: 69.7%
Official language: Ukrainian
Religion: Christian

45 UNITED KINGDOM

Area: 94,058 mi² (243,610 km²)
Capital: London
Population: 64,430,428
Population growth rate: 0.5%
Urban population: 82.6%
Official language: English
Religion: Christian

NORTH AMERICA

1 ANTIGUA AND BARBUDA

Area: 171 mi² (443 km²)
Capital: Saint John's
Population: 93,581
Population growth rate: 1.2%
Urban population: 23.8%
Official language: English
Religion: Christian

2 THE BAHAMAS

Area: 5,359 mi² (13,880 km²)
Capital: Nassau
Population: 327,316
Population growth rate: 0.8%
Urban population: 82.9%
Official language: English
Religion: Christian

3 BARBADOS

Area: 166 mi² (430 km²)
Capital: Bridgetown
Population: 291,495
Population growth rate: 0.3%
Urban population: 31.5%
Official language: English
Religion: Christian

4 BELIZE

Area: 8,867 mi² (22,966 km²)
Capital: Belmopan
Population: 353,858
Population growth rate: 1.8%
Urban population: 44.0%
Official language: English
Religion: Christian

5 CANADA

Area: 3,855,103 mi²
 (9,984,670 km²)
Capital: Ottawa
Population: 35,362,905
Population growth rate: 0.7%
Urban population: 81.8%
Official languages: English,
 French
Religion: Christian

6 COSTA RICA

Area: 19,730 mi² (51,100 km²)
Capital: San José
Population: 4,872,543
Population growth rate: 1.1%
Urban population: 38.6%
Official language: Spanish
Religion: Christian

❼ CUBA

Area: 42,803 mi² (110,860 km²)
Capital: Havana
Population: 11,179,995
Population growth rate: –0.3%
Urban population: 77.1%
Official language: Spanish
Religion: Christian

❽ DOMINICA

Area: 290 mi² (751 km²)
Capital: Roseau
Population: 15,957,223
Population growth rate: 1.6%
Urban population: 20.7%
Official language: English
Religion: Christian

❾ DOMINICAN REPUBLIC

Area: 18,792 mi² (48,670 km²)
Capital: Santo Domingo
Population: 10,606,865
Population growth rate: 1.2%
Urban population: 79.0%
Official language: Spanish
Religion: Christian

❿ EL SALVADOR

Area: 8,124 mi² (21,041 km²)
Capital: San Salvador
Population: 6,156,670
Population growth rate: 0.3%
Urban population: 66.7%
Official language: Spanish
Religion: Christian

⓫ GRENADA

Area: 133 mi² (344 km²)
Capital: Saint George's
Population: 111,219
Population growth rate: 0.5%
Urban population: 35.6%
Official language: English
Religion: Christian

⓬ GUATEMALA

Area: 42,042 mi² (108,889 km²)
Capital: Guatemala City
Population: 15,189,958
Population growth rate: 1.8%
Urban population: 51.6%
Official language: Spanish
Religion: Christian

⑬ HAITI

Area: 10,714 mi² (27,750 km²)
Capital: Port-au-Prince
Population: 10,485,800
Population growth rate: 1.7%
Urban population: 58.6%
Official languages: French, Creole
Religion: Christian

⑭ HONDURAS

Area: 43,278 mi² (112,090 km²)
Capital: Tegucigalpa
Population: 8,893,259
Population growth rate: 1.6%
Urban population: 54.7%
Official language: Spanish
Religion: Christian

⑮ JAMAICA

Area: 4,244 mi² (10,991 km²)
Capital: Kingston
Population: 2,970,340
Population growth rate: 0.7%
Urban population: 54.8%
Official language: English
Religion: Christian

⑯ MEXICO

Area: 758,449 mi² (1,964,375 km²)
Capital: Mexico City
Population: 8,174,527
Population growth rate: 1.2%
Urban population: 79.2%
Official language: Spanish
Religion: Christian

⑰ NICARAGUA

Area: 50,336 mi² (130,370 km²)
Capital: Managua
Population: 5,966,798
Population growth rate: 0.99%
Urban population: 58.8%
Official language: Spanish
Religion: Christian

⑱ PANAMA

Area: 29,120 mi² (75,420 km²)
Capital: Panama City
Population: 3,705,246
Population growth rate: 1.3%
Urban population: 66.6%
Official language: Spanish
Religion: Christian

⑲ SAINT KITTS AND NEVIS

Area: 101 mi² (261 km²)
Capital: Basseterre
Population: 52,329
Population growth rate: 0.8%
Urban population: 32.0%
Official language: English
Religion: Christian

⑳ SAINT LUCIA

Area: 238 mi² (616 km²)
Capital: Castries
Population: 164,464
Population growth rate: 0.3%
Urban population: 18.5%
Official language: English
Religion: Christian

㉑ SAINT VINCENT AND THE GRENADINES

Area: 150 mi² (389 km²)
Capital: Kingstown
Population: 102,350
Population growth rate: –0.3%
Urban population: 50.6%
Official language: English
Religion: Christian

㉒ TRINIDAD AND TOBAGO

Area: 1,980 mi² (5,128 km²)
Capital: Port of Spain
Population: 1,220,479
Population growth rate: –0.2%
Urban population: 8.4%
Official language: English
Religion: Christian

㉓ UNITED STATES

Area: 3,796,742 mi²
   (9,833,517 km²)
Capital: Washington, D.C.
Population: 323,995,528
Population growth rate: 0.8%
Urban population: 81.6%
Official language: English

SOUTH
AMERICA

❶ ARGENTINA

Area: 1,073,518 mi² (2,780,400 km²)

Capital: Buenos Aires

Population: 43,886,748

Population growth rate: 0.9%

Urban population: 91.8%

Official language: Spanish

Religion: Christian

❷ BOLIVIA

Area: 424,164 mi² (1,098,581 km²)

Capitals: La Paz, Sucre

Population: 10,969,649

Population growth rate: 1.5%

Urban population: 68.5%

Official languages: Spanish, Quechua, Aymara, Guarani

Religion: Christian

❸ BRAZIL

Area: 3,287,957 mi² (8,515,770 km²)

Capital: Brasilia

Population: 205,823,665

Population growth rate: 0.8%

Urban population: 85.7%

Official language: Portuguese

Religion: Christian

❹ CHILE

Area: 291,933 mi² (756,102 km²)

Capital: Santiago

Population: 17,650,114

Population growth rate: 0.8%

Urban population: 89.5%

Official language: Spanish

Religion: Christian

❺ COLOMBIA

Area: 439,736 mi² (1,138,910 km²)

Capital: Bogotá

Population: 47,220,856

Population growth rate: 1.02%

Urban population: 76.4%

Official language: Spanish

Religion: Christian

❻ ECUADOR

Area: 109,484 mi² (283,561 km²)

Capital: Quito

Population: 16,080,778

Population growth rate: 1.3%

Urban population: 63.7%

Official language: Spanish

Religion: Christian

7 GUYANA

Area: 83,000 mi² (214,969 km²)
Capital: Georgetown
Population: 735,909
Population growth rate: 0.2%
Urban population: 28.6%
Official language: English
Religions: Christian, Hindu

8 PARAGUAY

Area: 157,048 mi² (406,752 km²)
Capital: Asunción
Population: 6,862,812
Population growth rate: 1.2%
Urban population: 59.7%
Official languages: Spanish,
    Guarani
Religion: Christian

9 PERU

Area: 496,225 mi²
    (1,285,216 km²)
Capital: Lima
Population: 30,741,062
Population growth rate: 0.96%
Urban population: 78.6%
Official languages: Spanish,
    Quechua, Aymara
Religion: Christian

10 SURINAME

Area: 63,251 mi² (163,820 km²)
Capital: Paramaribo
Population: 585,824
Population growth rate: 1.1%
Urban population: 66.0%
Official language: Dutch
Religions: Christian, Hindu

11 URUGUAY

Area: 68,037 mi² (176,215 km²)
Capital: Montevideo
Population: 111,219
Population growth rate: 0.3%
Urban population: 95.3%
Official language: Spanish
Religion: Christian

12 VENEZUELA

Area: 352,144 mi² (912,050 km²)
Capital: Caracas
Population: 30,912,302
Population growth rate: 1.3%
Urban population: 89.0%
Official language: Spanish
Religion: Christian

About the Author

Stephen F. Cunha is the chair and professor of geography at Humboldt State University in California. He is also the state coordinator for the National Geographic Bee and co-author of *Our Fifty States,* a children's reference book published by National Geographic. He and his family live near Redwood National Park.

Since 1888, the National Geographic Society has funded more than 12,000 research, exploration, and preservation projects around the world. The Society receives funds from National Geographic Partners, LLC, funded in part by your purchase. A portion of the proceeds from this book supports this vital work. To learn more, visit natgeo.com/info.

NATIONAL GEOGRAPHIC and Yellow Border Design are trademarks of the National Geographic Society, used under license.

For more information, visit nationalgeographic.com, call 1-800-647-5463, or write to the following address:

National Geographic Partners
1145 17th Street N.W.
Washington, D.C. 20036-4688 U.S.A.

Visit us online at nationalgeographic.com/books
For librarians and teachers: ngchildrensbooks.org
More for kids from National Geographic: kids.nationalgeographic.com

For information about special
discounts for bulk purchases, please contact
National Geographic Books Special Sales: specialsales@natgeo.com

For rights or permissions inquiries, please contact
National Geographic Books Subsidiary Rights: bookrights@natgeo.com